D0875194

Accounting Classics Series

Publication of this Classic was made possible
by a grant from Price Waterhouse Foundation

Suggestions of titles to be included
in the Series are solicited and should
be addressed to the Editor.

FIVE MONOGRAPHS ON
BUSINESS INCOME

by
Sidney S. Alexander
Martin Bronfenbrenner
Solomon Fabricant
Clark Warburton

and Discussion

Scholars Book Co.
4431 Mt. Vernon
Houston, Texas   77006

Reprinted 1973 by Scholars Book Co.

with special permission
of the American Institute of Certified Public Accountants

Library of Congress Card Catalog Number: 73-84377
ISBN: 0-914348-00-0
Manufactured in the United States of America

CONTENTS

———

FOREWORD

This pamphlet is the third in a series published under the auspices of the Study Group on Business Income, organized by the American Institute of Accountants in 1948. The first two papers were prepared at the request of the Study Group, analyzing business income concepts and the problem of measuring business income, especially under changing price levels. The point of view is that of the economist: Mr. Sidney Alexander, formerly Assistant Professor of Economics at Harvard University, is on the economic staff of the International Monetary Fund; and Mr. Martin Bronfenbrenner is Associate Professor of Economics at the University of Wisconsin and is at present on leave of absence in Japan on General MacArthur's staff.

Mr. Alexander's paper on "Income Measurement in a Dynamic Economy" demonstrates how business income, a relatively simple, single concept in a "static" economy, becomes an exceedingly complicated family of concepts in an economy characterized by change in general price levels, technology and all the other factors that engender uncertainty. In such a "dynamic" economy, he suggests, choice of the concept of business income depends upon the purpose to which the measure of income is to be put. Mr. Bronfenbrenner's paper on "Business Income Concepts in the Light of Monetary Theory," carrying the discussion along, considers some of the purposes to which current measures of business income have been devoted by various groups. He then analyzes the validity, in these uses, of two "rival" concepts of business income.

To help round out this economic discussion of business income, we have added two brief papers by Mr. Solomon Fabricant, Professor of Economics at New York University and a member of the Study Group. These were presented by him before meetings of the American Institute of Accountants and the Institute of Trade and Commerce Professions. They are devoted primarily to that concept of business income most appropriate for inclusion in

i

measures of national income, a basic index of the nation's economic welfare.

The fifth monograph, by Mr. Clark Warburton, a member of the Study Group, was prepared to present a different point of view to that of Mr. Bronfenbrenner and is entitled, "Monetary Theory and the Price Level Trend of the Future." Mr. Warburton is an economist of the Federal Deposit Insurance Corporation. We are very glad to have this contribution to complete this series.

Following the monographs is a discussion of them which took form at a meeting of the Study Group on May 13, 1950.

The authors assume sole responsibility for their respective views. This pamphlet, like the others in the series, is circulated by the Study Group in order to stimulate thought and discussion of the important subject with which it deals.

PERCIVAL F. BRUNDAGE, *Chairman,*
Study Group on Business Income

INCOME MEASUREMENT IN A DYNAMIC ECONOMY

By Sidney S. Alexander

CONTENTS

INCOME MEASUREMENT IN A DYNAMIC ECONOMY

SUMMARY

A year's income is, fundamentally, the amount of wealth that a person, real or corporate, can dispose of over the course of the year and remain as well off at the end of the year as at the beginning. The arbitrary choice of a time period of one year raises certain difficulties in income accounting because many transactions relate to several different years. The elaborate developments of the art of accounting are principally designed to handle the problems raised by the attempt to assign to each year a share in the flow of income which is associated with the activities of many years. With these difficulties connected with the attempt to decompose the income of a corporation's entire life into the income of individual years, the present monograph has little to do.

Another set of problems, which concern the question of what is meant by "as well off at the end of the year as at the beginning", is the principal subject of the present monograph. It is here argued that in a dynamic economy, when values are changing both because of changes in prices and changes of expectations of future earning power, there is no unique well-defined ideal concept of income against which can be compared the actual practice of income measurement. Instead, many variant concepts can be conceived, each of which has certain advantages for a particular purpose. Consequently, in any dispute over how income should best be measured, it is only rarely that the question can be settled by appeal to the fundamental income concept. More frequently, the several different methods of income measurement under consideration are all consistent with the basic concept of income, but each puts a different interpretation on the elementary notions of which the basic concept is composed. In particular, important variations in the practice of income measurement are related to different interpretations of what is meant by a person's being as well off at the end of the income period as at the beginning.

Because different interpretations are possible, and because any concept of income is justified only by the use to which it is

1

put, the only criterion by which a choice may be made among various methods of measuring income is the relative effectiveness of the different methods in serving the purposes for which income is to be used. But income is in fact used for many different purposes, so it is only natural that the measure of income best for one purpose should not be well suited to another different purpose. That means that either a compromise measure must be devised, fairly suitable to several purposes but ideal for none, or a different measure is to be constructed for each purpose. Both these lines have been followed in actual practice.

Choice among various concepts of income is not governed only by considerations of which measure serves best the ends in view. Another very powerful factor operating on the development of accounting methods has been the attempt to reduce the accountant's responsibility for the human judgments which must be made in passing from a consideration of the accounts to the conduct of business affairs. This attempted avoidance of responsibility has led accountants to set up two requirements for sound accounting that somewhat limit the choice of methods. These are the requirements of objectivity and conservatism. To the extent that accountants have achieved objectivity and conservatism they have transformed the measurement of income into a safer activity but one which yields a result that only partially achieves the end sought. Anyone using the accountant's measure of income, particularly the businessman, must then adjust it into accordance with reality by himself making the subjective judgments which the accountant has avoided.

This division of function is probably well justified; the formation of the subjective judgments necessary for a final evaluation of income are more in accord with the activities and responsibilities of the businessman than with those of the accountant. It is certainly not suggested that the accountant should assume these responsibilities. But it should be recognized that income, as measured by the accountant, does fall short of the ideal appropriate to any particular purpose because the subjective judgments, inherent in the measurement of income, are avoided.

2

The economist's concept of income is designed primarily to fit the case where the future is known with certainty. Strict application of that concept would mean that a corporation which each year paid dividends equal to its income would always have the same level of income. Year to year variations of income are inconsistent with the economic concept of income under conditions of certainty. When the future is reasonably certain as in the case of a bond or annuity, the accountant shares the economist's point of view, but in the measurement of business income that viewpoint is abandoned, presumably because of the uncertainties inherent in business operations. In order to make a meaningful comparison between the economist's and the accountant's concept of income, the economist's concept must somehow be extended to the case of uncertainty concerning the future. This can be done by the introduction of the concept of variable income which is elaborated in Chapter IV. Variable income is defined as the receipts for the year minus a pre-determined adjustment; it can be taken as representative of the application of the economist's concept of income to conditions of uncertainty and can be contrasted with income as conventionally measured by accountants.

The principal respect in which the accountant's measure of income departs from the economist's concept is associated with the quest for objectivity. The accountant's practice consists of matching historical costs against historical revenues, it deals therefore in recorded events, and the only difficulties are the traditional accounting problems of just how to match up those recorded events in relation to any particular time period. Changes in good will or going value, which are not recorded events but judgments of the future course of events, are not in general permitted to enter income records of accountants. From the economist's point of view, changes in going value should be counted in income since they do influence the amount that a person can dispose of and be as well off. Furthermore, most of the purposes for which income is measured would be better served by the inclusion of changes of going value. Its exclusion in practice can be justified on the basis of the need for objectivity, but, it is here

3

argued, attempts to justify the exclusion of changes of going value from income on grounds of principle are ill-founded.

A second characteristic which differentiates the accountant's concept of income from one more nearly in accord with the viewpoint of economic theory, is that the accountant accepts the money measure of values, while economic reasoning most frequently runs in real terms, i.e., in terms of what the money can buy. It should not be thought that there is a body of economic doctrine that says it is wrong to measure income in money value when price levels are changing. But the whole orientation of economic reasoning is towards dispelling the money illusion and encouraging measurement in real terms. The most hotly contested points of dispute in the measurement of income depend fundamentally on whether income is to be measured in money terms or in real terms. In particular, the issue of whether depreciation should be charged on the basis of historical cost or of replacement cost hinges on whether income is to be measured in money or in real terms.

Since the ultimate criterion governing the definition of income is the purpose to be served, choice between the real and money measures must depend on what purpose is in view. The question of which procedure to use cannot then be settled on the basis of principle, but only on the basis of which procedure works best in the application in hand. One method is superior to the other if it works better, and appeals to general principles may obscure the issues of social philosophy or practical expedience which govern the choice. There is no reason why income for any purpose can not be so defined as best to serve the general welfare and the interests of those concerned. When those interests are in conflict the issue must be resolved by a comparison of the merits of the various claims and interests, and not by recourse to a "true" concept of income, independent of the ends served by the use of the income measurements.

Another unsettled question is whether capital gain should be counted as income. This question can be somewhat clarified by breaking capital gain into two parts; one, like the gain in value of

4

an appreciation bond, can clearly be recognized as income; another, like a change in market value of an asset, is in a more debatable position. The second component of capital gain may be called unexpected gain. The principal argument for its exclusion is that an unexpected gain is not a measure of how much better off a person has become, but is merely a revision of a valuation of how well off he is and has been. Even if this argument is accepted, however, it means that at some time in the past an asset was acquired that is now recognized to be worth more than was then believed, and what is more to the point, is worth more now than it cost then. Consequently, the unexpected gain must be counted as income of some period and the principal respect in which it differs from other types of income is in the difficulty of associating it with any particular time period within the time during which the asset has been held.

The two questions, should income be reckoned in real or money terms, and should a capital gain be counted as income, are both embodied in the controversy over whether depreciation should be based on original or on replacement cost. Current accounting practice, which bases depreciation on original cost, implies that income is to be measured in money terms and capital gains on assets used in the business are to be counted as income. That is, the difference between the current year's income as based on historical cost depreciation and as based on replacement cost depreciation can be regarded as the capital gain in money terms on that part of fixed plant and equipment which has been charged against the current year's revenues. If the principle were adopted that capital gains should not be included in income, then replacement cost should be used as the basis of the depreciation charge. If a real rather than a money measure of income (even including capital gain) were to be used, then the depreciation charge should be adjusted for changes in the general price level, rather than in the replacement cost of the specific assets owned. If, however, it is desired to include capital gains in income, and to use a money measure of income, then the current practice constitutes an elegant and automatic way of distributing the money-measured capital gain on a depreciable asset over the useful life of the asset.

5

I. The Conceptual Basis of Income

Use of the Income Concept

The determination of income is the principal task of the business accountant. The final result of his calculations is used in a variety of ways with important consequences for the individual firm, the business community and the economy as a whole. In particular, income is used as the basis of one of the principal forms of taxation. It is used in reports to stockholders or the investing public as a measure of the success of a corporation's operations and as a criterion for the determination of the availability of dividends. It is used by rate regulating authorities for investigating whether those rates are fair and reasonable. It is used for the guidance of trustees charged with the responsibility of distributing the income from property to one person while preserving the principal for another. Probably the most important use of income is, or should be, as a guide to the management of enterprise in the conduct of its affairs.

Because of the practical importance of the measurement of income in so many everyday affairs, extensive and complicated rules for the determination of income have been developed. These rules have come from academic and practicing accountants, from courts of law, from tax authorities, from regulatory bodies such as the Interstate Commerce Commission or the public utilities commissions of the several states, and from supervisory agencies such as the Securities and Exchange Commission. It should not be surprising that rules emanating from so many different authorities should be at variance with one another, since each has used income for purposes of its own and has adjusted its concept of income in accord with that purpose. All concerned, however, have looked to the accountant for the basic formulation of the rules for income determination.

The accountant in his turn has tried to eliminate the element of subjective judgment from the determination of income. He has tried to establish as nearly as possible hard and fast rules of calculation in order to eliminate the guesswork and to introduce precise measurements. But in a dynamic world subject to unforeseen changes of prices and business conditions, it is not possible to avoid guesswork in the determination of income. To the extent that the accountant can eliminate guesses, he is substituting something else for income. That something else will be a good approximation to income in a fairly static situation when prices and business prospects do not change very much; the approximation will be very poor in a highly dynamic situation when prices and business prospects are fluctuating violently.

It is the purpose of the present discussion to analyze the income concept from a purely theoretical point of view and to compare the results of that analysis with income as conventionally measured by accountants. The object of the analysis will be to clarify what happens to income as actually measured in periods of changing prices or changing prospects.

Such an inquiry is necessary because in his quest for certainty the accountant has come to assume certain values as constant which are in fact variable. In particular, the value of the dollar has been regarded as constant and the measure of all other values. No increase in value of any other asset has, in general, been recognized until its credentials are validated by its being "realized", i.e. being exchanged for dollars. Such unquestioning faith in the monetary unit must indeed have been shaken by the great rise of prices in this country during and after World War II. In other countries, where at various times the currencies have declined even more in value, a rejection of the local monetary unit has been common and accounts have been kept in gold or in foreign monetary units—ironically enough, frequently the dollar. In our country, no serious attempt to reject the monetary unit has been made, but numerous suggestions have been directed toward adjusting income computations to take account of changes in the price level.

The procedures of accounting are everywhere permeated by the assumption that the monetary unit is the only reliable measure of value. Once that assumption is thrown into doubt, it is not possible to repair the theoretical structure by some superficial

7

adjustments of dollar values according to changes in price levels. A complete reexamination of the income concept is required, a reexamination that may serve as a guide to the interpretation of figures derived from conventional accounting operations, and possibly as an aid to those accountants who are trying to bring their practices into closer accord with a unified theory of income.

In the present study, the subject will be approached from the viewpoint of economic theory. Parallel studies of the same subject have been made from the viewpoints of the accountant[1] and of the lawyer[2]. One disavowal must be made immediately. Economic science has no single universally accepted body of doctrine that need only be translated into non-technical language in order to tell the layman what "the economist" believes. Different economists believe different things and use different concepts, frequently with the same names. That is the basis of many a great controversy, and the subject of income and capital has been especially rich in controversy among economists. It would accordingly be arrogant for anyone to present "the economist's view of income." What is here presented is, at best, the view of one economist.

Nevertheless, the approach of most economists to the concepts of income and capital differs from that of most accountants in several important respects. The economist is accustomed to thinking of income in real terms while the accountant usually measures income in terms of money. Secondly, the economist usually considers an asset value as measured by the present worth of associated future net receipts, while the accountant has come to value assets largely in terms of historical costs adjusted for that part of original cost already charged to past operations. Finally, and most important of all, the economist regards income as the change in the recipient's entire command over goods and services over a given period. The accountant singles out certain transactions and confines his attention to the profit and loss on these transactions

---

[1]George O. May, *Business Income and Price Levels; An Accounting Study* (New York: Study Group on Business Income, American Institute of Accountants, July 1949).

[2]Arthur H. Dean, *An Inquiry into the Nature of Business Income Under Present Price Levels* (New York: Study Group on Business Income, American Institute of Accountants, February 1949).

rather than measuring the net change in the income recipient's entire command over goods and services. There are, of course, exceptions to these rules, but they do hold in broad measure and so we must expect a difference in income and capital as conceived by the economist and by the accountant respectively.

It is no mere accident that these differences exist. The most perplexing and perhaps insoluble problems in defining and measuring income and capital arise out of the economist's attempt to take account of changes in the values of assets or in the purchasing power of money. So long as the accountant can avoid these problems he can operate with relative confidence in a world of certainties. But to ignore the world's uncertainties does not get rid of them, and to the extent that the real value of money does change and it is necessary to revalue assets, the accountant will be presenting a false and misleading picture. Faced with a choice between precision of operation and precision of concept, the accountant has chosen the former, the economist the latter. That is, the accountant has chosen a concept of income which permits precise measurements but which yields misleading results under conditions of fluctuation and uncertainty. The economist has sought to construct a concept that would stand up under fluctuating conditions but such a concept cannot easily be applied in practice.

If prices did not change, and if the cost of an asset, adjusted for depreciation, should generally be fairly equal to the present value of the associated future stream of receipts, there would be no difference between the economist's and the accountant's concept of income and capital. But when prices do change and when historical costs are out of line with present values of future receipts, there will be divergence between income and capital as measured by the economist and as measured by the accountant. The nature of that divergence and the consequences of the use of one concept rather than the other are the principal objects of the present study.

The study will be complicated by the fact that the economist has bitten off more than he can chew. Those conceptual problems

9

which the accountant, ostrich-like, avoids by digging his head in the sands of monetary measurement and historical costs cannot easily be solved. Perhaps they cannot be solved at all. But something may be gained by considering rather than ignoring them.

The Concept of Income

Income is a familiar notion in everyday life. But as in the case of many other familiar objects, it is not customary for those who use the notion to get down to its fundamentals. For most people, certain simple rules of calculation suffice to guide the measurement of income for all practical purposes, and it is not necessary to inquire further as to what income really is or should be.

Since the widespread practices of income determination are very seldom referred back to a fundamental concept of income it is almost certain that all the practices cannot be consistent with a single basic concept of income. Each man conceives of income as he is accustomed to measure it, and there may be no common concept that governs all practices. We may begin, however, by trying to infer from the general practices of income determination what fundamental ideas are implied, and then, after refinement of these ideas, we may use them as a basis of criticism of the very practices from which they were, in a sense, abstracted.

Two notions in general use may be considered as lying behind the income concept. One is a man's income for a year, the other is a businessman's profit from a particular operation. These two are certainly inter-related. Indeed, we may presume that the second was a stage in the determination of the first. But since the two different basic approaches lead to concepts of income which differ in practical applications, we may consider them separately.

Income for a Year

A man's income for any year is generally recognized to denote roughly the amount which has become available for his expenditures during that year. It may be distinguished from his wealth,

10

which is defined as the total amount available for his expenditure or consumption at any given time. Wealth is a stock of value, income is a flow of value. That part of a man's income that he does not spend, he saves, that is he adds it to his wealth. In general terms, his wealth at the end of any period is equal to his wealth at the beginning of the period plus the difference between his income and his consumption.

These rough notions are suitable for the loose conversation of everyday life, but they are too vague for precise analysis. They do serve, however, to illustrate the essential nature of the income concept. The basic notion involved is that each man desires certain experiences which are afforded him by the use of material objects or by actions performed by himself or by other people. We may call the desired experiences satisfactions. Material objects whose use afford satisfactions are called goods, actions affording satisfactions are called services. If we could measure a man's satisfactions, we might then immediately define his total income for a given year as the amount of satisfactions over which he has gained command during the year. A man may be said to have gained command over satisfactions when he has gained the legal right to receive the goods or services which can afford the satisfactions.

If we call a man's command over satisfactions at a given moment his well-being at that moment, then we can define his total income for a given year as the net amount of well-being over which he has acquired command during that year. The word net is introduced here in order to take account of any element of well-being which has been given in exchange for another element of well-being.

When a man actually enjoys some of the satisfactions at his command, he may be said to consume the good or service which affords the satisfaction. His command over the satisfaction is exercised, and his well-being is then reduced by a corresponding amount. Therefore, the net change in his well-being over any year is his income minus his consumption. We can turn this obvious statement around to get an alternative phrasing for the defi-

11

nition of income; a man's income in any year is equal to his consumption plus the net change in his well-being.

In order to make the picture complete, we might conceivably take account of unpleasurable experiences (dissatisfactions) undergone during the year. In particular, account might be taken of the work the man has had to do to gain the well-being he has acquired during the year. This is not usually done, however, in the determination of income.

There is then an asymmetry in the concept of net income, as between the treatment of the exchange of one good or service for another and the treatment of the exchange of unpleasurable activity for a good or service. Thus if a man sells his car for $1500 and uses the proceeds to take a trip to Europe his income, as usually measured, is unaffected by this transaction. If, however, he sells an extra month's work for $1500 and spends the proceeds on a trip to Europe, then we say that both his income and his consumption are the larger by $1500. The surrender of the motor car must be set against the satisfaction of the trip to Europe. The surrender of a month's leisure is not taken into account. This is a peculiarity of the concept of the income of an individual that does not carry over to the case of a business enterprise.

The foregoing definition of income is advanced to indicate the basic ideas that lie behind the concept of income. This concept may be approached in theory, but cannot be attained in fact because of the impossibility of providing an objective measure of satisfactions and hence of well-being. A second approach might then consist of defining a man's income and well-being not in terms of satisfactions, but in terms of goods and services that afford these satisfactions. The goods and services need not be measured in common units so that a man's income could be thought to consist of the difference between two collections of goods and services. From this point of view, a year's income would equal the collection of goods and services consumed over the year plus the goods owned and the services commanded at the end of the year minus the goods owned and services commanded at the beginning of the year. If the catalog were complete, this

12

definition of income would closely approach the basic concept of income, but it would probably not be useful for any of the purposes for which a measure of income is desired. Those purposes require the measurement of income not as a complex relationship of heterogeneous objects and actions, but as a single measure in a well defined unit.

In order to achieve such a measure, it is necessary to do further violence to the concept of income and to eliminate from our definition those goods, and more particularly those services, which are not usually exchanged for money. Command over the remaining class of goods and services customarily exchanged for money may be called wealth, which is the *economic* component of well-being. A man's wealth may be defined as the aggregate of those goods and services at his command which are "directly capable of a money measure."[3] Because the elements of wealth are capable of a money measure, the aggregate of wealth is also capable of a money measure. It is this fact which, in practical operations, leads us to use wealth rather than well-being as the basis of income measurement.

It is probably obvious to most people that market value is the appropriate measure of well-being associated with each item of wealth in a man's possession. If one man feels that some of his possessions mean more in terms of his well-being than their market value, and others less, he is free to buy more of the first type of goods and sell some of the second type until market values and well-being are matched so far as he is concerned.[4] A man's economic income, as distinguished from his total income, can accordingly be defined as the net increase in the wealth available for his consumption in a given period. An equivalent definition of a man's economic income in a given year is his consumption of wealth over that year plus his wealth at year's end minus his wealth at the end of the previous year.

According to this line of thought, the essence of the income concept is the amount that a man can consume over the income

_____
[3]Alfred Marshall, *Principles of Economics* (7th Ed., London: Macmillan, 1916) p. 57.
[4]For exceptional goods and services it may be possible to buy but not to sell, or vice versa, but these are complications which need not concern us here.

13

period and be as well off at the end of the period as at the beginning. For practical purposes, the phrase "as wealthy" is substituted for the phrase "as well off" and a corresponding change is implicitly made in the concept of consumption. The latter is no longer to be regarded as the sum of all satisfactions enjoyed by the income recipient in the period under consideration but as the value of money-measurable goods and services used up in affording those satisfactions which did arrive from the destruction of wealth in consumption.

The foregoing concepts are highly academic; they are of value mainly to indicate some of the principles involved that will be of aid in discussing practical questions far from the abstract contemplation of the nature of well-being or of wealth. It is important to note that economic income measured in terms of wealth is only a rough approximation to a more fundamental but unmeasurable concept, income in terms of well-being. The most troublesome problems in the measurement of income arise when the measures of wealth we are using can no longer be regarded as sufficiently close approximations to the concept of well-being. In particular, in periods of shifting price levels, the money measure of wealth may be a poor basis for the determination of income.

Once we have limited the income concept to wealth, we need no longer confine our attention to the income of an individual, but we can speak of the income of an asset. Any particular bundle of property of an individual represents a certain amount of his wealth. If further accessions of wealth are connected with his ownership of the asset, we may call such accessions, net of any change in the value of the asset, the income of that asset. A business or a corporation may be regarded as an asset and indeed the growth of the business corporation was probably the major factor leading to a clear distinction between income and capital.[5]

Taking our cue from the definition of income for an individual, we may, as a first approximation, say that the income of any asset is equal to the net accession to the value of the asset over the period considered, including in that accession all receipts

---

[5]See Littleton, A. C., *Accounting Evolution to 1900* (New York: American Institute Pub. Co., 1933), p. 206.

14

attributed to the asset. If we needed the income measure only for the determination of the income of the individual who owns the asset, we could refine the definition by reference to considerations governing the concept of income of the individual. Thus, for example, a change in the value of the asset in exact proportion to a change in the general price level could not be regarded as an accession to the well-being of the individual, and therefore might be excluded from the concept of income.

Since the concept of income of that most important type of asset, the corporation itself, is used for so many purposes other than reporting its income to its stockholders, it may not always be desirable to transfer the rules appropriate to the measurement of an individual's income to the income of a corporation. For example, there may be some purposes for which corporate income is used which would be better served if gains from changes in the general price level are included in income. This question will be investigated in detail below.

Because we are here interested primarily in business income, we can avoid some of the problems in the determination of income of the individual that arise from the personal equation of the individual as a human being. We may define the income of a corporation in a given year as the amount the corporation can distribute to the owners of equity in the corporation and be as well off at the end of the year as at the beginning.

For a corporation to be as well off at the end of the year as at the beginning must mean that the value of the owners' equity at year's end equals the value at the beginning of the year. This is frequently expressed as "maintaining capital intact". It is then immediately apparent that the problem of measuring income is inseparable from the problem of measuring changes in the value of equity or of capital.

From the starting point of the income of an individual for a given year we have approached the income of a business enterprise as the difference between the net worth of its equity at the beginning and end of the period, with any distribution of wealth to equity holders during the year counted into year-end equity.

15

This general type of income concept we may call an equity change concept, so emphasizing the importance of the valuation of assets and liabilities at the beginning and end of the period. Such periodic valuation is necessary in order to find out how well off the equity owner is at the end of the period compared to the beginning and so to determine how much he could consume during the period and still be as well off at the end as at the beginning, in accordance with the basic notion of the income of an individual for a given year.

Profit from an Operation

Another approach to the basic concept of income stems from the analysis of the profit or loss on operations performed during the year. Thus, a merchant might inquire what profit his sales for a given year have brought him. To answer his question he must determine the cost of the goods sold. Once he has done this to his satisfaction, then by deducting the costs from the revenues he can compute his profit from the sales of a given period. Along this analogy, we can then characterize another general type of approach to the determination of income, namely the operating profit approach. That approach, in counter-distinction to the equity change approach, proceeds from a matching of costs against revenues or against products of a specified operation.

We have used sales as a particular example of the sort of transaction which can be used as a strategic point in the conduct of a business at which profit can be measured, but other types of operation might conceivably be chosen. For example, production rather than sales might be the basis of a computation of an operating profit. From the value of the product of the operations performed in a year can be deducted the cost of those operations, and the result will be a profit on goods produced. In that case, inventories of finished goods would be valued at market rather than at cost,[6] and operating profit would be reported on goods produced but not sold.

---

[6]Allowance should, of course, be made for any additional costs that must be incurred in selling the finished goods.

16

The equity change approach is considerably broader than the operating profit approach in that operating profit is merely one, although usually the most important, of the components of the change in equity. That is, the change in equity over any period is the sum of operating profit plus net changes in assets or liabilities not entering into the cost or revenues associated with the operation selected as the point of measurement of operating profit.

Of course the two approaches can coincide but they will do so only under highly special conditions such that no change in equity takes place except through the selected operation. This requires, for example, that no asset held by the firm lost or gained value during the year except to the extent that it entered into costs of operation, or benefited from the product of operations. The importance of distinguishing the two approaches derives from the fact that the actual practice of accountants and businessmen follows fairly closely the operating profit approach in such a way as to get results markedly different from those that would be obtained from the equity change approach if equity were independently revalued annually.

We have accordingly to deal with two broad groups of concepts of income. The one regards income as the net change in equity over the income period. The other regards income, or as we may say to keep it distinct from the first concept, profit, as the difference obtained when certain costs are deducted from revenues or value of production of the period. Our next task is to analyze each of these groups of income concepts in greater detail.

II. Variant Concepts of Income

A simplified example may help to clarify the differences between the two approaches to the income of a corporation as well as to illustrate some of the all too many different concepts of income. The complexity of this highly oversimplified case may serve as an excuse for the unrealistic assumptions made, since greater realism could be achieved only at the cost of overwhelming complications.

The Neverlose Manufacturing Company is engaged in the manufacture of gadgets. At the beginning of 1949, it was expected that throughout all future time the company would be able to manufacture a hundred thousand gadgets a year and sell them for $100,000 at a total cost of $90,000 including all charges,[7] so affording an annual profit of $10,000 indefinitely into the future. The current long term interest rate is at 5%, and so the value of the equity in the company is $200,000, the present value of $10,000 a year indefinitely into the future.

During 1949, however, the company actually manufactured 130,000 gadgets at a total cost of $104,000, or $.80 each, the cost of all material and services being measured as of the time of purchase. Under prices as of the time of manufacture it would have cost $117,000 to produce the 130,000 gadgets actually produced in 1949 for $104,000 historical cost.

In 1949 the company sold 107,500 gadgets at $1.00 each. The cost of goods sold, including all charges, taxes, etc., was $86,000. Under conditions as of time of sale, the goods sold would have cost $96,750.

The company paid dividends of $21,500 on December 31, 1949.

As of January 1, 1950 it is expected that in the future the company will be able to sell 120,000 gadgets a year at $1.00 each and will be able to produce 120,000 gadgets a year at an annual cost of $109,000. Therefore, the year-end value of equity after dividends is the present value at 5% interest of $11,000 a year, or $220,000.

Appraisal of the company's assets and liabilities at beginning and end of year shows an increase of tangible net worth (before dividends were paid) of $25,000 when year-end inventories of finished goods are valued at cost, or $30,000 when finished goods are valued at market.

---

[7]These costs are assumed to have been determined according to accepted accounting practice. They include the items normally charged to "cost of goods sold" plus interest charges, income taxes and other charges normally deducted in the process of obtaining net income after taxes. No charges for revaluation of fixed assets or inventories are assumed entered into "cost of goods sold," except to the extent such factors enter into predetermined allowances for depreciation, obsolescence, bad debts, etc.

The following, then, are some possible measures of the income of the Neverlose Manufacturing Company for 1949.

Equity Change Approach:

1) Mixed Economic Income (comprehensive equity change income) $41,500.

    a) Pure economic income $11,500.
    b) Unexpected gain   30,000.

2) Tangible equity change income

    a) Finished goods valued at cost   25,000.
    b) Finished goods valued at market   30,000.

Operating Profit Approach:

3) Accountant's income, mixed profit on sales,   21,500.

    a) Pure sales profit   10,750.
    b) Price gains to date on items charged to cost of goods sold   10,750.

4) Mixed profit on production   26,000.

    a) Pure production profit   13,000.
    b) Price gains to date on items charged to cost of goods produced   13,000.

Each of these four major types of income, and some of the subtypes have a claim to be considered for the title "The Income" of the corporation. There are many other possible concepts, some of which we mention below, but we must be content to investigate only those listed above, which should give us sufficient variety.

Mixed economic income is the most simple and direct form of the equity change approach to the concept of income. It is simply the change in the corporation's equity over the year. Of course, any dividends which have been paid should be included with the year-end equity. In the case of the Neverlose Co. the year-end net worth is $220,000 after dividends, and $241,500 before dividends. Year-beginning net worth as estimated at January 1, 1949 was $200,000, so that the company's mixed economic income for 1949 is $41,500. This is the amount the corporation might have paid out in dividends (assuming it to be legally permitted) without reducing year-end net worth below what it was believed to have been at the beginning of the year.

But it might be objected that should the Neverlose Company actually pay a dividend of $41,500 it would be worse off thereafter than it was at the beginning of the year. For the beginning of the year, valuation of the equity at $200,000 was too low. From what is known or believed at the end of the year, the beginning-of-the-year equity can be revalued. In fact, it should equal the end-of-the-year equity of $241,500 discounted back to the beginning of the year. That is to say, on December 31, 1949, the company's equity is judged to be worth $241,500. A fair value of the equity on January 1, 1949 would then be such an amount as would equal $241,500 by December 31, 1949, if it earned 5% interest over the year. That value comes to $230,000.

From this point of view, the company's income in 1949 was $241,500 minus $230,000 or $11,500. That amount may be called the pure economic income of the Neverlose Company in 1949. It is the difference between the year-end value of net worth and the year-beginning net worth, both valued according to the knowledge and beliefs current at year's end. Pure economic income is also the amount that could be paid out in dividends this year with the expectation that in future years an equal amount can be paid annually. That is, if this year $11,500 had been paid out in dividends, the remaining $10,000 of the $21,500 actually paid out might have been invested, presumably at 5%, and so would yield $500 per year. This plus the $11,000 expected annually from operations would lead to the expectation of dividend payment potentiality of $11,500 a year.

In paying out a dividend of $21,500, the company has impaired capital relative to the beginning of the year at least from this point of view, for net worth has been reduced from $230,000

20

to $220,000. The fact that net worth was on January 1, 1949, believed to be only $200,000 is argued to be beside the point; the difference between the $230,000 we now believe the equity to have been worth at the beginning of the year and the $200,000 we then believed it to have been worth is merely a correction of an estimate. From this viewpoint, it should not be regarded as income. It may be given a special name of its own, say "unexpected gain."

Given the rate of interest and the equity as valued at beginning and end of year, mixed economic income can always be broken down into pure economic income and unexpected gain. Whether the unexpected gain should, or should not, be counted as income is a controversial question we shall discuss later.

The definition of tangible equity change income is formally quite similar to that of mixed economic income but the concept is markedly different. Tangible equity change income is the change over the year in the value of the corporation's equity exclusive of the capitalized value of its own expected future earning power (going value).[8] In subsequent discussion we shall use the term "going value" to denote the difference between the capitalized value of the future dividend payments and the tangible equity however measured. That is, once someone has specified a measure of tangible equity, we can find the corresponding going value as the difference between the capitalized value of future dividends and the specified tangible equity.

The fact that future prospects of the Neverlose Company have improved over the year 1949 is not taken into account in the measurement of tangible equity change income unless the changes in prospects are reflected in the valuation of physical assets. This concept of income thus requires some method of appraising the value of the corporation's assets other than by future earning power. Market values are the most likely basis

---

[8]In order to preserve the subsequent discussion from undue complications, intangible assets other than going value are ignored. The expression "tangible assets" or "tangible equity", unless qualified to the contrary, will in subsequent discussion refer to assets or equity exclusive of going value. Going value is here defined as simply the difference between the tangible equity of the corporation and the capitalized value of its future disbursements to owners.

for the appraisal of some of the assets, but more mystical bases are used for others.

However little theoretical justification there may be for excluding intangible asset changes while including tangible asset changes, the practical reasons for doing so are very powerful. Accountants and business men would be surprised and shocked to find a business carrying an increase of going value to income account. We shall later consider how well founded such an attitude is. At present, we may note merely that tangible equity change income can be computed in a manner that is conceptually simple. It is merely necessary to appraise the tangible equity at the beginning and end of the year, and take the difference. The result, plus any dividends paid out during the year, is tangible equity change income.

Since there are many different ways of appraising assets, there are many different ways of estimating tangible equity change income. Of these many ways, two have been entered in the table above. The first, 2a, includes finished goods valued at cost. The second, 2b, includes finished goods valued at market prices minus expected selling cost. The difference between these two concepts is very similar to the difference between profit from sales and profit from production to be considered below.

Accountant's income is the income that would conventionally be reported for the corporation for most purposes. It is the profit gained on this year's sales, computed as $21,500 by deducting from the proceeds of this year's sales, $107,500, the total cost of goods sold including all charges, $86,000. Any item of cost that entered goods sold was valued at the price paid for it at the time of acquisition of the item by the company. Had costs been based on the prices of raw materials and other cost items as of the time of sale, the cost of goods sold would have been $96,750.

The accountant's income can accordingly be broken down into two components, pure sales profit and price gain respectively. Pure sales profit is the difference between sales revenue and cost of goods sold when both costs and revenue are valued at prices prevailing at time of sales. The difference between sales profit as usually measured (mixed sales profit) and pure sales profit is the element of price gain contained in mixed sales profit. That price gain is equal to the difference between the value of the items of cost charged to sales at prices ruling at time of sale and the corresponding value at prices ruling at the times of acquisition of the various items of cost.

In brief, accounting income, here identified with mixed profit from sales, is composed of the difference between sales revenue and cost at the time of sale plus the profit or loss from the changes of the value of cost items between time of acquisition and time of sale.

The concept of mixed production profit is formally similar to accountant's income except that it is applied to production rather than to sales. Certain specified actions performed by people connected with the business enterprise may be designated as production. Usually the actions so designated are considered the principal business of the enterprise. Just as it is possible with some degree of arbitrariness to assign all costs incurred by an enterprise to the sales of various time periods, it is also possible to assign all costs to the production of various time periods. Then the mixed production profit of any time period, say a year, will equal the value of the year's production minus the costs assigned to the year's production.

For the Neverlose Manufacturing Company mixed production profit for 1949 may be computed as $26,000, the difference between $130,000, the value of goods produced, and $104,000, the total cost of that production. Just as mixed sales profit can be broken down into pure sales profit and price gain, so can mixed production profit be broken down into pure production profit and price gain on cost items charged to production. Pure production profit, $13,000, is the difference between the value of goods produced, $130,000, and the total cost of goods produced at current prices, $117,000. The price gain component of mixed profit on production, $13,000, is the difference between the current value of the cost of production, $117,000, and the actual historical cost of production, $104,000.

If each year's entire production were sold in the same year, we should expect mixed profit from sales (accountant's income) and mixed profit from production to be equal. Similarly, pure profits from sales would equal pure profits on production, and the price gain components would also be equal. Differences arise to the extent that sales in a given year may be based partly on the production of other years, and the product of this year's operations may be sold partly in this year and partly in other years.

All these different measures of income are measures of money income. To each there corresponds a measure of real income which takes account of the fact that the value of the dollar has changed in purchasing power as between the beginning and the end of the year, and as between time of acquisition of cost items and time of use or sale. It is not necessary to investigate in detail the manner in which the money income measures can be adjusted to obtain real income measures. But it would not, in general, be appropriate to try to convert any of the money measures into real measures merely by dividing by the price level. For each measure is the difference between two money quantities. To get the corresponding real measure each of the two money quantities must first be converted into real quantities by dividing by the appropriate price level, and then the difference may be taken. To take the money difference first and then to deflate by the price level produces a misleading result.

The operating profit approach to income is more narrowly limited than the equity change approach in that equity can change either as a result of operations or for other reasons. But that does not necessarily imply a superiority of the equity change approach over the operating profit approach. For some purposes the equity change methods may include more than is desired. Similarly for some methods the pure operating profits may be more useful than the mixed operating profits which include price gains. No one of these concepts can be proclaimed as the *true* concept of income. Each has certain advantages and disadvantages. Furthermore even the advantages and disadvantages cannot be clearly identified because that which is good for one purpose may be bad for another. We want to use a measure of income for several different purposes, and it should not surprise us to learn that a measure which is good for one purpose is not good for another.

III. Income Under Conditions of Certainty

Of all the variant concepts of income mentioned above, that which we call economic[9] is the one most immediately related to the notion of income as the amount that the recipient can consume and remain as well off at the end of the period as he was at the beginning. For the corporation, equity is the appropriate measure of well being. Mixed economic income is the amount that can be paid in dividends while keeping the value of equity intact. But other concepts of income satisfy the same condition, at least formally, provided equity is defined and valued appropriately. Thus, if equity is valued on the basis of original cost, accountant's income will also correspond to the basic notion of income. Some question may be raised, however, as to how good a measure of well being is equity based on original cost. In any case, the essential feature of economic income is to be found in the way in which equity is valued under that concept. The basic tenet of economic income is that equity is an asset of its owner, and it should therefore be valued according to the principles applied to other assets.

The Value of an Asset

The value of any object can usually be explained in terms of supply and demand, an explanation which is useful only to the extent that we can actually describe the operation of the factors which govern supply and demand. Supply, at least of reproducible objects, is governed by the cost of production, or more fundamentally, by the circumstances influencing those costs. Demand for an object is governed by different factors depending on whether the object is desired for consumption or for procuring

---

[9]In the previous section a distinction is made between pure economic income and mixed economic income. That distinction is appropriate only under conditions of uncertainty. In the present section, in which uncertainty is assumed away, we need refer only to economic income.

25

other objects. Demand for consumption goods is governed by consumer preference backed up by purchasing power. But, in the case of capital assets, as we may call those assets held not for consumption but for eventual use in procuring other assets, the demand is governed by what the assets are expected to procure in the future.

The very nature of capital assets involves an evaluation of future receipts. Such an evaluation is complicated by three serious difficulties. First, and most important, the future receipts are not known, but can only be estimated. Secondly, a dollar in the future is not worth a dollar today even if the purchasing power should remain constant; this is reflected in the phenomenon of interest. Finally, the purchasing power of money does not remain constant. It is from these three circumstances that the interesting and important problems in the measurement of economic income and the corresponding concept of capital arise. We may first make some simplifying assumptions that will permit us to see how the value of capital may be measured when these difficulties do not plague us.

Let us assume that the future receipts associated with the asset are known with certainty, that we have a set of rules for determining the present value of a sum of money to be received at any specified future date, and that the general price level remains constant. Then it is quite easy to measure the value of the asset. It is the sum of the present value of the future receipts.

For brevity, we may call that very important set of rules which we use to convert future payments into present values "the rate of interest." It must be recognized, however, that we are dealing with a whole set of rates of interest, one for each possible time span. The way in which the structure of interest rates is determined is very complicated and remains highly controversial. Fortunately, we need not concern ourselves with that problem. We may take the rate structure as given, determined by market forces. Then, to measure the value of any asset, we need merely capitalize its future receipts; that is, find the sum of the present values of those future receipts.

The Value of Equity

The simple and obvious method of valuing owner's equity in a corporation would seem to be to take the difference between the aggregate value of the corporation's assets minus the corporation's liabilities. If this were done in the conventional manner, the result would be inappropriate for our present purposes since there would be no guarantee that owner's equity as so measured would equal the present value of future payments to ownership. The conventional measurement of balance sheet items does not aim toward that end. That is why a corporation's income cannot appropriately be measured by the changes entered on the balance sheet.

Even though we could measure the value of almost all the assets and liabilities of the corporation independently of the value of the corporation as a whole, that would not help us in the determination of the net worth of the equity of the corporation. For the corporation has a going concern value different from the sum of the values of its assets that can be independently measured. This difference can itself be expressed as an asset called "going value" but that asset cannot be measured independently of the total value of the corporation as an entity. So if we substitute a value of equity obtained by addition of independently valued assets and deduction of liabilities, then we are mis-stating equity from the economist's point of view. This is recognized every day by businessmen and investors who ignore book values in valuing a corporation but look to future receipts.

Only if an appropriate value is entered for going value can owner's equity be measured from the balance sheet in accord with the economic concept of the value of that equity as an asset of the owner. To enter any increase of going value as a part of income would shock most accountants, yet the going value is the one asset which most clearly embodies the economist's concept of asset value since the going value asset is most clearly capitalized earning power.

From the economist's point of view, the owner's equity in a corporation may be valued like any other asset as the present value of the stream of future receipts. There are many possibilities open to the management of a corporation of varying purchases and sales and operations. To each possibility there can be associated certain time patterns of disbursements to the owners of equity throughout the future. Each of these time patterns may be considered to stretch forward endlessly, though from some particular time onward in each pattern, receipts and disbursements may be steadily zero.

It is at least in theory the job of corporate management to choose those policies with which there is associated that time pattern of disbursements to present stockholders which has a greater present value than of any of the other possible time patterns. This maximum present value is the value of the equity. To calculate that value we should need to know not only all the possible time patterns of disbursements but also the rates of interest that should be used in converting a disbursement to the owners of equity at any future date into present value. Of course, if management does not act so as to maximize present value, the value of equity will be the present value of the disbursements that will in fact be made.

Some readers may feel that this concept leaves out certain vital elements. It may be argued, for example, that not only disbursements but what is left in the corporation must be taken into account. That argument is false. For whatever is left in the corporation must either some day result in a disbursement to ownership or else it should not be counted in equity, for the present value of a dollar now invested which will never be paid back is zero. Only if a definite length of time is taken and broken off at some future date, say five years from now, must we take account of what is left in the corporation. For then the value of equity must be defined as the present value of disbursements over that five years plus the present value of equity five years hence. But the value of equity five years hence must depend on the future disbursements as of five years hence and forever after.

A definition which requires knowledge of all future circumstances is obviously of little practical use. It is presented here for conceptual clarification only. It is interesting to note that most of the concepts of accounting are not required for this definition. Neither costs nor revenues, assets or liabilities as such, or depreciation, are mentioned. All that is needed to determine the present value of equity is the present value of future disbursements to ownership. If this were actually known, however, and future rates of interest were known, the future income of the corporation would also be known for all time to come as would the equity of the corporation at all future dates.

Is Our Definition Circular?

It may be objected that we have now involved ourselves in a circular definition. Income has been defined as the amount that can be disposed of in a given year while leaving the corporation as well off at the end of the year as at the beginning. Income so defined has been declared equivalent to the net change in value of owner's equity over the year. But owner's equity is from the owner's point of view an asset and it must be valued in terms of future receipts like any other asset. If those receipts were themselves income, we would be engaged in formulating a circular definition. But fortunately for our purposes the receipts need not be income but can be a mixture of income and return (or reinvestment) of principal. The objection of circularity is based on a confusion of receipts with income. In order perfectly to measure this year's income we do need to know all future receipts, we do not need to know all future incomes. The latter can be computed from the former, if the rates of interest are known. The process is better described as: given all future receipts and rates of interest to calculate present and future income.

Thus, suppose we are valuing the equity of a very simple corporation whose net dividends are expected to be $103.00 next year, $106.09 two years from now, and $109.27 three years from now with no further dividends thereafter.

If the appropriate rate of interest is 3%, the present value of each of these annual installments is $100 and the present value of the equity is $300. This can be computed directly from the scheduled receipts without distinguishing income from return of principal. Capital can be measured from the anticipated inflow of receipts and then the measure of capital so obtained can be used in the determination of income. Therefore there is no circularity in our definition of income.

Pure Economic Income

In the above example, at the end of the first year the owner of the asset can expect $106.09 one year later and $109.27 two years later. It may easily be computed that the asset is then worth $206 which in addition to the $103 cash just received makes $309. So by our definition income of that year is just $9 or 3% of the $300 value of the asset at the beginning of the year. Income is $9.00, $6.18 and $3.18 in the first, second and third years respectively.

It is no coincidence that the income so determined shows a yield on the value of the asset just equal to the rate of interest. The process of calculating the present value of an asset consists of breaking down a stream of receipts into two parts, income and return (or investment) of principal, in such a way that income in any period will represent a yield on principal still invested just equal to the rate of interest. It is always possible to do this by a simple mathematical procedure and so there is no circularity in our definition of income.

But this same reasoning then implies that unless there is a change in the interest rate, income from a given amount of capital will remain constant so long as that capital remains intact. Therefore, we may now formulate a rather odd definition of income which is equivalent to that previously formulated. This year's income is the amount that can be disposed of in the year with the expectation that an equal amount can be disposed of indefinitely in the future so long as the rate of interest remains unchanged.

30

Ideally defined then, if a firm did not reinvest earnings, its income would be constant except for changes in the rate of interest.

Similarly, the income of an individual if properly measured, must, under the assumed conditions of certainty and stability of interest rates, be constant over his lifetime except to the extent that he consumes or builds up capital.

A conclusion so contrary to the practice of income determination deserves further study. In the conventional measurement of a person's income, no account is taken of the capital value of the person's earning power. Suppose a man receives $10,000 salary this year, but can expect to receive only $5,000 a year henceforth into the future. Is it then appropriate to say that the man's income this year is $10,000 or something less? This question can be translated into the question of whether if the man spends $10,000 this year, he will be as well off at the end of the year as at the beginning. The answer of the conventional accountant would be, "Yes, he can spend the $10,000 he receives and he need not cut into his capital at all." The answer of economic theory is "No." The prospect of receiving $10,000 this year is part of the man's capital. His income is an amount such that, if consumed this year, the prospect remains of consuming an equal amount in the future. Let us suppose that for $4,500 the man can purchase an annuity of $500 for the rest of his life, excluding the current year. Then the income of this and each subsequent year may be calculated at $5,500. The $10,000 he received this year should be considered as $5,500 income and $4,500 return of capital. If the $4,500 return of capital is reinvested in the annuity, it will increase his annual income by $500 a year. If it is consumed, then he is consuming the capital represented by the capitalized value of his future earning power as of the beginning of the year.

The contrary conclusion of conventional accounting shows that it is not customary for individuals to use the economic concept of income but rather a tangible equity change concept or an operating profit concept.

31

It makes little practical sense to apply the economic concept to a man, since as a general rule, no one is interested in changes in the capitalized value of a man's earning power. The contrary is true in the case of a business enterprise, however. A corporation that earns $10,000 this year and $5,000 in all subsequent years (according to conventional accounting) can quite appropriately be said to have had income of less than $10,000 this year. Suppose there are a thousand shares of common stock in the corporation, these constituting the entire issued stock. Suppose that each year the corporation pays dividends equal to earnings as reported by the accountant. Then a share of stock will receive $10 this year and $5 per year in each subsequent year. Given a 5% rate of interest and perfect certainty as to the future, such a share would be worth about $105 at the beginning of this year and $100 ex-dividend at the end of the year so that the net income from the share will be the $10 dividend minus the $5 decline in capital value or about $5 this year, and the income will continue to be $5 a year in successive years.

We might of course say that the income from the share was $10 but that there was also a $5 capital loss when the market value declined from $105 to $100. But this merely raises the question to be discussed later of whether a capital gain or loss should be treated as income. It would certainly seem that if the owner of a share of the stock is intent on preserving his capital intact he should consider only $5 of the $10 received as income available for consumption.

The economic concept of income then does make sense in the case of a business enterprise because in that case a great deal of importance attaches to the capitalized value of future receipts. The fact that accountants do not measure economic income but something closer to operating profit is one of the important points of departure of the accountant's concept of income from that of the economic theorist.

As a matter of fact, when economists get into the actual business of measuring income as in the measurement of national income, they follow the practice of businessmen and accountants

32

rather than the dictates of economic theory. Measures of national income are certainly not based on the economic income concept as here defined. In large part this is necessary because the national income estimate must be built up from private income reported by businesses and individuals. These are based on a concept much closer to tangible income than to economic income. But more fundamentally it is doubtful that economists want to measure national income on a capitalized basis which would mean that each year's income as currently reported would be adjusted for changes in the present value of future incomes. As will be indicated below, the economic income concept tends to gloss over the particular causes of variation of receipts from year to year that are sometimes the principal object of interest in income measurement.

We may briefly summarize the nature of economic income under conditions of certainty of future receipts, interest rates and constant prices.

Given a specified stream of future receipts and a set of interest rates, it is always possible to compute for each period:

1) The income of the period, and

2) A receipt or payment on account of capital, such that:

a) The period's receipts equal income plus the receipt on account of capital or minus the payment on account of capital,

b) The receipt on account of capital is equal in amount to the change in the capitalized value of future receipts over the period, but is of opposite sign,

c) The income of the period is equal to the receipt of the period plus the change of capitalized value of future receipts over the period,

d) The income of the period is equal to the capitalized value of future receipts at the end of the previous period, times the rate of interest.

33

Income so defined is equal to economic income.

We may illustrate the difference between an accountant's and an economist's concept of income under conditions of certainty by a simple example. Suppose it is known that, according to the best rules of accounting, a certain corporation's future profits will be zero and $10,250 in alternate years forever into the future. Assume that dividends are accordingly paid of $10,250 on December 31 of every second year and no dividend paid in the intermediate year.

If the appropriate rate of interest were 5% an economist would disagree with the accountant and say that the income was $5,000 and $5,250 in alternate years rather than zero and $10,250, as reported by the accountant. Furthermore, if equity of the corporation was originally acquired for $100,000, the accountant would presumably continue to carry it at a value of $100,000 since all profits earned are paid out in dividends. The economist, however, would say that on January 1 of alternate years the corporation was worth $100,000 and $105,000 respectively. If the owner were thinking of selling, he would be well advised to go by the economist's rather than the accountant's valuation. For at the end of the year of zero receipts, the owner of the corporation according to the accountant has an asset that will pay off $10,250 at the end of the year and will be worth $100,000 after the payment. To sell such an equity for $100,000 when interest is at 5% would indeed be foolish.

If the asset under consideration were an annuity, not a corporation, however, the accountant would come around to the economist's point of view. What explains this remarkable double standard of action? The accountant will agree with the economist in valuing the annuity for in that case the accountant is willing to grant the assumption of knowledge of the future. But in measuring the income of a corporation, the accountant is not willing to act as if the future were known and for very good reasons.

To those accustomed to the accountant's concept of income, the idea that variations in a corporation's income from year to year

34

represent errors of measurement may come as a shock. One year's income of a corporation is frequently compared with another's as a gauge of the skill and success of management. This comparison lacks justification from the viewpoint of economic income. How then does the accounting concept of income differ from the economic concept in such a way that variations in income regarded as normal from the accountant's point of view must be considered errors of measurement from the point of view of the economist?

The accountant's basic concept of income is similar to the economist's. A year's income is the amount of wealth that could be distributed to the owners of equity over the year and still leave equity at year's end equal to equity at year-beginning. But this basic concept lies so far behind the accountant's operations that it is frequently lost from sight. More immediately there is substituted another concept of income which is equivalent to the economic concept only under highly special circumstances. Instead of basing income on the difference in the value of assets, accountants usually base it on matching costs and revenues.

It would be possible so to define costs and revenues as to insure that the difference between the two would equal economic income as defined above. If, for example, revenues were defined as any increase in assets (or decline of liabilities) and cost as any decline in assets (or increase in liabilities), then the difference between revenues and cost would be the net change in equity provided going value is included among the assets annually revalued.

But accountants do not try to keep accurate account of all changes in the value of assets and liabilities. Only those increases of assets which are specially secure are counted as revenues; and costs are counted, not as actual changes in the value of assets, but as methods of matching certain past or future payments to particular sales receipts. In both cost and revenues, primary emphasis is given to money payments. Gains are frequently not recognized as such until they are realized, that is converted for however short a period into money. Costs too, are

35

usually based on the money exchanged for the asset, but here exceptions are sometimes made as in valuing inventories at the lower of cost or market.

The principal difference between the accountant's and the economist's approach to income then is the accountant's refusal to take account of certain changes of value of the assets held by the corporation as they accrue. Only some of the gains and losses accrued, not realized, are recognized by the accountant. On the other hand, the economic definition of income requires that all accrued gains and losses be recognized, even gains and losses of going concern value. The result is principally a difference in timing, for eventually accrued gains and losses will be realized as the relevant assets are disposed of either through direct sale or through use in the production of goods and services which are eventually sold. Over the long run, therefore, the two measures will tend to yield the same results, but over short and intermediate periods there will be considerable differences. Even in the long run, however, so long as the business is not sold, increases of going value will not enter into accountant's income.

In the following discussion, it is frequently desirable to contrast an economist's definition of income with that of an accountant. This contrast is, at times, fairly complicated, and it would be unduly so if a complex set of accounting rules were to be reviewed at each step. Accordingly a strict historical cost concept of income will be used as representative of the accountant's point of view. This is, of course, a caricature of accountancy. In actual practice revaluation of assets by market value and other modifications of historical cost methods may enter into accounting practice. But, for simplicity, such modifications will in general be ignored.

Income based on historical costs, or more briefly, historical income, might be computed as follows. The value of all assets except cash at beginning and end of year can be measured by the cost of their acquisition in cash or its equivalent minus such portion of that cost as has already been charged to cost of goods sold. The value of cash is its face value. Liabilities can be measured or estimated directly from the books of the company. Equity can be computed as the difference between assets and liabilities. The change in equity so measured from year beginning to year end represents historical income, or as we shall call it, "accounting income."

An alternative method, and that usually used, is to start with revenues. In the simplest case revenues may be the proceeds of sales. Costs can be matched to these revenues according to established rules in such manner that all costs incurred can be assigned to those periods deemed most appropriate. Accountant's income for any period is the revenue of that period minus the costs assigned to that period.

Of course, in actual practice, great problems arise under this method as to how much of the costs incurred in the past, or expected in the future, is to be charged to this year's operations. But these problems, the traditional problems of accounting, do not concern us in this investigation. We need merely know that this method does provide some formula for assigning all costs to operations of particular periods. Such a method will be contrasted with the economic concept. In applying that concept we need not try to measure costs and revenues at all but we must compare equity at year beginning with that of year end in terms of future receipts rather than past expenditures. Roughly speaking, the historical cost method values an asset (except cash) at what it cost to acquire it minus that part of past cost that has already been charged to operations; the method of economic theory values an asset at the present value of what it can expect to receive in the future. The two methods would be equivalent only if the cost of an asset not yet charged to operations should always just equal the present value of its future receipts.

Accountants seldom attempt to charge to the costs or receipts of any year changes in going value. This follows first from the general accounting practice of charging a change in an asset's value to revenue or cost only as it is disposed of by use or by sale. In rare cases, usually when it has been purchased for cash or equivalent, good will or going value may be charged off as a cost

37

in annual installments. But never is a year to year variation in the value of good will or going value permitted to enter a sound income account. This means that accountant's income approaches tangible income rather than economic income as defined above.

Accountant's income then differs from economic income in two important respects: it excludes gain or loss on going value and it excludes gain or loss on those tangible assets not entering directly or indirectly into the current year's sales.[10] Tangible equity change income (or more briefly tangible income) accordingly lies half way between economic income and accountant's income. Like accountant's income, it excludes gain or loss on good will and going value, but unlike accountant's income, tangible income includes gain or loss on tangible assets accrued but not realized through the period. Differences among the three concepts can then be expressed in the following relationships.

Under conditions of certainty:

Economic income = change over the period in capitalized value of dividends of this and future periods.

Tangible income = economic income − change in value of good will over the period, = total change in the value of tangible equity.

Accountant's income = tangible income − change in value of tangible assets not realized in this period, + changes of value of tangible assets accrued in other periods and realized in this period = proceeds of all assets sold − costs assigned to these assets.

The choice between the economic concept and the accountant's concept of income must depend principally on whether or not it is appropriate to include going value change in income and whether it is better to count gains and losses as accrued or as realized.

---

[10]On this point accounting practice is far from uniform. Some revaluations are occasionally carried to surplus, sometimes through earnings, sometimes directly (See George D. Bailey, "Concepts of Income," *Harvard Business Review*, Vol. XXVI, No. 6, Nov. 1948). In any case it is not accountants' practice to revalue assets annually in conjunction with the determination of the year's income.

There may be some question how going value can change under conditions of certainty. There is a good deal of merit in the question since uncertainty is one of the most important factors leading to changes in going value. But even under certainty, going value can vary as it is, in a manner of speaking, realized. We may illustrate by a simple example.

Consider a corporation with tangible equity valued at $100,000, and with dividend payments expected with certainty of $10,250 at the end of the current year and $5,000 a year thereafter. Given a 5% interest rate, the present value of equity in this corporation is $105,000 and going value is therefore $5,000. After this year's dividends of $10,250 are paid, the capitalized value of future receipts will be $100,000. If the value of tangible equity is maintained at $100,000, then going value has been reduced to zero. Economic income for the first year is $5,250. The other $5,000 received in dividends is only a repayment of that part of the capital represented by going value. The tangible and the accountant's income in this case would be $10,250. We may then say the difference between the accountant's income and the economic income in this case is that economic income takes account of the $5,000 decline in going value while the accountant's and tangible income ignore this decline.

Since the treatment of going value is one of the most important respects in which accountant's income differs from economic income, it is necessary to go into considerable detail in investigating why it is included in one and excluded from the other. It is particularly important to find out whether the exclusion by the accountant is based on principle or on practicality. For if based only on practicality then we would have to carry the reservation that in interpreting the accountant's measurement of income, we must make allowance for the degree to which that measure departs from what it should be in principle. In short we must find out whether economic income is an ideal from which accountant's income differs only to the degree that the ideal is practically unobtainable, or whether accountants would not want to measure economic income even if they could do so.

It is easier to say why the economist includes the net change of going value in income than why the accountant excludes it. The economist's concept of the value of any asset is based on capitalized earning power, and that is in particular true of the equity in a corporation. To say this does not of course answer the question but just pushes it one step further back, from the income statement to the balance sheet. Why does the economist in valuing equity insist on measuring capitalized value of its future receipts? Why can he not accept a tangible measure of value? The economist's reply is that such a measure of value is unacceptable because it simply isn't what the equity is worth. The owner would be foolish to sell the equity for its tangible value if the capitalized value of future earnings were higher. A purchaser would be foolish to buy at tangible value if capitalized future earnings were lower. After all, an object's value is supposed to represent what the object is worth.

The accountants grant that the capitalized earning power is the only proper basis for valuing equity for purchase or sale and the courts apparently have also come to accept this view. If then it is universally agreed that the proper basis for valuing equity when buying or selling it is capitalized earning power, that must also be the proper basis for maintaining equity intact. If accountants use a different basis they must, in measuring what they call income of a corporation, be interested in something else than in determining the amount to be distributed as dividends while preserving equity intact.

Fortunately, the accountants can speak for themselves in this controversy. In the *Accountants' Handbook*[11] are set out the arguments supporting the "General Accounting Rule" which implies the exclusion of going value from accountant's income except for the amortization of intangible value actually acquired at cost.

---

[11]W. A. Paton, ed., *Accountants' Handbook* (3rd ed.; New York: Ronald, 1947) p. 841.

"Goodwill and other intangibles should not be recognized except where they are supported by costs actually incurred, in terms of transactions between essentially independent parties, and then only to the extent of the cash or equivalent cost. Intangible value so recognized should never be appreciated, but should be amortized as circumstances indicate."

We may examine in detail the supporting arguments adopted in part from Yang, *Good Will and Other Intangibles.*

"1. It is the *function of accounting* to show as assets the costs incurred in acquiring plant and other necessary elements (adjusted to allow for the effect of operation and passage of time) and to show as income, when realized, the earning power, in the particular setting, of such assets. To set up the capitalized value of an estimated element in earning power is inconsistent with this general function and tends to obscure the actual situation, from the standpoint of the owners of the particular enterprise, rather than to clarify it. On the other hand, where a special investment is made by the present owners in estimated future earnings, as in the purchase of goodwill, it becomes entirely consistent with the purposes of accounting to recognize such investment as an intangible asset, an asset on which, in the case of a perpetual earning power, the special element in earnings, as it materializes, is a return, or which, in the case of a terminable earning power, is recovered or liquidated through the realization of such earnings.

"2. While it is recognized that the validity of the book values of typical tangible assets, particularly specialized fixed assets, depends in considerable degree upon the presence of *earning power,* most of the tangible assets have some market value apart from their use in the business, whereas the intangibles have as a rule no economic significance except in terms of the going concern as a whole. Further, the tangible assets are in general more determinate in amount, stable in value, and realizable than the intangibles. These considerations make the general measurement and accounting recognition of intangibles, where not specifically purchased, impracticable.

41

"3. Recognition of nonpurchased intangibles is unnecessary from the standpoint of *managerial purposes*. Aside from the question of the sale of the enterprise as a whole, there is no question of managerial policy to be affected by such recognition. Setting up estimated intangibles does not affect cost of production in the strict sense, creates no basis for a shift from one method or policy to another, bears no relation to general planning and budgeting. In this connection, it is worth noting, the case for the recognition of appreciation of fixed tangible assets is much stronger than the case for the recognition of intangibles.

"4. Since the value of intangibles is merely an expression of differential earning power, such value, if recognized, would require *continuous adjustment* up and down, as earning power fluctuated over a period of years. Further, the fluctuating surplus created by capitalization of estimated differential earning power would in no sense be true surplus and might constitute a misleading and improper figure in the balance sheet.

"5. Earning power should in general be expressed in terms of *return on investment* or cost values, not such values plus the capitalized value of an estimated element in earning power itself. For example, to capitalize *proprietary skill* and efficiency, often a factor in building up goodwill, is illogical and confusing from the standpoint of the owners, as it means the placing of objective costs and implicit elements which are validated commercially only by the appearance of superior earning power itself, in the same category. Hence the capitalization of intangibles, without purchase, tends to create an improper relationship between balance sheet and periodic income report.

"6. *Rational comparisons* between enterprises, far from being promoted by a general attempt to set up estimated intangibles as assets, would be rendered more difficult. Carried to a logical extreme it would mean that in a particular field no concern would show a rate of return on asset values in excess of the normal or representative rate—which would be an absurd situation. In other words, it would create, artificially, a dead level of earning

42

rates in the particular industry below which individual concerns might fall but above which it would be impossible for any enterprise to appear. Likewise comparisons between periods in a single enterprise would be made less satisfactory by such a process of capitalization.

"7. Capitalization of an intangible, aside from purchase, assumes that it is possible to impute the effect of an element of earning power to one or more intangible factors. In view of the composite nature of business income such an *imputation*, in the absence of the commercial test of actual cost incurred, is sheer hypothesis. Further, setting up a reservoir of intangible value to express the difference between capitalized estimated earning power and the conventional book values of other assets, as has sometimes been advocated, involves the unwarranted assumption that the book values of such other assets, as factors in income determination, are correctly stated.

"8. Adoption of a policy of estimating and recording intangible values from period to period would not only obscure important relationships and run counter to the essential purposes and functions of accounting, but it would tend to encourage juggling and misrepresentation and would result in balance-sheet totals little if any more significant and stable than those which might be obtained by the continuous introduction into the statements of capitalized values as shown by the market for outstanding securities."[12]

Let us examine these arguments point by point:

"1. It is the *function of accounting* to show as assets the costs incurred in acquiring plant and other necessary elements ... and to show as income, when realized, the earning power, in the particular setting of such assets. To set up the capitalized value of an estimated element in earning power is inconsistent with this general function. ..."

Whether or not it is the function of accounting to show as assets the (adjusted) costs incurred in acquiring necessary assets

---

[12]*Accountants' Handbook,* pp. 841-843.

43

is itself an open question which can hardly be used as the basis for settlement of the matter at issue. Whether the accountant should, in the balance sheet, carry assets at adjusted cost rather than at economic value is by no means clearly settled in principle in favor of cost. There may be strong *practical* considerations in favor of the use of cost, but this establishes no *principle* that it is the function of accounting so to do. Are there then independent reasons for carrying assets at adjusted costs so strong that they can be extended to require exclusion of going concern value from the balance sheet (except as acquired by incurring costs) and changes therein from the determination of income?

This question sends us back in the *Accountants' Handbook* to the discussion of the "Case for Adherence to Cost" "as the basis of accounting." There it is stated as a paraphrase of Paton and Littleton, *Introduction to Corporate Accounting Standards:*

"Recognition of inadequacy of recorded cost (or cost less accrued depreciation) as a continuous expression of market value should not lead to conclusion that accounting based on cost is unsound and should be replaced by an accounting for values. The primary purpose of accounting is the measurement of periodic income by means of a systematic matching of costs and revenues. Substitution of estimated current market values for recorded cost factors on the way to assignment to revenue would constitute a radical change in the standard scheme of income determination; periodic net income would then include the effect of all write-ups and write-downs of cost factors involved.

"There seem to be no convincing reasons for the assumption that accounting would more adequately meet the needs of the parties concerned if estimated replacement costs or other evidences of current values were regularly substituted for recorded dollar costs. Costs are objectively determined data; current values are largely matters of opinion and for some types of cost factors are very unreliable. Hence a shift from costs to estimated values would generally mean the presentation of less dependable income figures. Such a shift, moreover, would result in income reports less satisfactory from the legal point of view—a

44

matter of importance in connection with income-tax determination, dividend policy, security retirements, etc."[13]

The defensive tone of this argument hardly seems consistent with the contention that "it is the function of accounting" to use the cost basis and therefore going concern value should be excluded. It seems from this argument rather that current values would in principle be preferable to cost as the basis for accounting, but that practical reasons militate against this improvement in principle. These practical reasons are that there would be a change in the scheme of income determination, a subjective element would be introduced, and the results would be less satisfactory from the legal point of view. These are certainly arguments of expediency, not of principle.

More fundamental is the contention that "there seem to be no convincing reasons for the assumption that accounting would more adequately meet the needs of the parties concerned if estimated replacement costs or other evidences of current values were regularly substituted for recorded dollar costs." This last statement furnishes the key to the whole problem. For it implies that whether costs or current values are to be used as the basis of accounting depends on which serves best the purposes for which a measurement of income is required. That makes the question of whether or not income should include change of going concern value anterior to the consideration of whether to use cost or current value as the basis. Clearly if the primary function is to determine income, we must first agree on the nature of income. Then we can decide whether a cost or current value basis is the more appropriate. The accountant's first argument against inclusion of going concern value puts the cart before the horse. We must decide directly from the basis of the use to which the income concept is to be put whether or not income should be based on going concern value. The use of cost by accountants cannot be appealed to as an argument for the exclusion of going concern value as that use of cost is itself dependent on the question at issue.

---

[13]*Accountants' Handbook,* pp. 805-806.

"To set up the capitalized value of an estimated element in earning power is inconsistent with this general function and tends to obscure the actual situation, from the standpoint of the owners of the particular enterprise, rather than to clarify it."[14]

The economist would merely reply that this statement is the opposite of the truth where capitalized value can reasonably be estimated. The actual situation is clarified by showing the value of the concern's equity and not by omitting an important part of it. The only possibility of obscuring the situation lies in the practical difficulty of estimating future earnings. This may be granted, but it does not affect the theoretical question here involved.

The argument in paragraph 2 on page 41 may be granted as one of practicality, which may be compelling to the accountant's practice but does not affect the question of principle. In any case the argument is rather trivial because the considerations mentioned, that tangible assets have determinable values and that they have value apart from their earning power in the business, are irrelevant to the determination of income for this business. This is shown by the fact that accountants avoid using the values which the tangible assets have for purposes outside the business and carry them at another conventional figure, their adjusted costs. The argument that tangible assets do have some outside value which is objective but irrelevant to the determination of income for purposes of the corporation hardly serves to dismiss the use of going concern value from the determination of income.

"3. Recognition of nonpurchased intangibles is unnecessary from the standpoint of *managerial purposes.*"

This statement may be challenged. Capitalized present value of the concern is not only a consideration for management, it is *the* consideration. An extreme but vivid example may serve to illustrate the point. Suppose the manager of a billion dollar corporation knew that by undertaking a certain deal he could add a million dollars to his tangible equity, i. e., to his profits for

---

[14]*Accountants' Handbook,* p. 841.

this year as measured by the accountant; but the corporation would then have to go out of business. He would certainly be justified in setting the prospective loss of going value against the prospective gain of tangible value. More precisely, it is management's duty to weigh any opportunity to increase tangible assets against any possible adverse effect on earning power. The usual statement that it is the duty of management to maximize profits is true of economic income but not of accounting income. Management must consider the effect of any action on future as well as present profits. That is exactly what is meant by being long sighted. But the future profits are precisely the content of going concern value. A dollar's worth of tangible assets is neither more nor less valuable than a dollar's worth of going concern value.

The case for recognition of appreciation of fixed assets mentioned later in paragraph 3, page 42, is not stronger than that for capitalized earning power. For if capitalized earning power is recognized, it is not only unnecessary to recognize changes in tangible fixed assets, but it is unnecessary to recognize explicitly even revenues from sales or costs of those sales.

That is, it is not necessary to match costs against revenues at all. Merely measure dividend distribution this year and the change in the capitalized value of future distributions. It is true that proceeds of sales and costs are relevant to the estimation of what dividends can in fact be paid this year and in the future, but this is a basic task of business management. In forming such estimates they are well advised to depart from the results of accountants' operations.

"4. . . . the value of intangibles . . . if recognized, would require continuous adjustment . . . the fluctuating surplus created . . . would in no sense be true surplus . . ."

The adjustment required would be of two sorts. One would be the result of changes of expectations of future earnings. This sort of adjustment will be considered in detail later when we come to discuss income under uncertainty. But, under certainty, the only adjustment required in the capitalized value of future receipts (or dividends) is the difference between this year's

47

receipts and this year's income. It is true that in measuring going concern value an adjustment is necessary for the difference between change in the capitalized value of future receipts and the change in tangible assets.

That either of these adjustments is required is not a defect of the concept of going concern value. The concept is useful precisely because it introduces the corresponding adjustments into income. The fluctuating surplus resulting would, the economist argues, be the only true surplus and the accountant's is the false one. For the economist's surplus represents the difference between the admittedly true present value of the equity and the stated capital. The accountant's figure for surplus is the difference between a conventionalized book value of equity and stated capital. That book value is out of touch with any value that we would be well advised to call the true value of equity. The adjustments are accordingly desirable although perhaps impractical.

"5. Earning power should in general be expressed in terms of *return on investment . . .*"

Why should earning power be expressed in terms of return on investment? It would seem most useful for most purposes to express earning power in terms of present value of future receipts. What the historical investment has been is a matter of antiquarian interest except in utility rate cases where the historical interest may be carried to the point of valuing an asset at the time it was first devoted to public service. It is, of course, not necessary and possibly not desirable to capitalize particular factors believed to explain good will or going concern value. It is necessary merely to capitalize the future dividend distribution of the corporation as a whole, not the earning power of particular factors tangible or intangible. As shown above, income can then be calculated directly as the current year's dividends plus or minus the change in capitalized value of future dividends as between beginning and end of the year.

48

"6. *Rational comparisons* between enterprises . . . would be rendered more difficult."

Far from being more difficult, rational comparisons among enterprises would have more significance on a capitalized earning basis than on historical cost book value. For to compare two enterprises, it is sufficient for almost all purposes to know the present value of the future earnings of each. It is true that it would be circular to compute rates of return on capitalized earnings—the result would be the number you first started with, namely the rate of interest used for capitalization. But by the same token, there is no need to compute a rate of return at all, for capitalized value gives you the same information.

If it is desired to compare the success which different corporations have had in making the most of their investment, then the ratio of present value of equity to capital funds invested is quite as good as (and equivalent to) the return on capital funds invested.

The dead level of earning rate on capitalized value would indeed be created, and if the going concern value were permitted to be negative, where that is appropriate, individual firms would neither fall below nor rise above that level. That just means that the rate of return would lose significance if the denominator is to be capitalized earnings. Taitel has found that there is sufficient revaluation of book values in actual practice to rob the rate of return on book value of any validity for long term comparisons of success in exploiting investments.[15] He was forced to make large adjustments to book value in order to estimate actual investment.

It is true that, under conditions of certainty, comparison of the income of different periods would lose interest if equity were valued as capitalized earnings. For then income would be constant from year to year except as the value of investment in the business, or the rate of interest, changed over time. But under conditions of uncertainty comparisons between periods would be

---

[15]Martin Taitel, *Profits, Productive Activities and New Investment,* Monograph No. 12, U. S. Congress, T. N. E. C., [Washington] 1941, Chapter III.

equally significant when equity is based on capitalized expected earnings as when equity is based on historical cost. However, a different concept of economic income, to be discussed in the next chapter under the name of variable income, would be appropriate for such year to year comparisons.

"7. Capitalization of an intangible . . . assumes that it is possible to impute the effect of an element of earning power to one or more intangible factors."

In capitalizing future dividends no imputation of earning power to particular factors is necessary, nor is it even necessary to value the tangible assets at all. If, by any process whatsoever, the accountant does value the tangible assets, then the economist can, conceptually at least, keep the picture straight by computing going concern value as the difference between the value of equity (capitalized dividends) and tangible equity as measured by the accountant. The assumption that the book values of assets other than going concern value are correctly stated as factors in income determination is indeed unwarranted, nor is it involved in the use of going value. It is more accurate to say that the use of going value is motivated precisely by the fact that book values do not represent factors of income determination, so a residual item is thrown in to make the sum total of assets correct even though the individual elements are not correctly valued on the basis of their earning capacity.

"8. Adoption of a policy of estimating and recording intangible values from period to period would not only obscure important relationships and run counter to the essential purposes and functions of accounting, but it would tend to encourage juggling and misrepresentation. . . ."

The argument that use of intangible values would obscure important relationships and violate the fundamental purpose of accounting has been answered under points 1 and 6 above. The encouraging of juggling and misrepresentation is a practical difficulty which we need not evaluate here since we are interested in whether there is justification in principle for elimination of

50

intangibles or whether that is based solely on practical considerations. The significance of introducing intangibles has been amply discussed above. The instability has been discussed in point 4. The example of marketable securities raises the question of great variability of capitalized earning power under uncertainty which we will discuss later.

A fallacious argument frequently levelled against the inclusion of changes in the capitalized value of future earnings as income is that to do so is double counting. It is time, the argument runs, to count the future receipts when they are received, but they should not be counted twice. Hatfield argues, for example, as summarized in the *Accountants' Handbook:* "An orchard of trees as it increases in growth from year to year undoubtedly becomes more valuable, but it is more valuable primarily because the larger trees yield a larger supply of fruit. The increasing yield is a cause of larger income. It in itself constitutes the larger income and this income can be distributed or divided or conserved by the owner. The increased value of the orchard as such is a reflection of this increased income but practically it is the crop income which is available as dividends and not the increased value of the orchard. . . . Indeed to consider both the increased receipts and the capitalization of the receipts as available for dividends to a certain extent is giving double recognition to a single factor."[16]

This argument is an exact parallel to that advanced against the alleged double taxation of savings. If income is taxed and $100 is earned and reinvested to earn $5 a year, not only will the original $100 be taxed, but the $5 a year will also be taxed so there will be a double tax on savings. This argument ignores the fact that the $5 annual interest is additional to the $100 and not just a repayment of the $100. It would indeed be unfair to tax as income all of a fifteen year annuity of $10 a year purchased for $100. Part of each year's receipts would then be return of principal. But in the case of a perpetual bond the purchaser was $100 better off for originally earning the $100. He is in addition $5 a year better off for investing the $100 rather than having consumed

---

[16]*Accountants' Handbook,* p. 122.

it when earned. Any time that he wants to sell his bond for $100 he can do so, consume $100 worth of goods as well as having consumed $5 worth annually paid for from the interest payments during the time he held the security. The point is that the annual income is additional to the increase of the capital value rather than a repetition of it.

On the other hand, it is argued that the man in the year he received the $100 net of taxes has a choice of consuming $100 worth of goods immediately or contracting to receive $5 a year indefinitely, which would permit a consumption of $5 a year indefinitely. Since the interest rate is assumed to be 5%, these two choices represent equivalent value. Yet if he chooses the $5 a year he will subsequently have to pay taxes which he will not have to pay if he chooses to spend the $100 immediately. In this sense then, the taxation of savings is a double taxation. One of two otherwise equivalent choices is burdened by taxation while the other is not.

Similarly, in this sense there is some double counting in the concept of income but this double counting is not peculiar to a case of change in the capitalized value, but is characteristic of all income. That is, it might be argued that in purchasing a perpetual bond paying $5 a year a man exchanges $100 right now for its equivalent value—$5 a year in perpetuity. There is accordingly no accession to his wealth as he receives the $5 annually, and the $5 should no more be considered income than should a suit of clothes bought and paid for in one period and delivered in the following period. The $5 a year has similarly been bought and paid for in a previous period and represents nothing more than payment for value received. Adoption of this point of view would destroy the income concept completely. Any set of receipts over time that we should be tempted to call income can be capitalized to a certain value at an arbitrarily chosen initial period, and then can be regarded as deliveries over time of the value of the stream of receipts in the initial period. Consequently all income payments could come to be regarded as a sort of return of capital, it being understood that the equivalent value of sums of money at two different times is to take into account the rate of interest.

Suppose, for example, that we accept the doctrine that the purchaser of the perpetual bond of $5 annually should not count the annual $5 payments as income, but should count them as repayment of capital. If he is to maintain his capital intact he would have to reinvest his annual payments, and so the current money value of his capital would grow at 5% a year. As a result of the adoption of this concept of income, we should be forced to conclude that in order to maintain capital intact it must grow at the going rate of interest per year! This would destroy the phenomenon of income completely.

In Hatfield's example, suppose that an orchard acquired at a cost of $1,000 will just meet expenses for the first year and thereafter can be expected to yield $52.50 per year over expenses forever into the future. Hatfield implies that the income available for dividends should be zero the first year. Given a 5% rate of interest the orchard is worth $1,050 at the end of the first year. Hatfield would deny that the $50 increase in capitalized value of the orchard's earnings should be considered as available for dividends. Actually, we are here arguing that the $50 should be considered as income retained in the business. Theoretically a small part of the orchard might have been sold for $50 and the proceeds might have been distributed as dividends. The remainder of the orchard would presumably yield $50 a year thereafter. Or $50 could be borrowed in perpetual loan at 5% interest so that $50 could be paid as dividends in this and all succeeding years. If no dividends are paid the first year, it is not double counting to say that income the first year was $50 which was reinvested in the business. Income in subsequent years was $52.50 or $2.50 more than if that $50 first year's income had not been reinvested in the business.

Our conclusion must be that no valid principle has been advanced to warrant the exclusion of going value from the determination of income. One possible exception is the argument that inclusion of going concern value obscures comparisons

53

between periods. The only fundamental question remaining then is: do we want an income concept that shows changes in our wealth from period to period or one that measures how much the events of a particular period contributed to our wealth? The difference will be discussed below as the difference between economic income and sales or production profit, which is here called activity profit.

Accrued Versus Realized Gains and Losses

Implicit in the historical cost approach to income is the refusal to recognize any gains other than realized gains. For if unrealized but accrued gains were recognized, the corresponding asset would no longer be carried at cost of acquisition but rather at value at the time of revaluation. However the structure of assets is transformed, no profit is deemed to arise under the accountant's income concept until an asset is exchanged for cash. That is, every asset except cash is assumed to be worth what the corporation gave for it. Cash on the other hand has a face value. So the cash asset has the unique characteristic of not being valued by historical cost, i.e. by the value of the asset that was given for it, and so profit can creep in only in a transaction in which an asset is exchanged for more cash than the cost of the asset.

The refusal to recognize a gain until it has been realized reveals the accountant's prejudice in favor of cash over other assets. The economist argues that a man is better off as of the moment when his asset gains in value and not as of the moment it happens to be sold. The accountant might grant the validity of the economist's point. But an accrued but unrealized gain is uncertain and cannot be objectively measured. An appraisal must be made and different appraisers might give different appraisals. It seems best therefore to wait until the asset is sold before taking account of any income from its appreciation. If the asset is not sold directly, but is used in the productive operations of the corporation, the gain will be realized as part of the difference between the asset's cost and the proceeds of the sale of the object in which it was embodied.

54

Economists count gains when accrued, accountants usually count gains when realized by sale of the asset on which the gain has been made. However, accountants are frequently, if not always, willing to accrue costs and losses in agreement with economists. This difference in the treatment of gains and losses is exemplified in the widespread practice of valuing inventories at cost or market whichever is lower. Under this system, decline of inventory values is immediately charged against income, increase of inventory value is counted only at the time of sale of the appreciated item or the product in which it is embodied. This dual standard indicates that the treatment of accruals is not dictated by the conceptual nature of income but rather by practical considerations summed up in the term "conservatism." Conservatism in accounting consists principally of counting gains only when realized but anticipating costs and losses as soon as possible. But conservatism is rarely carried so far as to charge declines in value of fixed assets (other than those associated with depreciation and obsolescence) to current income. That is, there is no standard treatment of fixed assets similar to the "lower of cost or market" treatment of inventories.

In spite of the conspicuous exception in the case of inventories, we may say that in general accountants do operate on a realized gain basis. "Among accountants the rule that 'profit belongs to the period of sale' is almost axiomatic."[17]

Why do economists insist upon accrual and accountants on realization? Once more we may ask if the difference is one of principle or practicality. Economists' insistence on accrual stems from the fundamental idea of income as a difference between wealth at two different times. If a corporation has more valuable assets at the end of the period than at the beginning this is an increase in wealth whether a sale has taken place or not. The accountant may reply he cannot be sure the gain has been made until the sale has taken place. "Making of the sale furnishes objective evidence of the profit. That is, after the sale has been effected, the profit no longer depends merely on the opinion of

---

[17] *Accountants' Handbook*, p. 111.

the proprietor; it is manifested by an enforceable contract."[18] Furthermore, "The sale is generally considered to be the most decisive and *significant event* in the chain of transactions and conditions making up the stream of business activity."[19]

There are then two principal arguments for the accountants' practice of counting income realized rather than as accrued. The first, that sale affords an objective measure, is an argument of convenience. This argument would be consistent with the view that in principle income is earned as accrued, but in practice it is more convenient to measure it as realized, otherwise we must depend on the proprietor's opinion rather than on the judgment of the market. The objective nature of sale as contrasted with the subjective estimation of accruals constitutes a *practical* argument for the use of realized rather than accrued profits.

The second argument, that sales are the most significant events in the operation of an enterprise may have greater theoretical weight. For if sales do represent the major difficulty facing an enterprise, so that an item produced but unsold cannot, in view of the uncertainty of sale, be valued at anything over the cost of production, then there would seem to be strong arguments for waiting until the sale is made to count the profit. But then there is probably some error in carrying the product at cost, for if sold at prevailing prices, there will be a profit, but if unsaleable, there will be a loss.

Of course, the economist does not argue that the product should be carried at sale price. From the point of view of economic income, there is no need to value individual assets whatsoever. Only the change in the total equity need be valued and that depends only on current and future dividend payments.

If in fact the sale is a critical stage in achieving a profit from the operations of an enterprise, it would seem appropriate to recognize this in the process of accruing value to the product. Part of the difference between cost and selling price can be accrued during the period of production and another part in the

---

[18]Hatfield as paraphrased in *Accountants' Handbook*, p. 111.
[19]*Accountants' Handbook*, p. 111.

period of sale. In practice, however, this would be very difficult, and it is doubtful whether any useful end would be served thereby. It is much more convenient to confine the profit to the period of sale. This argument applies to ordinary operating profit, but not to gain in value of assets held in the business.

Although the accountant's use of realized rather than accrued gain is based principally on convenience, there is some justification in principle to the extent that sales are the main limitations on profits. But the application of the realization criterion is far broader than could be covered by this justification. We must conclude that the realization rule is based principally on the tenet that only money gains should be counted, a tenet itself based on the accountant's search for objectivity.

Fluctuating Versus Stable Income

Although the accountant's departures from the economic concept of income are motivated principally by practical considerations, they are so basic as to constitute a different type of income concept. This is vividly illustrated by the frequently stated requirement that a measure of income should be useful in comparing one year's operation with another's. Such a requirement is clearly antithetical to the concept of economic income, which starting from a fluctuating set of receipts breaks them down into a relatively stable stream of income and a fluctuating sequence of payments on account of capital.

A year to year comparison of the success of a company's operations under conditions of certainty requires a measure of operating profit rather than of economic income. Because the phrase "operating profit" has a meaning for accountants somewhat different from what we mean by it, I shall reluctantly abandon that phrase and use instead the phrase "activity profit."

Activity profit is the difference between the value of the results of certain specified operations performed over the year and the costs of those operations. It may be contrasted with economic income which is the net increase of the value of the owners' equity in the corporation over the period other than that arising from

57

additional investment by the owners. The economic income concept is attached to the given year in that it deals with differences between beginning and end of the year. The activity income concept is attached to the year only in that the transactions selected for inclusion are those that reached a specified stage during the year. The transaction as a whole may contain other stages which were reached either in the same or in other years.

Economic income is then related to comparison of assets at two different times, activity profit to the matching of revenue or output on the one hand with cost on the other. The basic idea of economic income is how much better off has the corporation become over the period. The basic idea of activity profit is how much better off is the corporation for having performed certain activities which are somehow associated with the period.

The accountants' rejection of going value as an element of income is consistent with the concept of activity profit but inconsistent with the very essence of the economic concept of income. For, having eliminated going value, the accountants no longer measure changes in the value of equity, if the latter is to be defined as the present value of future dividend payments. The accountants' use of time of realization as the criterion of the period to which a gain is to be assigned implies that sale rather than some other operation is to be the critical activity for the measurement of activity profit. That is, the adoption of the realization rule implies that accountants' income will be the same as profits from sales. The relative merits of sales profits as against economic income as *the* income concept can be judged only on the basis of what need the concept must satisfy. We may postpone consideration of that fundamental question however until after we have considered these measures of income under conditions of uncertainty. It suffices for the present to point out that a concept of income which serves as a measure of the success of a particular year's operations as compared with other years is, under conditions of certainty, inconsistent with the definition of income as a net change in equity over the period. For, under conditions of certainty, net change in wealth over the period will not fluctuate at all but will always be equal to interest on equity at the beginning of the period. Under conditions of uncertainty, however, it may be possible to bring the two concepts closer together.

IV. Income Under Uncertainty

Objectivity Versus Relevance

So far we have assumed stable price levels and interest rates, and perfect certainty as to future receipts. Let us drop the assumption of perfect certainty. This makes no difference for accounting income; that concept does not depend on future receipts but only past costs and current sales. It is true that in estimating certain costs, such as depreciation, obsolescence, amortization of deferred charges, etc. accountants do have to make some judgments of the future, but this is done on a rule of thumb basis rather than as a genuine prediction. The error introduced into accountant's income by basing depreciation on a necessarily fallible estimate of the useful life of the equipment will be infinitesimal compared to the error introduced into economic income by the uncertainty of future receipts.

The very basis of economic income is the present value of future receipts. Since these are uncertain, economic income is uncertain. In practice, equity must be valued as the capitalization not of the future dividends that will actually be distributed but of *expected* future dividends. But whose expectations are to be used? Each person in valuing equity must, of course, use his own expectations so that the valuation process becomes subjective, a condition abhorrent to accountants.

The non-objective character of economic income under conditions of uncertainty is not alone sufficient basis for its rejection in favor of some more objective standard. For the fact is that future receipts although unknown are the most important measure of the value of an asset, and so the most appropriate basis for the determination of income. Original cost is advocated as a substitute method of valuation largely because original cost

59

can be objectively measured. In so far as it is objective it is an objective measure of the wrong thing.

When any decision has to be made on the basis of a corporation's income, it will always be wiser for the decision maker to base his judgment on the best estimate of economic income he can make, however subjective that judgment may be, rather than to rely on the perfectly objective measure of income based on historical cost, which is irrelevant except as an approximation to economic income or as a subject for idle curiosity. It is better to act on the subjective evaluation of the relevant factors than on a perfectly objective measure of irrelevant factors. An example was given above of the folly of acting so as to increase accountant's income when economic income is decreased. For a reduction of economic income means a reduction of wealth and it is foolish to try to increase operating profit if in so doing one reduces one's wealth.

Changes of Expectations

The non-objective character of income based on expectations is, however, only the beginning of the difficulties we meet in applying economic income to conditions of uncertainty. Since future prospects are uncertain, we may from time to time change our expectations. Each such change implies a change in our valuation of equity, the capitalized value of expected dividend payments. Economic income has been defined under conditions of economic certainty as the change in equity over the period. Is it appropriate to include in income a change of equity resulting from a change in expectations?

The economic concept of income so far developed can give no answer to this question. That concept is based on the criterion of being as well off at the end of a period as at the beginning. We are now facing the problem that arises when at the end of the period we have changed our opinion as to how well off we were at the beginning of the period. Under such circumstances which valuation shall we use, that of the end of the period, that of the beginning of the period, or some mixture of the two?

60

If, as in the example of the Neverlose Manufacturing Co. mentioned above, expectations change so that an owner's equity valued at $200,000 at the beginning of the year is valued at $241,500 at the end of the year, should we say that the owners are $41,500 better off at year's end, or that they just didn't know how well off they were at the beginning of the year?

One point of view was mentioned above, according to which only $11,500 of the $41,500 should be considered income. This figure was obtained by subtracting from the year-end value of the equity of the Neverlose Co. the hindsight value of the equity at year-beginning. The hindsight value of equity at year-beginning is calculated by discounting the year-end value of equity back to the beginning of the year. Income computed as the difference between equity at year-end and hindsight value at year-beginning may be called pure economic income. It equals the current rate of interest on hindsight value of beginning of year equity.

The difference between the hindsight value of year-beginning equity and year-beginning equity as valued at the beginning of the year may be termed "unexpected gain." We must choose between the alternates of considering unexpected gain as an actual increase in wealth or as a mere revision of an estimate of wealth. As an actual increase of wealth, it should be included in economic income, as a revision of an estimate, it should be excluded.

The first viewpoint is based on the assumption that a man is as well off as he thinks he is, and not as well off as someone with superior knowledge either now or later may know him to be. If he owns a plot of agricultural land originally believed to be worth $1,000, which upon the discovery of oil beneath it is then believed to be worth $100,000, he is according to this view $99,000 wealthier for the discovery of the oil. This $99,000 could accordingly be spent for consumption leaving him with $1,000 or just as well off as he considered himself at the beginning of the period. Therefore, the $99,000 unexpected gain is income.

The second view is that the land was really worth about $100,000 at the beginning of the year; the owner simply did not know

61

it. Upon discovering the oil, the owner should merely revise his estimate but should not regard the revision as available for consumption. Should he consume any of the value of the land, say $10,000 worth, then he will be worse off at the end of the year than at the beginning of the year by that amount, for at the beginning of the year, he held an asset actually worth $100,000 whatever he may have thought it was worth. Now, if he holds an asset worth only $90,000 he has consumed $10,000 of his capital. Because a man has changed his mind as to what his capital is worth does not justify his consuming that part of the capital.

We obviously cannot use the definition of economic income to settle this argument since the difference concerns the meaning of a phrase in that definition. The two views disagree on what is meant by "as well off at the end of the period as at the beginning" under conditions of uncertainty. The issue must be deferred until we examine in detail the purposes for which an income measure is needed. Then we may consider which of the two points of view serve those needs best.

For the present then, we may merely distinguish pure income and unexpected gain as two components of what we must now call mixed economic income.

The Concept of Variable Income

There is one possible approach to economic income under uncertainty which comes a great deal closer to accountant's income than does pure economic income. We may introduce this approach by some rather bizarre examples.

Suppose that in a certain country where the long term interest rate is 5% the government has issued a perpetual bond sold for $100 with the following arrangement. Each year a coin is tossed. If heads appear the bondholder is paid $10; if tails appear no payment is made for that year.

Under this arrangement the income will be variable without affecting the principal. So long as the interest rate remains unchanged at 5%, the bond should be worth $100 on January 1 of each year. Consequently, whatever is received as payment each

62

year can be counted as income even though an equal amount cannot be expected in each future year. This example certainly comes closer to the actual facts of business than does the assumption of perfect knowledge of the future.

In any case, it would be highly inappropriate to say that such an asset each year earns income equal to interest on the capital value. It has an expectation of such income, but the expectation will sometimes be exceeded and sometimes disappointed.

There is some question of whether in a year in which $10 is paid, part of that $10 might not be considered unexpected gain. In general, unexpected gain arises whenever an asset is found to be more valuable than it was previously valued. In a year in which $10 is paid, the bond will have been found at year's end to have been worth at the beginning of the year about $5 more than it had been valued at that time. But the bond was at the beginning of the year truly valued because there was then only half a chance of getting the $10.

Now, suppose, that another sort of security is on sale in our mythical country. Like the first bond this pays either $10 or nothing at the end of each year, depending on the toss of a coin. But it is good only for twenty years from issue. In this case the security declines in value each year so that the net income of each year is either $10 or zero minus the appropriate deduction for loss of value of the asset.[20] This arrangement begins to look more like an asset as assets really exist.

Finally, consider another arrangement which yields each year a payment which may be anything over a fairly wide range depending on some game of chance. Any particular part of that range may be deemed to have a certain probability, but these probabilities are not well known and can only be roughly estimated. If it is not believed that the probability distribution of payments varies from year to year, the payment actually made in any particular year may be considered income for that year. The applica-

---

[20]That appropriate deduction varies from year to year. In the nth year it is equal to $\$5/(1.05)^{21-n}$ on the assumption that the interest rate is 5%.

63

tion of these considerations to business income may be illustrated by yet another example.

Suppose, in a period of stable prices, a retailer sells only one type of product, say candy at $1.00 a box. He buys the candy for $.75 a box, rents a store for $1,000 a year and pays a clerk a salary of $4,000. He has no other expenses. He averages $40,000 sales a year with considerable fluctuations from year to year.

The accountant would report his income as varying according to sales volume so that when he sold $60,000 worth of candy, his income would be $10,000. When he sold $20,000 worth, his income would be zero. Can we not reformulate our economic definition of income so as to agree with the accountant at least in this simple case and still not sacrifice our basic economic principles? This can be done in line with the procedure followed with respect to the perpetual bond whose payments depended on the toss of a coin.

We may say that this candy dealer has an expectation of sales of $40,000 a year, and therefore of $5,000 net receipts per year. Here we may define net receipts as the difference between aggregate receipts and aggregate costs paid out. Furthermore, we may add that this expectation is not altered by the experience of any particular year. If the interest rate is 5%, his business is worth $100,000 year in, year out. In any year in which he sells $60,000 worth of candy and has net receipts of $10,000, he is well justified in counting that $10,000 as income even though in subsequent years he can expect net receipts of only $5,000 annually. For at the beginning of the year he had an asset worth $100,000. At the end of the year he still has an asset worth $100,000 plus $10,000 cash from his net receipts.

Once we have abandoned the fiction of certainty of future receipts, it no longer seems reasonable to impute hindsight values to beginning of year's equity as is done in computation of pure economic income. Yet if this is not done an inconsistency apparently arises. For given an asset worth $100,000 at the end of the year just after the owner has received $10,000 as this year's dividend, while the interest rate is 5%, it seems inconsistent to

64

say that the asset was worth only $100,000 at the beginning of the year. Surely, it now seems one would have been well advised to pay more for it at that time. But at that time, this year's receipts as well as the value of the asset ex-dividend at the end of the period were uncertain. In view of the uncertainty, it may be maintained, $100,000 was indeed the correct value of the asset as measured by the then present value of expected future receipts.

The existence of uncertainty, therefore, opens the way to variable income in that it breaks down the rigid relationship between the beginning of period value of equity and end of period value of equity, plus receipts. Once we regard each year's net receipts as a quantity subject to chance variation then we are justified also in regarding each year's income as subject to chance fluctuation.

The concept of income which is suggested by this line of thought may be called "variable income." It is equal to the expected income of the period, plus or minus the amount by which the actual receipts exceed the expected receipts.

In most practical cases, no particular receipts are expected but rather any value in a whole range may be expected with a different probability for each part of that range. It is accordingly appropriate to define variable income not in terms of *expected* income and receipts but in terms of *expectation* of income and receipts. Such an expectation is the average of the various possible values expected, each weighted by its probability. When, as is usually the case, these probabilities are not formulated exactly, the expectation may however be formulated directly on the basis of the owner's or investor's judgment. An investor may judge that a certain corporation has the expectation of earning net receipts of $100,000 a year even though the investor would not wish to estimate whether this expectation was made up of an even chance of $200,000 or nothing or of $150,000 and $50,000.

Thus, in the case of the perpetual bond paying $10 on heads, zero on tails, the receipt expectation is $5 a year and the income expectation is also $5 a year. If in a particular year $10 is received, then the excess $5 is also counted as income. Similarly, in the case of the candy merchant there is an expectation of annual net receipts of $5,000 and an expectation of annual income of $5,000.

It may appear from these examples that variable income is always equal to net receipts and that the matter is unduly complicated by the use of two concepts instead of one. Consider however the security mentioned above that pays either zero or $10 a year for twenty years, depending each year on the toss of a coin, and after the twentieth year the arrangement terminates. Its expectation of receipts each year is $5. But its expectation of income is somewhat less because the security loses value from year to year. At issue, the security is worth $62.70 assuming an interest rate of 5%. One year later it is worth $60.42, and two years later $58.34. If in the first year heads appear and the second year tails, then variable income for the two years is $8.12 and —$2.08 (loss) respectively. That is, expected income in the two years was $3.12 and $2.92 respectively and the expectation of receipts was $5 each year. Actual receipts exceeded expectation by $5 the first year and fell short by $5 the second year.

It is unfortunate that the concept of variable income depends so heavily on expectations. The reason for this dependence is the necessity of getting beforehand an appropriate adjustment to receipts as they appear. The objection to considering these receipts as income is that they may be related to some change in value of the asset itself. If, for example, a large receipt for this year reduces the value of the asset, it is inappropriate to consider the receipt entirely as income; part of the receipt must be regarded as repayment of principal. If now we conceive of the receipts as fluctuating according to chance circumstances or to skill of management and we wish to include these chance fluctuations in income, we must have some method of distinguishing between that part of the receipt which is the result of the chance fluctuation that does not affect capital value and that part which is associated with change in capital value.

The solution to this problem embodied in the concept of variable income is that an adjustment factor for a period is selected at the beginning of the period. Then however net receipts of the period fluctuate, variable income will be the difference between the net receipts and the predetermined adjustment. *This procedure is justified if, and only if, a larger than average receipt in one period is not at the expense of a receipt of a later period.*

If part of the receipt for this year is at the expense of a reduced receipt of a future period, it is appropriate to count into income only the difference between what is gained this year and the discounted value of what is sacrificed from the expectation for future years.

We may now redefine variable income as the net receipt from any asset over any period, plus or minus a predetermined adjustment factor, provided full account is taken of the effect of the present period's receipts on the receipts of future periods. The predetermined adjustment factor is the difference between the value of the asset at the beginning of the period and its expected value at the end of the period ex-dividend on the basis of the expectations current at the beginning of the period.

Variable Income and Unexpected Gain

Changes of expectation introduce serious difficulties into the concept of variable income. Provided we can distinguish a given period's receipts from the main body of the asset, we can separate variable income from a concept of unexpected gain correlative to variable income.

Suppose a perpetual bond that pays either $10 or nothing depending on the toss of a coin, in a particular year is, at the close of the year, voluntarily modified by the issuer so that in the future it will pay $12 or nothing depending on the toss of a coin. If the interest rate is 5%, the value of the bond has been increased from $100 to $120. If in this year heads appear, the variable income of the bond is $10 and the corresponding unexpected gain is $20.

Or suppose this year that the candy merchant mentioned above improves his position in the market so that in the future he expects to average $44,000 sales per year and so net $6,000 a year over costs instead of $5,000. If this year the sales were $50,000 worth of candy netting $7,500 over cost, he may say that his variable income was $7,500 and his unexpected gain (given an interest rate of 5%) $20,000. The latter is the difference between the $100,000 value of the business when it was expected to have annual net receipts of $5,000, and the $120,000 value when it is expected to have annual net receipts of $6,000 a year.

The sum of variable income and the correlative concept of unexpected gain is equal to the total change in the value of the equity from the beginning to the end of the period, including in the end of the period equity any disbursement to ownership over the period. But this total is exactly the same as mixed economic income, which in turn is the sum of pure income and pure unexpected gain. So the difference in the two concepts, pure income and variable income, can be explained in terms of the sort of unexpected gain that is eliminated from mixed economic income. If from mixed economic income is subtracted the unexpected gain as measured by comparing beginning of period value of equity with hindsight value, then pure economic income is the remainder. If from the same total is subtracted unexpected gain computed as the difference between the value of the main body of the asset at the end of the period and what that value was expected to be as of the beginning of the period, the remainder is variable income.

If in any period, receipts match expectations and expectations of future receipts do not change, then in that period variable income, pure income and mixed economic income will all be identical. The principal difference between variable and pure income is that any excess of the current period's receipt over expectations are included in variable income, but excluded from pure income.

We have now achieved a concept of income which satisfies the economic definition and yet reflects the year to year variation in the skill or luck which has attended the firm's operations. For variable income is the amount the corporation can distribute in dividends and be as well off at the end of the year as at the beginning. The predetermined adjustment is designed to make

68

this true. Yet variable income will fluctuate from year to year with the fluctuation of the firm's net receipts.

The principal difficulty in applying the variable income concept to a corporation is in the separation of this year's receipts from the main body of the asset and from the unexpected gain. This difficulty can appear even in the case of a share of stock where it may be seen more easily. Suppose a share of stock is purchased at the beginning of the year for $100 in the expectation that it will pay a $5 dividend and be worth $100 at the end of the year. The latter valuation is based on the expectation of a $5 annual dividend indefinitely into the future. Suppose the stock actually pays $3 this year but rises to $103 on the expectation of a $5.15 dividend indefinitely into the future. (We assume a 5% rate of interest.) It would be inappropriate to say that variable income was $3 and unexpected gain $3 if the fact that the dividend was $3.00 and not $6.00 was the reason for the increase in future receipts. How then shall we draw the line between variable income and unexpected gain? The answer must be that only by a consideration of expectations can we measure unexpected gain. We do not have any objective measure of expectations that will permit us to separate the appreciation of an asset that is the result of forbearing to distribute income from the appreciation that is the result of a favorable change of expectations. If we were willing to deal with mixed economic income, we could escape this dilemma, but if for certain purposes, we require an income concept that is free of unexpected gain, then we are in for trouble with expectations.

Measurement of Variable Income in Practice

Up to now we have talked of assets as if they were simple securities with the main body of the asset distinct from the receipts therefrom. But in a business enterprise, there is no clear line of distinction between the main body of the asset and the receipt. For the calculation of pure income, there is no need to make this distinction. The value of the asset can be taken as the capitalized value of expected future dividend payments and

69

dividend payments can be used as the relevant receipts. Then the interest rate can be used to separate income from return of capital and pure income from unexpected gain. For the computation of variable income, this procedure is obviously inappropriate. To make a year's income of a corporation depend on the dividend the directors decide to pay is clearly ridiculous.

It is most difficult to say what the receipts of a corporation are in any period as distinct from changes in its capitalized value. We may know what tangible assets the corporation had at the beginning and end of the year, we may estimate the going value of the corporation at the two different times and so may get the net change in equity. This is the mixed economic income for the period, but it must be broken down into variable income and the correlative unexpected gain. To do this we must make allowance for the change of expectations as between the beginning and end of the period.

An appropriate conceptual device for measuring variable income for the corporation is as follows:

1) Find the change in tangible equity (excluding going value).

2) Add to it the change in going value minus that component of the change in going value (or intangible assets) which is attributable to changes of future expectations not resulting from this year's actions.

That is, the variable income of a corporation is equal to the change in tangible equity (before dividends) adjusted for any change in going value not arising from a change in expectations.

In the practical measurement of business income, it is frequently possible to make an assumption that greatly simplifies the determination of variable income. That assumption is that if the value of the tangible assets of the corporation is maintained intact, the corporation's earning power will be maintained. Sometimes an even rougher assumption is made that if the physical assets of a corporation are maintained intact its earning power will be maintained. The latter form is frequently rejected however as shown by the allowances for obsolescence. Such allowances imply that in order to maintain earning power, it is necessary to do more than maintain physical assets since physical assets must be modernized as techniques change or else earning power will decline.

If it is assumed that the going value of a corporation will be maintained providing the value of its tangible assets, or more accurately the value of its tangible equity, is maintained intact, then the task of measurement of variable income is made very easy. Income of any period will be equal to the value of the tangible equity at the end of the period minus its value at the beginning of the period. This assumption, that the going value of the corporation is not subject to change except by change of expectations so long as tangible assets are unchanged, lies behind most practical measures of income. Where the assumption is true, tangible income will equal variable income.

To recapitulate, under conditions of uncertainty the variable income concept seems to be the most useful economic income concept that excludes unexpected gain from income. For a business corporation, variable income equals the change in tangible assets plus the change in the going value minus that part of these changes attributable to changes in expectations of future receipts. If we assume that so long as tangible equity is maintained going value will be unchanged then variable income is equal to tangible income.

Several observations seem appropriate:

1) The importance of verifying the basic assumption.

If the computation of income is to be based in principle on variable income, but in practice on tangible income, the validity of the procedure depends on the basic assumption that going value will not change. Therefore, special adjustments will have to be made whenever that assumption is not valid. In particular, if going value is built up at the expense of tangible assets, or tangible assets built up at the expense of going value, then ac-

71

count must be taken of these changes in going value since without this adjustment, tangible income will not equal variable income.

2) The function of depreciation.

In comparing the value of tangibles at different times, it is necessary to take account of changes in value associated with the passage of time or the rate of use of the tangibles. Our basic assumption can be turned around to be used as a guide to depreciation allowance. That is, insofar as we are free to choose a depreciation policy, let us choose that one which goes farthest to make the basic assumption true. In accord with this view, the annual depreciation allowance should be reckoned as the amount that would have to be reinvested to keep the going value of the concern constant in the absence of changes of expectations.

It may be that profit on sales is interesting in its own right, that there are some uses for which it is to be preferred to an income concept that is based on the notion of maintaining capital intact. But before going into that question, let us see under what conditions profits from sales will agree with variable income.

If all prices remain constant, and if a corporation which maintains the value of its tangible equity can be expected to maintain its earning power, then profit from production will equal variable income. Under these circumstances variable income will differ from profit on sales only by the difference between profit on sales and profit on production. That difference is one which need not concern us here. It will in general be small, and where it is large, as in the construction industry, business practice will usually be found to make some special arrangement for prepayments etc. and accountants will adjust the concept of income accordingly.

Under what circumstances in actual practice will profits from sales be a poor measure of variable income? We will postpone discussion of the effect of price changes and we may regard the difference between profit on production and profit on sales as generally of little importance. The really important possibility of divergence between sales profit and variable income arises when the activity of a given year has affected the sales profit to be ex-

72

pected in future years. Thus, if in a given year certain expenditures, say for advertising, charged as costs of the current year's sales, will in fact have the effect of boosting sales in subsequent years, the current year's variable income will in truth be larger than the sales profit by the present value of the future sales profit attributable to this year's action. Conversely if some of this year's sales are achieved at the expense of customer good will, such that future sales profit will be lower than if sales had not been pushed so far or hard this year, then sales profit for this year will be greater than variable income.

We may conclude that under constant prices, sales profit is an acceptable approximation to variable income except where:

1) There is a significant change in going value either as a consequence of some action in this period, or of an expected change in the corporation's future selling position. An unexpected change should, of course, result in an unexpected gain or loss rather than influencing variable income.

2) There is a divergence between profit on production and profit on sales due to a difference in timing of production and sales.

V. CHANGES IN PRICES

Real Income

Occasionally tremendous changes in the general price level demonstrate the instability of the monetary measure on which business accounts are based. In extreme cases of inflation the maintenance of capital intact in money value becomes a ludicrous preoccupation. If the concept of income is pushed back to the amount a man can dispose of and be as well off at the end of the period as at the beginning, it is clearly inappropriate to use money value as a measure of well being in a period during which money's command over goods and services is shrinking rapidly.

Under such circumstances it is appropriate to substitute a "real" measure of well being for the money measure. The

73

simplest way to convert a money measure into a real measure is through an accepted index of the general price level. No perfectly satisfactory index of the general price level exists, nor can one be conceived. It is not only that price indexes are imperfect because of poor price reporting and inadequate coverage, but even in theory it is impossible to construct a perfect price index no matter how much information one has.

The theoretical difficulty in constructing a price index derives from the fact that since all prices do not move together, it is necessary to use an average of different movements. That average must be weighted and the appropriate weights change as between the periods measured. Because of this difficulty, one of the leading contemporary economists has rejected the income concept entirely in advanced theoretical analysis.[21] But for practical purposes, the theoretical imperfection of index numbers need not worry us too much. We are willing to use a price index as a general measure of the purchasing power of money in many important affairs in spite of the fact that different indexes give different results, no one of which can clearly be said to be superior to the others.

The deflation of money wages by a price index to obtain a measure of real wages is a familiar operation. Unfortunately a corresponding deflation of money profits by a price index does not yield a measure of real profits as it would be sensible to define them. Suppose that this year the net worth of a certain corporation which has paid no dividends during the year increases from $1,000,000 to $1,100,000 so that the money measure of mixed economic income is $100,000. Suppose during the same period, the general price level rises from 100 to 110. In measuring the real income of the firm in the current year, it would not be sufficient to deflate the money measure of income ($100,000) by the price index (110) to get about $90,000, as the measure of real income.

That procedure will not indicate by how much the real value of owner's equity has changed over the year. In order to measure

---

[21]Hicks, J. R., *Value and Capital* (Oxford: Oxford University Press, 1939 and 1941) p. 180.

real income it is necessary to put both year-end and year-beginning equity into terms of dollars of equal purchasing power. If we compare them in terms of dollars of year-end purchasing power then the year-beginning net worth in current dollars (assumed to be $1,000,000) must be adjusted to the year-end price level (110% of the year-beginning price level). That is, in year-end dollars, the year-beginning net worth was $1,100,000 while year-end net worth in year-end dollars is also $1,100,000. The corporation has accordingly earned no real income over the year, the real value of its net worth was at year-end just equal to the real value of its net worth at year-beginning.

For most of the many possible concepts of income, there are several different ways of defining a corresponding real income concept. It would be a bewildering and thankless task to consider them all. We may confine our attention to a few of the more important concepts of real income. These are: real economic income, real variable income, contemporaneous sales profit, and pure sales profit. With each of these there will be associated a correlative concept of gain not counted as income.

It is most convenient to express any real measure of income in terms of dollars of purchasing power as of a specified time. In what follows it will be taken for granted, unless otherwise stated, that the real income of any year is expressed in dollars of purchasing power as of the end of the year.

Real economic income of a corporation is the real value of its equity at year end minus the real value of its equity at year beginning plus the real value of dividends paid over the year.[22] That is, in comparing year-end net worth with year-beginning net worth, account is taken of the change of purchasing power of the dollar. It is thus quite possible that a corporation which has earned money economic income has suffered a real economic loss. That merely means that although the money value of equity rose, it rose less than the general price level so that its real level declined.

---

[22]It is taken for granted here as well as elsewhere that any change of equity through increased investments from outside the corporation is not counted in change of equity for the purpose of income determination.

A real pure income could be defined but since we will have no need of this concept which implies conditions of certainty, we may pass on to the concept of real variable income. As before, that depends on receipts and expectations thereof. An adjustment to the current year's receipts can be computed on the basis of beginning of the year's expectations and expressed in dollars of beginning of the year purchasing power. That adjustment is the difference between the present value of the stream of receipts expected as of the beginning of the year and what it is expected to be worth at the end of the year after this year's expected receipts are taken out. That is, expected receipts minus the adjustment equals expected income. Real variable income is then the difference between the real value of this year's receipts and the real value of the adjustment. The variability is introduced by the fact that actual receipts may differ from expected receipts.

To this there is a correlative unexpected gain equal to the real value of the future stream of receipts at year-end minus the real value of that stream as expected at year-beginning. The sum of real variable income and the correlative measure of expected gain is real economic income.

We shall consider two different ways of translating money profit from sales to a real base. We may call these contemporaneous sales profit and pure sales profit respectively.

Contemporaneous sales profit is so called because it is based on matching revenues and costs in dollars of the same purchasing power, i.e. in contemporaneous dollars. That is, against the sales revenue of a given year is matched the costs of those sales with each item of cost revalued according to the movement of the general price level. Thus a raw material purchased for $1.00 when the price level was 100 is charged to cost at $1.10 when the price level is 110 at time of sale of the product to which it is charged.

The measure of contemporaneous sales profit so obtained may be contrasted with pure sales profit with which it is sometimes confused. Pure sales profit is equal to sales revenue minus cost, priced according to the particular prices of the cost items prevailing at date of sale. Only if the prices of the cost items used by a corporation have on the average moved in strict proportion to the general price level will contemporaneous sales profit and pure sales profit be the same. In general the two will differ according to the degree by which the prices of the cost items of the corporation have diverged from the general price level.

In brief, pure sales profit is based on replacement cost valuation of cost items. Contemporaneous sales profit is based on real purchasing power valuations of cost items. For inter-year comparisons, it would then be appropriate to deflate each year's contemporaneous or pure sales profit by that year's general price index just as wage payments are deflated to measure real wages.

Correlative to contemporaneous sales profit is temporal gain on sales. It is so called in order to indicate that it is that part of total money gain which is attributable to the fact that costs and revenues are not simultaneous. It is the difference between mixed sales profit and contemporaneous sales profit. It is equal to that part of mixed sales profit which is assigned to cover the allowance for change in the general price level.

Similarly, the difference between pure sales profit and mixed sales profit may be called price gain on sales. It is equal to the difference in value of the cost items as between time of acquisition and the time they are charged against sales revenue.

The relative merits of the various measures of income will be discussed after consideration has been given to the broader issues of whether a real or monetary measure is to be preferred for each important use. That issue is truly fundamental. Once it has been settled, the problem of which measure of real income or of money income should be used is largely one of practical convenience.

Real Versus Money Income

If we start with a general notion that income is the amount that can be freely disposed of while leaving capital intact, we must now inquire whether it is money value or real value of capital that is to be kept intact.

77

In the elementary use of the income concept by an individual the real value is the most appropriate. For money is merely the measure of what it can purchase. So, if a man buys an asset for $100 at the beginning of the year and sells it for $200 at the end of the year, and meanwhile the price level doubles, he has no real gain on the transaction. His $200 will buy no more at the end of the year than his $100 would have bought at the beginning of the year. It would clearly be a delusion to believe that he had gained $100 by the operation. Yet just this delusion does enter into conventional income accounting, which takes no heed of changes in the general price level.

For certain purposes, however, there is some justification for ignoring the general price level. Under the trust fund theory of the capital of a corporation, that the creditors are entitled to protection against reducing the value of owner's equity below a stated amount, it is appropriate to use a money measure rather than a real measure of capital. For under this doctrine, the creditors have a right to demand that a certain money amount of capital be preserved in the business. If the money value of the assets increases, the creditors can have no objection to the distribution to the owners of the equity of part or all of the increase in value since what is left will afford as much protection as before in money terms and the creditors' claims are for certain amounts of money rather than for a specified real value.

Correspondingly when the price level declines, the creditors can justifiably object to any attempt to reduce the money value of capital which must be maintained intact for their protection. It is clear that from this point of view a money measure of capital is appropriate, since a claim fixed in money terms is being protected.

For the purposes of taxation as well there is some justification for the use of a money measure. Consider the man in the previous example who worked up $100 worth of material into $200 worth of product while the price level doubled. Contrast him with the man who deposited $100 in the bank at the beginning of the year. In real terms the first man is just as well off at the beginning of

78

the year as at the end of the year. The second man has only 50% of the real value that he deposited at the beginning of the year. To tax the first man on his $100 money gain is in fact a capital levy in real terms but any tax on money income less than 100% leaves him better off than the man holding cash or a bank deposit. A general price rise is a capital levy on those holding money or claims to money. Equity may best be served if the increase of money value of any asset be subject to a tax since this makes the burden of the price rise more evenly spread.

Of course, equity would also be served if a real rather than a money measure were used throughout the economy. Then the man with the $100 bank deposit might claim a 50% loss on that account to be deducted from his other income for tax purposes. Such a procedure has, in principle, greater merit than the taxation of money rather than real profit. But it may be deemed impractical to carry the real income concept so far as to allow a loss deduction on all assets whose values have not increased in proportion to the general price level. In particular, if the holders of money and of government bonds are not to be indemnified for their real loss brought about by the rise in prices, those property owners who have escaped that loss by owning assets whose prices have risen may equitably be taxed on their money gain.

One argument commonly advanced in support of the money rather than the real measure of income as the basis of taxation is open to serious question. It is often said that in a period of rising prices, if corporations were to be taxed on their real rather than their money income, the tax base would be reduced, and if a given amount were to be collected, the tax rates would have to be increased. Nothing would be changed, the argument runs, in actual tax payments since the increase in rates would just balance the shrinkage of the base. This argument is true for all corporations taken as a group but not for individual corporations. Consider two corporations each with $100,000 money income. The first corporation has equity valued at $800,000 at year–1 beginning and $900,000 at year–1 end while the general price level rose from 100 to 110. Then its money income is $100,000, and its real income at year–1 end prices is $20,000, since $800,000 at the beginning of the year was equal in real value to $880,000 at the end of the year. The second corporation had owner's equity of $200,000 at the beginning of the year and $300,000 at the end of the year so its money income was also $100,000, but its real income was $300,000 minus $220,000 or $80,000. If then the alternatives are 40% taxation on money income or 80% on real income the total tax yield will be $80,000 in either case, but the tax payment of each corporation will be much different. With the 40% tax on money income, each pays $40,000, while with the 80% tax on real income, one pays $16,000, the other pays $64,000.

The choice between the real and the money measure of capital as the basis for profit determination is more complicated in activities such as public utilities subject to rate regulation. If the rates have been set so as to permit no more than a fair return, should an increase in rates be permitted upon a rise in the general price level? There are really several separable questions bound up together in this problem. In order to separate out the various issues, we shall consider certain simplified cases before attacking the problem in its full complexity.

Consider first a tunnel constructed at a cost of $1,000,000 in such a manner that it requires no maintenance expenditure and is expected to last forever. Rates have been set for the use of this tunnel which can be expected to yield a 5% return or $50,000 a year. Now the price level has doubled and the operators request a modification of rates so as to yield $100,000 a year. The justification advanced for this request is that the real value of $100,000 now is the same as $50,000 formerly; the price of everything else has gone up so that the tunnel rates should go up too. Furthermore, the present cost of construction of the tunnel would be $2,000,000.

To the extent that public regulatory authorities have rejected reproduction costs as a rate base it might be expected that this request would be refused. On the other hand if another parallel tunnel is required to handle the traffic, and investment is not forthcoming at less than 5%, then at least for the new tunnel, rates must be permitted that would yield $100,000 a year. Similarly, in ordinary unregulated business, the prices of products can be expected to increase with the general price level. Had the owners of the tunnel invested instead in commodities they would have doubled the money value of their capital. Had they held their $1,000,000 in a bank account however they would still have only $1,000,000. Whether or not the increase in rates should be permitted depends on whether the regulatory authorities wish to use the experience of the holders of cash or the holders of commodities as the norm for the treatment of owners of regulated assets.

Under the general doctrine of rate regulation that the rate should be sufficient to keep and attract capital in the business, it would seem appropriate to permit the increase of rates, that is, to recognize the real rather than the money measure of profit. At the same time then, it would be appropriate to tax the owners on their capital gain of $1,000,000 if the rate rise is permitted. For then (assuming an interest rate of 5%) their asset acquired for $1,000,000 has increased in value to $2,000,000, and as argued before, in fairness to those who hold cash, bank deposits, or government bonds during the price rise, the capital gain should be taxed.

The argument for permitting the rate increase applies more clearly to the case of depreciable assets. If the service is to be maintained, replacement of depreciable assets must be contemplated and it is then appropriate to permit depreciation on the basis of replacement cost. It might however be possible to delay the increase of rates until after the replacement has actually been made. But this would require different treatment of those with old and those with new assets. Precedent can be found for such different treatment, but the theoretical justification for it is weak. It is more consistent with the operation of the unregulated sector of economy (except for the holders of cash) to permit depreciation based on replacement cost, but to tax the capital gain represented by the difference between original cost and replacement cost.

Finally, there can be little argument against permitting rate increases based on increased operating costs which are the result of the general rise of the price level. We may conclude that the use of a real rather than a money measure of income as the standard for public utility rate regulation seems well justified by the principle of permitting rates that will induce the maintenance of capital and will attract new investment. However, the rate increases could be delayed by permitting different rates to be charged by the owners of new and old facilities, respectively. To do so puts the owners of old facilities on a par with those who own cash or government bonds during a price rise. Permitting rate increases based on a real measure of capital and income puts the owners of public utility equities on a par with owners of physical assets. It should therefore make them subject to taxation on the appreciation of their assets if such taxation is based on the money rather than the real measure of income.

There has recently been considerable public controversy over whether a real or money measure of profit is more desirable.[23] The discussion has not been couched in these terms however but has concentrated on the subsidiary topics of whether in the computation of profit, inventory and depreciation costs should be entered on the basis of historical cost or of replacement cost. In terms advanced here, the controversy was more narrowly focussed on pure sales profit versus mixed sales profit than on real versus money measures of profit in general.

Unfortunately, none of the protagonists in the struggle really got down to fundamentals. Most of the witnesses before the Joint Congressional Committee on the Economic Report implied that the use of a real rather than a monetary measure was appropriate, only a few said so explicitly, and none said why. The usual statement was to the effect that the use of historical cost overstates true profits when prices rise, that error is introduced when costs and revenues are measured in dollars of different purchasing power. It may then be inferred that these witnesses regard pure profit or contemporaneous profit from sales as true profit but why they do so, the record does not show.

---

[23]See *Corporate Profits.* Hearings Before The Joint Committee on the Economic Report, Congress of the United States, Eightieth Congress, Second Session, Pursuant to Sec. 5(A) of Public Law 304, Seventy-ninth Congress (Washington: 1949).

However, the implication is clear that most of the witnesses regarded profits as the amount to be distributed to equity owners and still leave the real earning power of the corporation intact. This was taken for granted rather than explicitly discussed. The heart of the whole matter is in fact whether equity owners are entitled to have their real equity maintained intact, or only the money value of that equity, as in the case of the owner of cash or of a government bond. Only a few questions of Senator Flanders in all the voluminous hearings raised this issue and so foreign was it to the temper of the discussion, that the learned witness did not seem to know what the Senator was driving at, nor did the Senator push his argument to its logical conclusion.

"Senator FLANDERS. The last question that I wanted to ask you, Mr. Pogue, was brought to my mind by your brief, and your practice there of expressing profits in terms of a dollar of a past time, saying that in comparing profits one should also take into account the purchasing power of the dollar.

"Now, what should the investor demand in that respect? The man who buys an evidence of debt like a bond does not expect to be repaid in any other terms than the dollar which he invested. There is no provision made for upping the return on that bond due to the change in the cost of living.

"Mr. POGUE. That is correct.

"Senator FLANDERS. Now, should a man who has invested his dollars in equity in the same concern properly expect that his returns should be on any other basis than the particular dollar originally invested when the stock was issued? Do you see any difference between those two things? If there is a difference, you tend perhaps to make a case for your conclusion that profits should be reckoned in terms of an older dollar for comparison. If there is no basis of equity in the two things, it seems to me that you would use the current dollar right along straight through.

"Mr. POGUE. Well, Senator, I do not see that.

"Senator FLANDERS. Why should we say that profits should be great enough to make the same basis of comparison with a

83

previous period in which the dollar was worth more? That is the question."

* * * * * *

"Senator FLANDERS. Looking at it this way, with regard to the uses of profits, there is no need for upping your profits to a depreciated value of the dollar for your servicing of the debt. That can be done in the old dollar. There is need for upping your profits for capital replacement, because that has to be in the new dollars.

"Mr. POGUE. That is right.

"Senator FLANDERS. Now, where does the need for dividends on common stock lie? We know where the needs of the holder of common stock are. He has got to pay more. Is the company whose stock he holds bound to recognize that need of the stockholder for more money to live on?

"Mr. POGUE. No; I would not think it would have to.

"Senator FLANDERS. That really reduces the need for reckoning profits in the new dollar, it would seem to me, to that area of capital replacement, where very evidently it is needed."[24]

Senator Flanders has in fact yielded too much, for if it is merely necessary to maintain the old money level of dividends, it is not necessary even to allow for replacement costs of capital assets. Thus, suppose a house-renting corporation has capital assets of ten houses of average value $10,000 each at original cost minus depreciation to date. Altogether then the ten houses are worth $100,000 and suppose they earn $10,000 a year after all operating costs and maintenance but before depreciation of $5,000 a year, so that net income is $5,000 a year. Now, suppose a doubling of all prices and rentals. Earnings before depreciation are now $20,000 a year. If replacement cost is used as the basis of depreciation, the annual charge can now be doubled to $10,000 a year and net income after depreciation would also be $10,000, or double what it was before. Eventually, if all income so computed were paid out in dividends and all houses replaced as retired, the company will have ten houses averaging $20,000 value each at original cost minus depreciation and earning $10,000 net.

---

[24]*Hearings,* pp. 188-189.

84

Real earnings will have been maintained and money earnings doubled.

If historical cost is used, however, depreciation will continue to be $5,000 a year as long as the old houses last, and during that time, net income will be reported as $15,000 a year. If net income as reported is paid out in dividends and only $5,000 a year reinvested in houses, then eventually the company will have only five houses at $20,000 value each, earning $10,000 before $5,000 depreciation, or $5,000 net income. In short, if it is merely desired to maintain the old level of money dividend, no retention of earnings to replace capital assets at higher cost is necessary. The physical volume of capital assets will then be reduced, but their money values and money earnings maintained.

Senator Flanders was accordingly in error when he thought that there were two different ways of looking at the matter, one in which it was considered whether or not the stockholders should have their money dividends increased in proportion to changes in the price level, and the other whether the allowances for depreciation should be permitted to increase in proportion to changes in the price level. One of these implies the other. That is, if stockholders are to have only a constant money income then it is not necessary to count depreciation at replacement prices. If, however, depreciation is counted at replacement prices, then stockholders will tend to receive higher money income so as to maintain the real value of the dividends.

The issue is not whether real or money capital shall be maintained. There is general agreement that for the social good, real capital should not only be maintained, but expanded. The question is quite a different one of whether such maintenance of real capital should be allowed for in the determination of income. For it is quite possible that income should be computed on a money basis while real capital can be maintained or increased largely out of reinvestment of income so computed. This is in fact what has been happening in the United States in the past few years. Under these circumstances, money income is greater than the corresponding amount of real income but part of the reinvestment of money earnings helps maintain the real value of capital intact.

Since pure profit from sales was almost universally taken for granted by businessmen as the true measure of profits, we may infer that it is the concept most acceptable to the businessman. The reason is not far to seek. The businessman is inclined to think of maintaining or of expanding the physical volume of his operations—the idea of obtaining a constant money volume of sales in a period of rising prices is repugnant to him. Although he is unaccustomed to thinking in real rather than in money terms in contemplating general economic developments, he is keenly aware of changes in the cost of replacing inventory or capital assets. It is only the more academic-minded who would suggest that if, for a given firm, its own costs, selling prices, and volume remain unchanged while there is a movement of the general price level that an adjustment should be made in its income for changes in the general price level. Consequently, in general, the businessmen implied at the Congressional hearings that pure profits were true profits while academic economists and accountants implied that contemporaneous profits were true profits.

This attitude of businessmen, that they wish to maintain physical volume intact with perhaps some expansion, or at least some upward adjustment for increasing efficiency and size of the market, indicates that for the internal purposes of the corporation, and perhaps for reports to stockholders and for director's decisions on dividend policy, a real measure of profit seems appropriate. Such a real measure might be based on the prices relevant to the corporation rather than on general purchasing power. That is to say, pure profit rather than contemporaneous profit seems to be the one thought of as ideal by businessmen. This is a matter of choice for those concerned. If the stockholders and officers of a corporation wish to have some measure of the funds disposable which will still leave the capital intact, they can choose what meaning to give to the phrase "capital intact" for their own particular purposes. The use of pure profits from sales in this connection seems well in accord with the aspirations and preconceptions of businessmen and investors.

Pure Profits Versus Mixed Income

Although businessmen are interested in an approximation to pure profits from sales primarily as a basis of a dividend and taxation policy that will permit them to maintain their place in the market, they are also interested in mixed profits from sales. As between two corporations or as between two time periods a more reliable measure of success is furnished by mixed profit than by pure profit. For it is certainly an important function of the businessman to buy and sell wisely. So if one corporation has in a given year a greater pure profit from sales than another, but a lower mixed profit, then the first corporation has not done so well as the second.

Of course, either one of these concepts is inferior to the mixed economic concept as a measure of how well the firm has done. Indeed sometimes the pure profit on sales is regarded as superior to mixed profit on sales because there is an expectation of the recurrence of pure profits in the future, but the price gain component of mixed profits, it is argued, cannot be expected to recur in the future. If the facts are as assumed, there is something in this argument. But in most cases, the facts will not be as assumed since it will not in general be true that pure profit will recur in the future. If a measure of profit is desired that will take account of expectations of the future, surely it should be so designed as to take explicit account of such expectations rather than to bring them in by the back door on the pretext that pure profits are more likely to recur in the future than are price gains.

It is sensible to value a corporation on the basis of expected future net receipts rather than on a mechanical projection of past profits however measured. It may be true that a measure of pure profits from sales furnishes more useful information on which to base a projection of future net receipts than does a measure of mixed profits from sales. But it would be folly to project pure profits into the future in the face of any information on the basis of which changes in the profit level can be expected. If no such information exists and current profit levels can be expected to continue into the future, then there will be no difference between pure profits and expected future net receipts, and pure income will become identical with mixed economic income.

There is no escape from the necessity of using expected receipts as the basis of a sound evaluation of a corporation. Any attempt to avoid the subjective nature of such expectations through the exclusive use of some objective measure of profit on past operations is likely to do more harm than benefit to anyone relying on the valuation. A valuation must be based on a judgment of the future, it can not be both sound and objective at the same time in a world of uncertainty.

In any case, as between two companies one with and the other without price gains, each with the same pure profit from sales, the one with price gains can generally be considered to have done better. We say generally rather than always because account must be taken of the effect of this year's activities on future earning prospects. That is, for inter-firm comparison, mixed profits from sales is superior to pure profits from sales but both are inferior to mixed economic income.

Lacey has maintained that in a period of falling prices, it is unreasonable to expect management to make a mixed profit on sales, and in a period of rising prices, management should be expected to make more than the normal rate of mixed profit on sales.

> "(1) The principal fault [with the existing method, i.e. mixed sales profit] is that the existing method of computing profits sets an unnatural standard for business management. If the amount spent on consumer goods is likely to vary with the movement of current industrial costs, i.e., with the money now being pumped into circulation by industry as income to raw material producers, employees, etc., then it is inappropriate to judge business success by reference to recovering a margin over the actual cost of goods now being sold from stock; these goods were produced weeks or months ago and their cost has already determined the income of an earlier period. When money costs are rising, the earning of a reasonable profit over actual cost is easily achieved, with the result that a false optimism is induced. And when costs are falling, managements are set an impossible task in attempting to recover the earlier and

88

higher costs of goods sold out of stock, together with a margin for a normal profit, and at the same time to maintain the volume of sales. As already indicated, industry cannot in ordinary circumstances expect to recover in sales proceeds more than is being currently paid out in costs."[25]

The implications of this objection to the use of mixed profits from sales are that primarily it is not the task of management to buy and sell well; it is merely the task of business management to produce as much as it can whenever there exists an advantageous difference between cost and selling price. With this view I must take strong issue. It is an important responsibility of management to make the value of present owner's equity as large as possible by whatever legitimate means is open to management. In particular, management should aim to time purchase and sales so as to get the most favorable prices consistent with volume. It is management's responsibility to form its best judgment as to the future movement of prices and to be guided accordingly. Decision as to purchases, sales and operations must be based on management's best judgment of price movements as well as upon other considerations such as volume of sales. To use a measure of business profits which completely disregards management's success or failure in buying and selling is to neglect a most important part of management's activity and responsibility.

There may well be an advantage for presentational purposes in separating out the two components of mixed sales profit, the pure sales profit on the one hand and the price gain on goods sold on the other. But both components must be considered in evaluating the success of a corporation in a given year. Of course it is true that in a period of price decline no management can be expected to avoid some price loss on goods sold since such loss could probably only be avoided by so curtailing operations as seriously to impair pure profits on sales. But the two must be taken together. It would be foolish to stimulate management to maximize pure profit from sales irrespective of the price losses

---

[25]K. Lacey, "Profit Measurement and the Trade Cycle," *The Economic Journal,* Vol. LVII, No. 228, December, 1947, pp. 456-474.

that might then be sustained. Management decisions should aim at the maximization of mixed profit from sales and not at either of its components exclusively. Such maximization must always, of course, be subject to an adjustment for the effect of any decision on future profits which comes around to saying that management must in the end try to maximize mixed economic income.

Contemporaneous Versus Pure Sales Profit

One of the greatest advantages of contemporaneous sales profit over pure sales profit is that the former is an adequate basis of inter-firm comparison, while the latter is not. As mentioned above, even if two firms have equal pure profits, one may have done better than the other if it made larger price gains. But any price gain over and above the movement of the general price level is included in contemporaneous sales profit and any price gain less than the movement of the general price level will appear as a loss in contemporaneous sales profit. If two corporations each have the same mixed sales profit but one has the greater contemporaneous profit that means that the other has purchased its goods at times when the general price level was lower so that the one with the smaller contemporaneous profit has also the smaller real profit because the real value of its costs were higher than those of the other firm.

The great advantage of contemporaneous profit is that it measures costs against the other opportunities for purchase at the time the cost item was acquired. Thus if two companies make the same amount of sales this year and have purchased the goods that have gone into cost at the same price then their mixed profits from sales will be equal. But if one of these companies has purchased its cost items in a year in which the purchasing power of money was very high, in other words when the real cost level was high, and the other purchased its cost items in a year in which the purchasing power of money was low, the second will have the higher contemporaneous profit because the second gave for its cost items less real value than did the first.

Contemporaneous profit is not a pure profit in the sense that it does contain the effect of price changes as well as the effects of differentials between costs and revenues as of a given time. But the adjustment for changes of the general price level assures us when we are matching costs and revenues that these are measured in uniform dollars even though the costs are incurred at price levels different from those at time of sale.

Another aspect of the difference between the two measures is the implication for the maintenance of capital intact. The contemporaneous measure implies that a corporation's capital is maintained intact when the money value of that capital has increased in proportion to the general price level. The pure sales profit concept implies that a corporation's capital is maintained intact when at the end of the period it can be exchanged for the same physical collection of goods as was owned at the beginning of the period.

Should Unexpected Gains Be Counted As Income?

Business and taxation practice has long distinguished between capital gains and income. One type of capital gain, the appreciation of an asset that corresponds to an interest payment, as in an appreciation bond, can clearly be recognized as income. Such capital gains are expected gains. That part of any capital gain over and above appreciation in lieu of interest or similar payment, is an unexpected gain, since if it were generally expected it would disappear. Thus an asset which is expected to be worth $110 one year from now will be worth about $105 now if the interest rate is 5%. If after a year it should be worth $115, then $10 of the $15 appreciation may be considered unexpected gain, the other $5 as expected gain in lieu of interest or dividend payment.

As agreed above, the expected gain should certainly be considered as income; should the unexpected gain as well?

Naturally, that depends upon the purpose for which the particular measurement of income is being made. For taxation purposes it certainly seems that the beneficiary of an unexpected gain

91

is thereby better able to bear taxation than one who has had no such gain. Yet in some countries capital gains are not subject to taxation as income. In the United States, however, taxes are imposed on realized capital gains. The practice of capital gain taxation has varied over the past, but currently capital gains on assets held longer than six months are taxed as the equivalent in income of only 50% of their amount with a maximum rate of 25%. The principal justification of such differential treatment of capital gains relates principally to the concentration in time of the realization of capital gains. If capital gains were handled on an accrued basis or somehow spread over the period during which the asset has been held, there would be less justification for treating them differently from income of other sorts. In short, the doctrine that gains are to be counted only when realized leads to the concentration of a capital gain into the time period in which the asset is sold, and so, with a progressive tax, would lead to an excessive tax burden in that period.

Even if spread over the holding period, a capital gain, or the unexpected portion thereof, differs from ordinary income in its nature as a revision of an estimate. Nevertheless there are strong arguments for considering capital gains as similar to other types of income, problems of timing aside. Even if we should agree that an unexpected gain is not income in the period when it is recognized but is merely a revision of an estimate of wealth, that implies that an equivalent income was earned and unrecognized in an earlier period.

Thus suppose a man bought some land for $1,000 at the end of 1949, and received during the year 1950 $100 in rental therefrom over all expenses and sold the land at the end of 1950 for $2,000, the interest rate being 5%. We may reasonably claim that his 1950 income should be unaffected by this sale since the unexpected gain is merely a revision of the estimate of his wealth. But then we must also grant that he bought in 1949 for $1,000 an asset that was really worth $2,000. Therefore even if we agree that the capital gain realized in 1950 should not be counted as income, we must also admit that a gain of $1,000 accrued in 1949 when an asset worth $2,000 was purchased for $1,000.

92

It is obviously inconvenient to tax capital gains as they accrue. There is, however, justification for the taxation even of unexpected capital gains because they partake of the nature of income according to the fundamental definition of income as the amount that can be consumed while leaving the income recipient as well off as before. The problem surrounding the taxation of capital gains are accordingly not basically problems of principle but problems of practical convenience. It is impractical to tax capital gains as they accrue, at least the unexpected component, and if they are taxed when realized in the same manner as any other income, an inequity may result under progressive income taxation.

Present methods of taxation do lead to the spreading of taxation of one very important class of capital gains over the period during which the asset is held and used. If depreciable assets used in the conduct of a business gain in value, this will be reflected in increased receipts from the sales of the products in whose production the assets are used. If the depreciation is based on original cost the profit as measured by the accountant will then contain each year part of the capital gain on the asset. Therefore, basing depreciation on original cost will in the case of assets which have increased in value, lead in effect to a steady inclusion of part of the capital gain in each year's reported profits until the asset is retired. That is, each year's reported profit, computed in accordance with standard practice of depreciation based on cost, will include not only pure profits on sales but also price gains on that part charged to this year's costs of any asset which has appreciated in value.

The accountant's procedure in matching costs of one period against revenues of another automatically includes in income the result of capital gains or losses on those cost items charged to the current year's operations. If then, depreciation were to be based on replacement cost, it would be necessary either to tax the capital gain accrued in the revalued assets or to let this capital gain escape taxation. The capital gain will not be realized through sale but through the use of the more valuable assets in the conduct of the business. Under the present system, such capital gains

93

appear as a component of ordinary income. If depreciation were based on replacement cost, such capital gains would not appear as any component of income subject to tax unless a specific tax was levied on the revaluation of the assets on which increased depreciation was claimed. This, of course, would defeat the purpose of claiming increased depreciation based on replacement costs, except possibly for timing considerations.

A distinction must be drawn here between an asset that appreciates more than the general price level and one that merely appreciates along with the general price level. In the first case there is a capital gain in real terms, in the second in money terms only. The considerations discussed in the previous section on the real versus money measure of income apply to this case as well.

Of course, similar reasoning applies to capital losses on assets whose value is charged to cost. If an asset suffers an unexpected decline in value, and depreciation continues to be based on original cost, then reported sales profit will be lower than pure sales profit and accordingly some tax allowance is automatically made for the capital loss suffered.

Conclusions

The principal differences among the bewildering number of concepts of income that may be conceived can be narrowed down to three major issues. These are the real versus the money measure, inclusion versus exclusion of capital gains, and accrual versus realization as the criterion for timing of a gain or loss. If decisions were reached on these three major issues, almost every one of the many controversial points concerning the measurement of income could be settled. But income is used for so many different purposes that a set of decisions on the three major issues appropriate to one use of a measure of income may very well be inappropriate to another.

A period of changing prices especially urgently poses the issue between the real and the money measure of income. If a real measure of values were used throughout the economy, strong arguments could be made for a real measure of income. But in an economy in which many contractual relations are expressed in money terms certain inequities would be introduced by measuring business income in real terms while government obligations, corporate bonds, and bank deposits were still fixed in money terms.

The accountant's rejection of accrued income, which implies among other things, excluding from income changes in going value, is based primarily on the practical necessity of making income an objective measure. But subjective valuations are inherent in any useful concept of income so that the user must make his own adjustments to the accountant's measure.

Capital gains can be recognized as a form of income, but a form which requires separate treatment from the point of view of most of the uses of income. The accountant's procedures do lead to the separate treatment of capital gains on earnings assets sold out of the normal course of the business, but capital gains on inventories and on other assets which are eventually charged to cost ultimately appear confounded with normal income.

BUSINESS INCOME CONCEPTS IN THE LIGHT OF
MONETARY THEORY

---

by MARTIN BRONFENBRENNER

CONTENTS

BUSINESS INCOME CONCEPTS IN THE LIGHT OF MONETARY THEORY

Mi chiamano Mimi, il perchè non sò. "La Boheme."

I. INTRODUCTION: MONETARY THEORY AS A BRANCH OF ECONOMICS

"Monetary theory" and "economic theory" are a difficult pair of concepts to distinguish. "Monetary theory," however, has come increasingly to refer to that part of economic analysis which treats of the economic *aggregates,* such as the national income and product, the general price level, the total volume of output and employment. Originally focused almost entirely about price level problems, it has been expanding steadily to encompass the other aggregates mentioned, and more in addition. A recent authoritative volume giving a clear idea of the scope of modern monetary theory is Professor Alvin Hansen's *Monetary Theory and Fiscal Policy.*[1]

Monetary theory is set off at times against "economic theory proper," which concentrates its attention on *relative* prices and on the production of single commodities and small groups of closely related commodities (complements and substitutes), meanwhile assuming the aggregates to remain constant.

Sometimes the distinctions between "monetary" and "economic" theory are put differently; a brief terminological excursus may be of some assistance to the reader who has not cared to remain abreast with the economists' professional patter. To many authorities, "economic theory" is a general term, with "monetary theory" and "price theory" the principal species thereunder. To others, what we have called monetary theory is known as "macro-economics," whereas relative price theory is "micro-economics;" the distinction uses the Greek words for "large" and "small" respectively. Since its emancipation from primary concern with price level measurement and determination, monetary theory has also become known as "aggregative economics" or " theory of income and employment." The terminology, like the content,

---

[1]New York: McGraw-Hill, 1949. See also George N. Halm, *Monetary Theory* (Second Edition; Philadelphia; Blakiston, 1946).

97

is in a state of flux; perhaps another generation may see it clarified or at least solidified.

The boundaries between monetary and economic theory, to return to the terms used in the Business Income Study, are nowhere defined with any precision, and with good reason. On the one hand, any really important fluctuations in the prices and production of a few basic commodities will have appreciable effects on the aggregates. For example, a changed wage rate for unskilled factory labor will have significant reactions on total income, employment, consumption, investment, and general prices. Or, to cite a more extreme example, some writers ascribe a major part in the over-all recession of 1927 in the United States to the action of a single major enterpriser, Henry Ford, in closing down his plants for conversion from Model T to Model A.[2] On the other hand, the relations between economic aggregates may differ according to the detail of their composition. Consider as an illustration the "consumption function," which is used frequently to summarize the relation between aggregate consumers' income and aggregate expenditures for consumers' goods. It is certainly conceivable and may be significant that the *distribution* of income between different classes of consumers will alter the total of consumption expenditures out of a given total national income[3]; changes in the *relative prices* of consumers' goods may have similar effects.

The two main branches of economics, unfortunately, have not yet been integrated in any completely satisfactory manner. There

---

[2]For brief discussions of the role of Henry Ford in the 1927 downturn see Elmer C. Bratt, *Business Cycles and Forecasting* (Third Edition: Chicago: Irwin, 1948), p. 273, and Thomas Wilson, *Fluctuations in Income and Employment* (Third Edition: London: Pitman, 1948), p. 138.

[3]A study by Harold Lubell, "Effects of Redistribution of Income on Consumers' Expenditures," presents the following tentative results on this point:

Type of Income Redistribution	Percent Increase in Expenditures	Percent Decrease in Saving
10% toward Equality	0.52	5.5
50% " "	2.87	30.5
100% " "	5.82	61.5

The level of income assumed is taken as constant in this study, which was published under the above title in 37 *American Economic Review* (March and December, 1947), pp. 157-170, 930. The table reproduced is found at p. 930.

sometimes arise actual or apparent contradictions between their results, particularly in some aspects of wage theory and of the analysis of international trade. Most of the better economists content themselves with working in both branches with as much insight and technical skill as they can command, and with checking the results obtained in each branch with the aid of the other.

II. THE TREND OF PRICES

One of the major concerns of monetary theory, or any of its modern synonyms, has always been prognosis of the long-term trend of prices under existing or proposed monetary institutions. Needless to say, it has not always been uniformly successful in its forecasts. At the present time, however, the weight of both authority and evidence seems to indicate a long-term trend of general prices rising erratically into the indefinite future, with each period of prosperity marked by price increases which will not be cancelled out completely in the succeeding period of slackness.

If this diagnosis of a ratchet under the price level is substantially correct, the definition of business income becomes a matter of persistent and important practical significance as well as an academic question for accountants, economists and statisticians.[4] If business income continues to be defined generally net only of reserves sufficient to replace capital instruments at their cost of production, with no allowance for systematic increase in their cost of replacement, at least three important consequences

---

[4]This should not be taken to deny the vital importance of the definition to particular companies and individuals in any wide price movements whatever, even about a constant long-term level. For the business world as a whole, Mr. Justice Stone was quite correct in his remark (*United Railways* v. *West* [1930], 280 U. S. 234) :

"Costs of renewals made during the present prolonged period of high prices and diminishing replacement costs tend to offset the higher cost of replacing articles purchased in periods of lower prices."

if one assume a stable long-run price level. He was certainly wrong for single companies or individuals, whose investments were concentrated at one period or another, or who were involved in complex legal relations involving estates for lives or terms or years, or remainders certain or contingent, in income-producing or upkeep-requiring property. Cf. Arthur Dean, *An Inquiry into the Nature of Business Income Under Present Price Levels* (New York: American Institute of Accountants, February, 1949), p. 84f.

will follow, in the absence of some offset equally potent.[5] First, the percentage of income so computed which is available for distribution to stockholders without impairment of their equity must decline below its customary value, with unfortunate consequences for amicable relations between stockholders and management. Second, the proportion which business income so defined bears to total business receipts and disbursements, including particularly industrial payrolls, must rise permanently above the proportion considered reasonable before World War II, with unfortunate consequences for amicable relations between business on the one hand and consumers and labor on the other. Third, any income or excess-profits tax liability ascertained on the basis of business income so computed will play in some measure the role of disguised capital levy in addition to its ostensible character of income or profits tax.

To justify our forecast of secularly rising prices, we rely primarily on historical and secondarily on analytical grounds. Secular inflation, it cannot be overstressed, is nothing new. Neither the New Deal nor the trade unions nor the Germans nor the Russians invented it. It has been rather the general trend of price history throughout the ages, pre-capitalist and capitalist alike. It has been the universal release from the dead hands of the rentier, creditor, and hoarder. It has nullified all our pretty preachments about the virtues of thrift and the mystic powers of compound interest. The century and a quarter (1815-1940) following the Napoleonic Wars was perhaps the longest period in history without marked upward trend of prices in the leading commercial nations; our historical and analytical insights have not

---

[5]Technical progress may but need not provide such an offset, as will be illustrated in the following hypothetical example. Suppose a machine, which produces 1000 units of output per year, to cost $10,000 and to have a working life of 10 years. At the end of this period, both the price level and the efficiency of the machine have doubled, so that the replacement now costs $20,000 but produces 2000 units of output per year. In terms of the physical productive power at his command, the owner of the machine will have suffered no loss so long as technical progress has kept pace with inflation. In terms of general purchasing power, he may still suffer a loss unless the price of the product also keeps pace with the general price level, which outcome is somewhat unlikely in a manufacturing industry benefiting from major technological innovations. Compare a comment by Senator Joseph C. O'Mahoney, at the *Profits Hearings* of the Congressional Joint Committee on the Economic Report, p. 65.

yet emerged from its spell sufficiently to realize how abnormal it was. Lord Keynes in a neglected passage of his *General Theory* has summarized the broad sweep of price history in a singularly clipped and masterly manner:[6]

> "The very long-run course of prices has almost always been upward. For when money is relatively abundant, the wage-unit rises; and when money is relatively scarce, some means is found to increase the effective quantity of money."

Secular inflation, however slow its annual average rate, cumulates over the generations in glacial fashion to a tremendously powerful force. "A rise of prices of only 2 per cent a year seems small," Slichter reminds us.[7] "But it will cause the price level to increase about 25 per cent in a decade, and to double in less than forty years." A few random illustrations from various countries will illustrate the efficacy of secular inflation over the centuries of debasement, repudiation, devaluation, and forthright monetization of debt.

To the Emperor Charlemagne (800-814) we owe not only the establishment of the Holy Roman Empire but also the establishment in this Empire of the *pound*, or *livre*, of silver as a monetary standard for most of Western Europe. Leaving to the antiquarians the minor differences between Charlemagne's pound and the present Anglo-American unit of weight, it is interesting to compare very roughly the present value of a pound of silver with the present value of certain European currencies based upon it. A pound of newly-mined domestic silver, at the (subsidized) U. S. Treasury price of $1.29 per ounce, is worth $20.64. Compared with this figure in excess of $20.00, the British pound sterling is valued at $2.80. Turning to Continental currencies, we find the Swiss franc[8] quoted at 23.6 cents, the Belgian franc at

---

[6]J. M. Keynes, *The General Theory of Employment Interest and Money* (London and New York: Harcourt Brace, 1936), p. 307.

[7]Sumner H. Slichter, *The American Economy* (New York: Knopf, 1948), p. 43.

[8]The name *livre* was changed to *franc* in French-speaking countries following the French Revolution, but the change of name itself involved no alteration in the metallic content or value of the coin involved.

2.16 cents, and the French franc at slightly less than ⅓ of a cent on the free market! Abstracting from changes in the price of silver relative to other goods, we can see in these figures evidence of depreciations over an 1100-year period ranging from 86 per cent for Great Britain to the legendary 99 44/100 per cent figure for France. The American monetary system of course shows no such direct historical link with Charlemagne's day, but its progress can be summarized in another of Slichter's conclusions:[9] "Today the wholesale price level in the United States is over three times as high as it was two hundred years ago, and over twice as high as it was a hundred years ago."

From time to time attempts were made, from considerations of morality or on behalf of creditors, to reverse the trend of secular inflation by the provision of new currency of standard weight and fineness. (We speak, needless to emphasize, of periods prior to the rise of modern deposit banking.) This new currency would disappear promptly, being worth considerably more as bullion than as coin, while the debased or under-weight or clipped currency would continue to form the active circulation and prices remained as high as ever. The futility of such efforts as these to turn back secular inflation gave rise to the aphorism "Bad money drives out good," ordinarily called Gresham's Law after an Elizabethan statesman and financier who enunciated it in Shakespearian English. (Earlier versions can be found in the writings of such men as the medieval French economist Nicole Oresme, the classic Greek dramatist Aristophanes, and the legendary Chinese philosopher Confucius.)

Evidence of secular inflation is also obtainable from the very names of monetary units. In Brazil, for example, the basic unit under Portuguese rule was the *real* (plural, *reis*). As inflation progressed over the 19th and 20th centuries, the purchasing power of the *real* shrank to a cumbersomely small quantity, and the basic Brazilian monetary unit is now the *milreis* of 1000 *reis*. When we consider subsidiary monetary units, in which most consumers goods were ordinarily priced at retail, we find country after coun-

---

[9]Slichter, *op. cit.*, p. 160.

try in which these have passed nearly or entirely out of existence as inflation has progressed. Examples are the French *sou* and *centime,* the Italian *centesimo,* the Greek *lepton,* the Chinese *cent,* or the Japanese *sen* and *rin.*

A long-term upward price trend such as we are forecasting, then, represents not a break with all past history but rather the resumption of a movement which can be traced back to classical antiquity. It is the century and a quarter of prices fluctuating widely around a horizontal trend, beginning after the battle of Waterloo in 1815, which becomes a hiatus in a history of rising prices, as much of a hiatus in its way as are the occasional hyperinflations which have accentuated the long-term trend.

Let us consider the hiatus of 1815-1940, when the trend of prices remained horizontal through a series of sharp cyclical oscillations, in slightly more detail, together with its accompanying monetary theory. The period was marked in most industrial and commercial countries by an unusually rigid adherence to a metallic currency standard, of uniform weight and fineness. On the goods side, there was a remarkable succession of innovational booms and territorial expansions which provided a singularly rapid growth rate of economic activity despite what many present-day writers would consider the binding restraint of its monetary arrangements. The ages of steam, railroads, steel, electricity, and petroleum overlapped both each other and the "expansion of Europe" to America, Africa, and the Far East. During this period, not only did general prices not rise, but price declines constantly seemed in the offing and actually prevailed over periods as long as a generation (1866-1896 in the U. S.). They were staved off more or less completely by such extraneous coincidences as new discoveries of precious metals (California, Australia, South Africa, Yukon), improved processes for extracting gold from low-grade ores, and most important, by the expansion of banking and credit institutions which increased the "velocity of circulation" of a given monetary base.

The conditions of 1815-1940, more particularly the limiting influence of the gold standard or sound money "religion," are dead

103

and gone, perhaps forever. The guiding fetish of monetary policy is no longer "sound money;" "full employment" has taken its place, and "stable prices" are lost in the struggle. Nineteenth century monetary theory, however, continues to exercise a great deal of influence on business thought and action, particularly on the older generation of business leaders, largely in the direction of anticipating price trends similar to those of the period 1815-1940.

During this "stable price" period, as we have said, price declines constantly threatened, and might conceivably have eventuated except for the effects of gold discoveries and innovations in economizing the use of the precious metals. The monetary theory of the period, operating so to speak in the shadow of the gold standard, stressed the possible consequences of long-term declines in general prices, or at least slighted the possible consequences of the opposite type of movement. Some writers, such as the influential Swedish economist Gustav Cassel, feared the deflationary outcome of a world-wide gold famine. Others, including Irving Fisher, perhaps the outstanding American monetary theorist of the first third of this century, proposed various modifications in the gold standard itself to forestall such a deflationary movement. A minority, who pointed out the desirable effects of falling prices on fixed-income consumers, were excoriated as tools of the creditor interests of Wall Street.

In the present Age of Full Employment, our thought remains centered, or at least returns periodically, to the price outlook appropriate to the Age of Gold. Why should this be? Part of the explanation, presumably, is sheer lassitude combined with hardening of the mental capillaries. Part is "cultural lag," which may be only an abstruse sociological expression of the same idea. In part, also, poignant memories of 1920-21 and 1929-33, when prices did indeed move downward with a certain inexorability and every appearance of permanence, are still with us, and we are overly addicted to comparisons between postwar periods simply as being postwar, without adequate consideration of differences between them.

III. THE PRICE RATCHET

Let us spell out in more detail the type of price movement which much contemporary monetary theory anticipates for an Age of Full Employment. It is definitely not a smooth or even rise, by a certain number of index or percentage points a year, like a curve of population or productivity. It is rather a series of upward jerks and starts, occurring at irregular intervals and uncompensated by downward movements of anything like equal intensity. It has been likened to a jack or a ratchet in its operation, being constantly susceptible to upward pressure but highly resistant to pressure downwards.

In the future as in the past, the purchasing power of money is expected to fall, and prices are expected to rise, under conditions of cyclical boom or of international conflict. Even with guaranteed full employment, we may be able to moderate the extent of future rises somewhat by monetary and tax measures, if these can be adopted early enough and with sufficient strength. Specific price controls of the OPA type, combined with rationing and allocations, may, under the same assumptions and if continued for a sufficiently long period, maintain the purchasing power of a *certain quantity* of each individual's money completely constant over rationed amounts of price-controlled goods. Price indexes weighted heavily with these goods would also remain highly stable. This statistical stability, however, like the mother younger than her son in *Iolanthe,* is usually spurious. When the purchasing power of one portion of a man's income, spent on the rationed amounts of price-controlled goods, remains approximately constant, what happens to the purchasing power of his other assets and the remainder of his income? It may shrink to zero in purchasing power (if the resources are blocked, and cannot be spent at all). It may fall precipitously (if spent on black markets or luxury goods not reflected in price indexes). It may shrink sharply, in ways not measured by price indexes, through induced expenditure on goods which a man does not particularly desire (lottery tickets, government bonds) rather than those which he

105

would prefer at existing prices.[10] Some fall in the purchasing power of money, in any case, we may fairly continue to anticipate in most boom or war situations, not necessarily so great as in the past but still fairly substantial, pending real improvements in the technique of devising and administering controls and "selling" them to a free electorate.

So much for periods of boom and war prosperity, where the link with the past is strongest. The break with the past is expected in what would otherwise have been periods of depression, recession, readjustment, or what have you. We shall not venture on the disputatious terrain of business cycle theory, except for a statement, to which most economists and business men will agree, that these downward movements will continue at irregular intervals in the future for some time. (We have not learned to eliminate them, although we can perhaps lessen their amplitudes and mitigate their effects.) Our claim is only that the price level cannot be expected to fall, or the purchasing power of money to rise, in such periods in the future to the same extent as it has done in similar periods in the past, or indeed to an extent sufficient to keep the long-term trend of prices on a horizontal level. The reason for this claim is the strength of what its friends call the philosophy and its enemies the fetish of Full Employment.

The process of deflation (downward price adjustment) is always painful and never welcome to the active business community. It decreases the market value of assets, and increases the real burden of debts and other fixed charges. Even when they accept the abstract proposition that general prices or the cost of living are too high, business men and workers resist any cuts in their particular prices and wages, fearing to "spoil their markets" in some sense. This resistance does not require collusive agreement of any sort to make itself effective, although open or tacit

---

[10]If a consumer is sufficiently poor as to afford to purchase no more than his rations, the purchasing power of his entire stock of money or his entire income is maintained by a price control and rationing system. As his status rises, so that less and less of the expenditures he can afford are provided by his ration, the purchasing power of his total money stock or income is progressively reduced. The price control and rationing system, therefore, operates strongly in the direction of overcoming inequalities in the distribution of money income and wealth, and preventing their manifestation in inequalities of real income. This effect, widely known and well understood in Europe and the United Kingdom, has received less attention in the United States.

collusion is frequently present as an additional support. When goods are not moving at existing prices, and price declines are being fought, the obvious method of resistance is to reduce production to the amount salable without price cuts, while awaiting an upturn in demand. Reduced production, in turn, leads with a relatively short lag to reduced employment of labor.[11] The process of adjustment is made more painful, and effective compromise with deflation is made more difficult, by consumers' expectations of price cuts and more price cuts. These expectations induce postponements of purchases, and prevent any but the most drastic price reductions from stimulating production and employment as much as one might otherwise expect. Once substantial unemployment develops, the situation becomes worse. Consumer buying power falls off, downward price and wage pressure is intensified, and a further cycle of production and employment cut-backs is required if prices and wages are to be maintained or if cuts are to be minimized.

Among the sharpest pains of price deflation are underproduction and underemployment. These develop initially, as we have tried to show, while price cuts are being resisted. Once they have developed, however, they are not eliminated immediately when the cuts are made. Since the price or wage which A pays is the income which B receives, successive cycles of price and wage cuts reduce purchasing power along with prices and costs, and do not go very far in solving the problem created by the original resistance to deflation.[12] They may very well make the problem worse, through generating anticipations of further cuts.

---

[11]"Guaranteed annual wage" and "severance pay" plans are devices to increase this lag. They are expected to induce employers to reduce employment less rapidly than production, and to keep their labor force intact despite reductions in their activity.

[12]The late Lord Keynes, in the famous Chapter 19 of his *General Theory*, went even further, and denied that price and wage cuts had any favorable effects on production and employment even in the long run. Without considering the subsequent controversy in any detail, this writer would like to dissent from so extreme a position. Price and wage cuts do, in his opinion, eventually generate a favorable effect on employment and output by increasing the purchasing power of money assets and fixed money incomes. Consumers are induced by the high purchasing power of their remaining assets both to spend more freely for consumption goods and to invest more freely in production goods. This, however, is a long-run adjustment, whose strength and timing are unreliable and which may be offset for long periods by the unfavorable anticipations and the reduction in deposit currency which depression brings with it. It is not of much use in the short period.

Consider this analysis from the viewpoint of a political-economic pressure organization, such as a trade union or a trade association. Labor, agriculture, commerce, and industry have become and are becoming better organized for economic and political pressure than they have ever been before. It is to their interest to exercise all the influence at their command to prevent price and wage declines, with the painful adjustments which accompany them.[13] "Full production," and "full employment," obviously good in themselves, serve admirably as slogans, especially when price and wage cuts can be shown so ineffective in bringing them about. To achieve and maintain "full employment" is to achieve and maintain immunity from the pains of price deflation. Unfortunately (to the consumer at any rate) it is also to achieve and maintain resistance to anything substantial in the way of price declines themselves. For why should prices and wages ever come down when demand falls off, if a beneficent Government can be prompted by pressure and magnanimity to provide supplementary demand in the interests of full production and employment?

The present Administration accepts the philosophy of guaranteed full employment and production, as do leading segments of the Opposition. Given its general economic philosophy, and given the pressures of business, labor, and agricultural organizations, this or any other electable Government is expected to choose full employment above lower prices whenever unemployment threatens in substantial measure. This is particularly true in the present (1949-50) international tension, when any domestic recession is seized upon by our Soviet and other opponents in the world-wide propaganda war currently raging. Government is expected to yield by supporting "demand" and "purchasing power", in the interest of full employment. In some cases this support will take the form of floors under the sagging prices (mainly in the agricultural sector). More usually, it will maintain demand and purchasing power in support of general prices through public works,

---

[13]This sentence of course requires some modification in the case of business and to a lesser extent agricultural organizations, who stand to gain by cost reductions if wage rates and raw material prices fall during any deflationary readjustment.

108

tax reductions, armament programs, foreign dumping, consumer subsidies, or other weapons in its ample arsenal—all of which, of course, maintain prices simultaneously with employment in one or more sections of the economy.

This is not the entire story, since it omits the threat of "unemployment inflation." Let unemployment be defined, in accordance with the usual practice, as inability to find work at going wages, whatever these may be. The way is then left open to wage inflation by unions who attempt to raise going wages to bolster their members' purchasing power when unemployment threatens, or even when it is present. This is "unemployment inflation." In a competitive labor market, unemployment inflation would be practically impossible. An individual refusing work at the market wage rate would be considered voluntarily unemployed, and no reasonable full employment policy would require concessions to him. Under trade unionism, however, organized labor can and does affect the going rates themselves by successful collective bargaining. Indeed, such is the essence of successful bargaining. With going or market wage rates subject to bargaining, and unions exempt from anti-trust prosecution in respect to their normal bargaining activities, the unemployment inflation problem is at least potentially a serious one.[14] Until checks to unemployment inflation are devised, any full employment program in a collective bargaining economy runs the risk of positive inflation even while the Government is engaged actively in bolstering the economy.

IV. STAGNATION AND UNDERCONSUMPTION

To show how significantly the pattern of our economic life may be changed under a regime of full employment and price

---

[14]May unemployment inflation also start from the price side? Yes, insofar as price rigging is exempt from anti-trust prosecution, or such prosecution is ineffective. No, on a competitive market.

Consider a small employer on a competitive market, who raises prices without prior wage increases in a depressed situation. He risks the loss to rivals, first of his market and then of his labor force, without arousing Government intervention on his behalf. A large employer or a trade association which raises prices under similar circumstances faces anti-trust prosecution with a dangerous *prima facie* case against it, unless, like a trade union or a farmers' co-operative, it is exempt from such action.

109

ratchets is the task of this excursus devoted to "stagnation" and "underconsumption", the twin bogeys of the 1930's, as yet incompletely exorcised either in labor or political circles.[15] We shall not consider in any detail the validity of these beliefs in a competitive, stable price economy, although our personal conclusion is negative. Our claim here is only that, with a rising price level, whatever danger of economic stagnation or chronic underconsumption may have otherwise existed is greatly reduced and perhaps eliminated entirely.

Stagnation and underconsumption are more closely related to business income in matters of policy than in matters of definition. If the American economic system in peacetime is indeed stagnating from insufficient mass purchasing power to buy back a full-employment output of consumption goods, what is more natural than to increase consumption by shifting income away from business toward labor, agriculture, and low-income consumers generally, and to advocate fiscal, price, and wage policies which will bring this result about? Opponents of the stagnation and underconsumption theses take more friendly positions toward business income and policies designed toward maintaining or increasing its relative share. Even in matters of definition, however, one would expect an economy threatened with stagnation and underconsumption to be less sympathetic to proposals which would effectively reduce the melon to be cut than an economy which is not so threatened.

In past periods of high prices and high costs, which were not expected to continue for much longer, individuals and business

---

[15]Useful and influential contemporary summaries of the "stagnation thesis" in different forms are to be found in Alvin H. Hansen, *Fiscal Policy and Business Cycles* (New York: Norton, 1941), especially chapter 14, and H. Gordon Hayes, *Spending Saving and Employment* (New York: Knopf, 1945). See also Benjamin Higgins, "Concepts and Criteria of Secular Stagnation," in L. A. Metzler *et al., Income Employment and Public Policy* (*Essays in Honor of Hansen,* New York; Norton, 1948) pp. 82-107. George Terborgh has attacked the thesis particularly sharply in his *Bogey of Economic Maturity* (Chicago: Machinery and Allied Products Institute, 1945), and the current trend of American economic thought seems to be away from it. The controversy itself goes back to Marx and beyond. Most of the great names in theoretical economics have participated; among English-speaking writers, John A. Hobson has been the leading storm center, and Lord Keynes leaned strongly in the Hobsonian direction in the last two chapters (23-24) of his *General Theory, op. cit.*

concerns felt safe and insured against depression when they held cash or gilt-edge debt securities (bonds) already in existence and promising fixed money income. The same alternative was open to them when rates of profit on venture or equity capital fell below "expected" or "normal" levels. Economists believe that shifts of investment away from equities and other types of risk capital to cash and debt securities have helped to bring booms and inflations to their end. They also believe that similar movements, continued during periods of falling prices after the boom is over, have intensified depressions.

If price declines of the magnitude of 1920-21 or the duration of 1866-96 can no longer be anticipated in this country, the motive to hold cash or gilt-edge bonds is weakened. When prices are rising secularly, holding of such investments entails almost inevitably a *loss* of purchasing power in the long run, although still a valuable cover against temporary downturns. It is now necessary for the investor to hedge in nearly all periods against both inflation and deflation, with the former almost certain to be dominant except during the very peak of a boom.

The foregoing analysis is a prelude to consideration of the stagnation and underconsumption theses, because shifts out of consumption goods and other investments into cash and debts are an important part of the mechanism by which stagnation and underconsumption allegedly affect the economic system. As the private economy approaches full employment, it is said, or after full employment has been reached fortuitously for a time, profit margins tend to fall. There are three principal reasons for this. In the first place, the total output of goods increases as existing capacity is utilized completely and new capacity comes into operation, but insufficient additional income (above the full-employment level) is available for their purchase at existing prices. This is generally accepted, even by many critics of stagnation and underconsumption; it is illustrated, for example, by the swelling of American industrial output in 1948 and the price weakness of 1949. In the second place, the demand for consumption goods, at least over the short period, increases less than proportionately to consumer incomes. Consumers, with their high full-employment incomes, tend to lay aside and leave unspent a larger proportion of these incomes than they laid aside out of their previous lower partial-unemployment incomes.[16] The generality of this rule is open to dispute, but an illustration can perhaps be seen in the rise of the "savings ratio" in the United States since 1948, although price resistance is a complicating factor. In the third place, profit margins are pinched from the cost side as well. "Marginal" workers and natural resources must be used, and overtime must be worked. Suppliers' prices and wage rates tend to rise. Interest and rent contracts cannot be renewed except at higher rates. In general, unit costs rise and break-even points move upward toward a higher percentage of physical plant capacity.

When profit margins fall, the comparative attractiveness of liquidity increases. Individual and corporate savers shift part of their funds from productive investment (capital goods and new securities) to holdings of cash, bank deposits, and high-grade bonds, or to repayment of debt outstanding. Demand for current output as a whole, consumption plus investment goods, will therefore decline just as output is expanding. (The decline in consumption-demand and the increase in total output were discussed in the previous paragraph. The shift of investment funds, accentuated by the completion of plant expansion programs, accounts for the decline in investment demand.) With the decreased demand for goods in general, either sales volume or prices or both weaken,

---

[16]The nature and stability of the so-called "consumption function" which relates total consumer incomes to total expenditure on consumption, has become a subject of increasing dispute among economists and statisticians since forecasts based upon it fell short of actual consumption in the period 1945-56, and contributed to the erroneous predictions of immediate postwar depression. Among the problems raised by the function is this: over an individual business cycle, the savings ratio, or proportion of income saved, usually rises with income. Over a longer period, however, it appears to be nearly constant from one cycle to the next, despite the upward trend in income. Of the increasing volume of literature on the consumption function, the following recent articles are worthy of particular mention: James S. Duesenberry, "Income-Consumption Relations and Their Implications," in Metzler *et al., Income Employment and Public Policy, op. cit,* pp. 54-81, and Franco Modigliani, "Fluctuations in the Saving-Income Ratio: A Problem in Economic Forecasting," 11 *Conference on Research in Income and Wealth* (New York: National Bureau of Economic Research, 1949), pp. 371-441. See also, for earlier developments, M. Bronfenbrenner, "The Consumption Function Controversy," 14 *Southern Economic Journal* (January 1948), pp. 304-320.

and profit margins fall further, producing another cycle of increased demand for liquidity. At the same time that demand for money, in particular, increases, "sound" commercial banking policy operates to decrease its supply. In situations of weakened demand and reduced profit margins, commercial banks' loan standards stiffen. They seek cash and Central Bank reserves above the legal minimum, and shift their own investments from loans, which create deposit currency, to bond purchases, which do not. The result is refusal to renew some loans as they expire, calling of loans that may be overdue, refusal to make new loans as old loans are paid off. The decline in bank loans brings about reduction in the volume of deposit currency, and increased monetary stringency. The tendency of sound commercial banks to reduce the volume of deposit currency, in the interest of their own liquidity, just when the demand for money in general increases, is part of what economists call the "perverse elasticity" of a fractional-reserve banking system like our own.

Facing falling profit margins and a tightening money market, business men reduce production and employment, liquidate such inventories as they can dispense with, and decline is on in earnest. The business community's urge for greater liquidity, given falling profits, is a fundamental step in the process. At such times, business men find it increasingly difficult to obtain liquid assets from the banks by borrowing, from the public by selling stock, or by liquidating inventory except at losses, and they encounter increasing demands for cash by their creditors. They can improve their position by shifting assets away from production and employment, and providing greater liquidity from their own resources. The effects on employment, income, expectations, and demand are all unfavorable, but what can the individual business man do?

This analysis has attempted deliberately to present the stagnation-underconsumption position plausibly and sympathetically. If, as it implies, prolonged full employment generates forces which bring it to an end, any private capitalistic economy is doomed to operate below full production and employment for the greater part of the time. This is precisely the charge of the stagnation and underconsumption theories. In the past, the argument continues, rapid population growth and expanding geographical frontiers provided additional investment opportunities based on future potentialities rather than present conditions, and concealed underlying tendencies toward stagnation for the greater part of the first century and a half of capitalism—until approximately 1914 according to some, or 1929 according to others. But with declining population growth, and with the closing of many major frontiers in capitalist countries, the situation was expected to become worse. Whether or not the standard of living under capitalism continues its secular rise, new savings will constantly seek investment in competition with old. In consequence, the volume of capital in existence would rise as well. The increasing volume of existing capital, competing with new saving, would lower steadily the rate of return on additional investment.[17] With a falling rate of return on active investment, hoarding would increase in attractiveness, and exert an increasing drag of depression and unemployment on the economy.

A number of economists, mainly of liberal and Socialist persuasions, have proposed various ways out of the stagnation-underconsumption difficulty. Most of these solutions react unfavorably on business income before or after taxes. One group, including John A. Hobson and H. Gordon Hayes, stress the distribution of income and wealth. They focus their attention on plans to increase consumption and decrease saving by redistribution of income, as by progressive taxation and social service expenditure, largely away from business and property in favor of lower income labor groups who are believed to consume a larger proportion of each additional dollar they receive. Such influential New Deal economists as Alvin Hansen of Harvard University and Leon Keyserling of the Council of Economic Advisers have proposed to supplement private investment for profit as a source of employment and production with government investment, sometimes

---

[17]This is the essence of the Marxian doctrine of the "falling rate of profit." "Profit," the above argument suggests, should continue to fall unless income declines (or the stock of capital rises) until new saving equals no more than depreciation allowances on existing capital.

114

for traditional public purposes (schools, highways, parks), but commonly competitive with some form of private business (low-cost housing, public electric power projects, additional steel capacity). A third group, including Mordecai Ezekiel, A. P. Lerner, and J. H. G. Pierson, think in terms of subsidizing full production and employment by guaranteeing consumer income or expenditures at a full-employment volume. They would use new money issues or permit a rise in the national debt, rather than extraordinary taxation, to finance whatever guarantees had to be made good, and are willing to risk inflation from any future increase in the rapidity of circulation of the expanded money supply or the monetizable national debt. Fourth and finally, the Marxists deny the practicability of any solution whatever, short of a Socialist revolution and a centrally planned economy on the Eastern European model.

Whatever validity these views may have—and we are not concerned with their criticism here—is reduced when the price level is undergoing a secular rise. If liquidity is certain to involve a loss in the purchasing power of one's principal, the incentive to invest in productive activity or investment goods at any positive rate of return, however small, will be much stronger than otherwise. In particular, durable and storable commodities (grains and metals) may replace cash and debt securities as sources of liquidity in the long run. This development may, if it comes, provide for industries producing durable and storable commodities the same sort of "lift" to these industries in depressed periods which the gold standard provides for gold mining and which the Graham-Graham "commodity reserve currency" proposal was designed to generalize to other raw material industries.[18] The urge to buy immediately, rather than at higher prices in the future, may also be important for some durable consumers' goods

---

[18]Commodity reserve currency proposals are associated in this country particularly with the names of Benjamin Graham of Columbia University and Frank D. Graham of Princeton University. See Benjamin Graham, *Storage and Stability* (New York: McGraw-Hill, 1937) and Frank D. Graham, *Social Goals and Economic Institutions* (Princeton: Princeton University Press, 1942). For a criticism, consider Alvin H. Hansen, *Economic Policy and Full Employment* (New York: Whittlesey House, 1947), ch. 18, especially pp. 219-21.

(automobiles) and for consumers' capital investments (houses and home repairs).

It is probably an exaggeration to forecast that the speculative motive for holding cash and high-grade bonds as bearish hedges will ever be eliminated entirely in a society such as ours. Even with an upward trend of prices continuing over a longer period than it has, and recognized more widely as such by the general public, there will remain occasional periods of price decline, minor and secondary if you will but still distinctly perceptible, such as the last quarter of 1948 and the first half of 1949. Holding of cash and bonds will remain eminently judicious at such periods, even if they be shorter than they have been in the recent past. All that can be said is that the speculative motive for hoarding and liquidity will be weakened rather drastically.

Furthermore, some possible hedges against inflation are like cash hoarding as a hedge against deflation, in that they cause little or no demand for current output, so that a shift of demand in their direction appears as stagnationist as hoarding in its implications. Undeveloped real estate or old houses are examples, as are equities already in existence. Gold coins, antiques, old masters, and other collectors' items will serve as illustrations of inflation hedges which involve relatively little demand for current output. Notice, however, that these are not of great quantitative importance, that any elasticity in their stock is benign and not perverse, and that current production may serve as a fairly adequate substitute for purposes of hedging against inflation. If, for instance, people wished to buy existing house properties as protection against inflation and bid up their prices sufficiently high, new houses employing current labor and capital will serve their purposes equally well. In jewelry and art objects as well, current production competes with the heirloom stock, although the latter is probably much larger quantitatively.

If we are correct in concluding, first, that the long-term trend of prices will be upward for an indefinite period, and second, that the problem of under-consumption and stagnation will be much less pressing with prices rising than constant or falling, we can expect public feeling against high business income to lose much of its force and vehemence. Admittedly, the proportion of business income which is saved, either as undistributed earnings of corporations or as personal savings of their stockholders, is considerably greater than the corresponding proportion for income as a whole. With an upward trend of general prices, however, this should lead not to hoarding of cash and debt securities but to increased investment in equities and commodities. If increased investment increases final output, or otherwise lowers the rate of return on venture capital, the result will not be under-employment and a flight to debts but an automatic correction, through permanently lower profit margins, of the very "maldistribution" of income which may have caused investment to expand so rapidly in the first instance. Controversy regarding the distribution of income and wealth will not be eliminated entirely by this development, but the economic argument about "maldistribution", centering as it does about the stagnation and underconsumption theses, will be weakened greatly, and future controversy will concern itself mainly with considerations of ethics and politics.

V. MEASUREMENT OF BUSINESS INCOME UNDER RISING PRICES

If we can accept the high probability of a continued upward price trend, with the more favorable philosophy it engenders toward business income or profits, we may pass on to considering the accounting and statistical problems involved in the definition and measurement of business income under these conditions. It is only with great diffidence that the present writer approaches this subject, since he is no acountant and has had little training and no experience on practical accountancy, which is the discipline primarily involved in this part of the study.

Controversy regarding the measurement of business income under rising prices relates primarily to the inventory and depreciation accounts:

1. When inventory is sold at the increased prices necessary to replenish it after prices have risen, should the increase be

117

included in business income or balanced by the corresponding expense item involved in inventory replacement?

2. Should reserves for depreciation and replacement of fixed capital equipment, computed on an original cost basis, be increased in recognition of increased cost of production and purchase of fixed capital items?

Neither of these questions, we should remark at the outset, is a matter of "price deflation" in the usual sense. On their answers depends the *number* of current dollars, however cheap or depreciated these may be, which business may be said to have available for tax payments, dividend distributions, wage increases, price reductions, and other claims upon it. To revalue these dollars for an estimate of "real" profits in dollars of constant purchasing power is a second step, which does involve deflation by a price index of some kind. No "double deflation" as a special dispensation to business income is involved, however, suspicious labor spokesmen to the contrary notwithstanding.

The principal "facts of life" as regards inventory and depreciation accounting may perhaps be considered as accepted by all parties to the current controversy, although their consequences are subject to widespread disagreement.

Conventional accounting practice, with a traditional conservative outlook on the monetary valuation of *assets,* though not necessarily of *incomes,* answers our two questions in roughly the following way:

1. Goods sold are identified, justifiably from the physical viewpoint, as the oldest portions of the firm's physical inventory, and valued accordingly at their cost price. (This is the first-in-first-out rule, or FIFO.) When prices are rising, the extra mark-up providing for the replacement of this inventory is treated as part of business income or profit, which is then considered as plowed-back in higher-priced inventory. These "inventory profits," it is pointed out, do not arise automatically when prices rise, but result from the conscious decision of the enterpriser to increase his normal

118

mark-up and therefore—so runs the argument—should be treated like any other profit items.[19]

2. Depreciation is computed on the basis of some formula based in turn either on the passage of time or the production of physical output, without regard to price changes.

If an affirmative answer to our two questions above be taken as permitting the inclusion in business expense (and the exclusion from business income) of the increased cost of replacing working and fixed capital when prices rise, traditional accountancy answers both questions in the negative. This is explainable in part by its historical conservatism, combined with its historical emphasis upon balance sheets rather than income statements as fundamental instruments.[20] Furthermore, accounting practice in England and America developed largely during periods of stable or falling prices, when the evasion of problems raised by changes in the monetary unit erred on the conservative side in measuring business income as well.[21] Even in the earlier period, price-level movements of a short-term character, as over individual business

---

[19]This traditional position has been supported forcibly by Professor Charles A. Bliss in his controversial article, "The Reality of Inventory Profits," 26 *Harvard Business Review* (Sept. 1948), pp. 527-542.

[20]The balance sheet has been described as "the oldest, and long the principal or only statement issued," whereas in more recent years of public investment in equity securities, "The growth of interest in accounts as a guide to the value of securities has resulted in increased importance being attached to the income account." Again, "the main emphasis has shifted from the balance sheet to the income account." George O. May, *Financial Accounting* (New York: Macmillan, 1943), pp. 240, 215, 47. The same authority has elsewhere defined "conservatism" in accounting as "a disposition to resolve doubts in the measurement of assets or profit on the side of understatement," [*Business Income and Price Levels: An Accounting Study* (New York: American Institute of Accountants, July 1, 1949) p. 7], a somewhat equivocal definition insofar as a single accounting procedure may simultaneously affect asset value and current income in opposite directions.

[21]"Our financial accounting . . . has been largely influenced by English practice. In England financial accounting of general business corporations grew in importance after the passage of the Companies Act of 1862, which has been called the Magna Carta of limited liability business. . . . the third of a century following that date was one in which the purchasing power of the pound was steadily rising, and . . . this fact may have a relation to the accounting emphasis on past costs since, in the circumstances, the use of cost was both convenient and conservative. . . Today, while it may still be convenient, it is admittedly the reverse of conservative both in England and America." May, *Business Income and Price Levels, op. cit.*, pp. 7, 8. Again, in a listing of fundamental "Accounting Principles and Postulates," May mentions specifically "The Postulate of Stability in the Monetary Unit," as underlying standard accounting practices, (*Financial Accounting, op. cit.*, pp. 46-49).

119

cycles, prevented complete satisfaction with the results, although a counsel of patience to dissatisfied parties appeared more rational in the last century than it appears at the present time.

Suppose a corporation, in a period of secular rise in prices, estimates its income by standard accounting procedures. Let us suppose that it pays taxes based on the standard rules, and subsequently distributes to its shareholders all income which it is permitted legally to distribute under these rules. Such a corporation would be a model firm in the eyes of many neo-liberal critics of American corporate enterprise. It would dodge no taxes. It would hoard no funds in "secret reserves." All its expansion would be financed externally, and subjected to the test of the markets. Its management would neither deprive its needy stockholders of the dividends they had earned, nor provide its wealthy stockholders with an "incorporated pocketbook" of undistributed profits beyond the reach of the Bureau of Internal Revenue. Now, having given our hypothetical corporation a clean bill of social health, let us consider its economic condition.

The firm will be able neither to replace its inventories as they are sold, or its fixed capital as it wears out, from its own reserves. It will be forced to seek funds from outside for these purposes, as well as for any expansion it wishes to undertake. How good a risk such a firm will be considered by potential lenders of funds or purchasers of equities I leave to the reader to estimate. If rights in its corporate property are divided between life tenants (or shorter-term interests) and remaindermen, the corporate policy will be admirable from the viewpoint of the life tenants but will exhaust progressively the real capital of the remaindermen. If the corporation is engaged in a regulated industry, such as a public utility, rates set by regulatory agencies on the basis of standard accounting practices will be too low to permit the corporation to earn the "fair return" which it is ostensibly guaranteed on the cost of its capital, while simultaneously replacing it at rising prices.

The accounting profession, speaking through recognized professional associations such as the American Institute of Accountants, has been understandably loth to initiate or recommend any sweeping changes or modifications in concepts or procedures which have stood the tests of time and experience, and whose mastery in full and complex detail forms part of the occupational stock-in-trade of the profession. Before any change will be in order accountants should be convinced, first, that the long-term trend of prices has actually shifted to a significant extent in an upward direction, and second, that some practical means of dealing with the situation exists which may meet eventually with the approval of the business community, the tax authorities, the leaders of labor, and the general public once it has been blessed professionally by the accountants themselves. Any modification of standard practices, in this writer's view, should possess at least the following desirable qualities:

1. It should be substantially more accurate in interpreting accounting data to business men, labor leaders, and the public in periods of changing prices.

2. It should be as simple as possible from the mathematical and statistical viewpoint, and avoid as far as possible ventures beyond the high-school level of algebra, although it is probably impossible to escape some increases in complexity beyond the present standard rules.

3. It should be consistent in its treatment of working and fixed capital, *i. e.* in its solutions of the inventory and depreciation problems. Standard "old fashioned" practice of FIFO inventory accounting and original cost depreciation satisfy this requirement. Certain "new-fangled" adjustments do not, which may explain in part the disfavor with which they are sometimes regarded. For instance, the use of last-in-first-out (LIFO) accounting for inventories may adjust not only for price level changes but also for changes of individual prices, while it is almost completely inapplicable to problems of fixed capital accounting. On the depreciation side, "accelerated depreciation," which is coming into increased favor, makes no price adjustments whatever but attempts merely, in violation of physical fact, to concentrate de-

121

preciation charges in a relatively small number of years when price increases and gross profits are expected to be unusually large. LIFO and "accelerated depreciation," then, are not a mutually-consistent pair of modifications.[22]

4. It should be consistent as between its applications to periods of rising and falling prices, even if (as we have claimed above) the former will be in the dominant position. Many participants in current controversy appear to violate this self-evident principle. Thus most business leaders will agree that conventional practice regarding depreciation results in overstatement of business income during periods of price inflation. They would like to see this practice modified, and in many cases have prepared for stockholders and the public supplementary income statements in which additional depreciation is charged *ad hoc,* largely on the basis of higher replacement costs,[23] although the Treasury has not yet recognized the additional depreciation charges for tax purposes. These same leaders did not, so far as we know, support or even accede to the assertion, made during the 1930's before the

---

[22]This report will not attempt to discuss either LIFO or accelerated depreciation at adequate length, but a few footnote comments may be in order:

1. LIFO accounting alters income statements in realistic directions over the business cycle or other periods of price change. It is, nevertheless, subject to at least two important objections. First, LIFO does not conform to the physical facts of inventory flow in commerce and industry. Second, LIFO tends to distort balance sheets by leaving the inventory account on the asset side evaluated at the prices of inventory initially acquired or inventory held when LIFO was introduced, which may be very different from current market values.

2. "Accelerated depreciation" does not deal with the problem of rising prices, but rather defers it. Let us, reverting to the example in note 5 above, consider a firm with a machine which cost $10,000 and has a 10-year working life, at the end of which its cost will have risen to $20,000. If the total amount of depreciation taken can be only $10,000, how is the issue met by concentrating the depreciation allowance into the first five years instead of spreading it over the entire ten? Insofar as the company can gain by this device, it is for reasons other than rising prices. For example, corporate income tax rates in the first five years may be higher than those expected in the second five, or the firm may expect losses in the second half of the period which it cannot carry back in full, or accelerated depreciation in the first five (profitable) years may prevent the granting of wage increases which will be a serious burden during the second five (unprofitable) period. These advantages may be very real in individual cases, but they do not grapple with the price level problem per se.

[23]Arthur H. Dean, in *Business Income Under Present Price Levels* (*op. cit.,* pp. 20-37), discusses a number of these adjustments used by leading American companies in their reports for 1948 and early 1949.

Temporary National Economic Committee and elsewhere, that the same conventional practice applied to the construction costs of the 1920's had understated business income during the Great Depression with its low prices. Their critics, may we hasten to add, stand on no firmer ground. During the 1930's they assailed conventional depreciation accounting for understating business income, and allowing accumulation of hidden tax-free reserves which permitted plant expansion to be financed internally instead of providing outlets or offsets for the public's saving.[24] In the 1940's, when conventional accounting has the opposite effect on business income, the critics become the purest of the purists.

We shall now pass to consideration of two rival concepts of business income. Each recognizes the same "facts of life" outlined above, and each satisfies the four criteria just considered. For want of titles more generally recognized, we may christen them the "venture" and the "continuum" concepts respectively, then proceed to differentiate them from each other and choose between them. Each is held, we hasten to admit at the outset, not only in its pure form but with various admixtures of advantageous if imperfectly consistent material.

The "venture" concept, beloved of the trade unions and their neo-liberal sympathizers, corresponds most closely to the traditional concept of the accounting profession.[25] It ignores changes in tax rates, interest rates, and industrial technique. According to this concept, each purchase of working or (especially) fixed capital instruments should be regarded as a separate venture of one or more investors. Conversely, each investor should be considered as contributing a certain sum of money to one or more

---

[24]See, in particular, the testimony of Dr. Oscar L. Altman, then of the Securities and Exchange Commission, 9 *T. N. E. C. Hearings—Investigation of Economic Power*, pp. 3675-3679, in which he concludes that concerns replacing in 1935 machinery for which depreciation reserves had been accumulated in 1929 "not only would have 12 percent of the original cost in cash but probably also a better machine" (p. 3702). If the year 1933 had been chosen to make the replacements, the saving would have risen to 20 percent (p. 3676).

[25]For example, clear statements of the venture concept can be found in the testimony of two of the labor representatives at the Profits Hearings of December 1948, Donald Montgomery of the United Auto Workers (*op. cit.*, pp. 430, 443) and Russ Nixon of the United Electrical Workers (*ibid.*, p. 460).

123

separate ventures. A company's earnings, over and above the amount contributed as the sum of the separate ventures, should be regarded as business income. Whether the money contributed by the original investors, when set aside in reserve by the company, does or does not in fact permit replacement of the real capital goods involved is completely irrelevant under this concept. For each such replacement or repurchase is viewed as a distinct second venture, for which funds should be raised quite independently on the open market. The function of depreciation accounting is to spread *past money* costs over time, not to raise funds for capital replacement. Prices should not be raised or dividends withheld to provide for replacement of capital instruments, but only for the return of money actually contributed. Shifts in the purchasing power of this money are to be treated as among the risks and uncertainties to be borne by corporations and their shareholders. Why, it is asked, should the equity investor, the risk-bearer personified, be better protected from price-level changes than the rest of the community who suffer them likewise and whose incomes are not justified under the rubric of "uncertainty-bearing?"

Opposed to this view is the "continuum" concept, which is held by most businessmen, and likewise by most economists. Under the "continuum" concept, a business enterprise should be considered as a going and unified concern rather than as a discrete series of separate and loosely-related individual ventures.[26] The investor, likewise, is seen as contributing some portion of the real fixed and working capital of the concern where he invests his funds, albeit his investment is made in money form and the particular item contributed is never identified. Perhaps his investment can be regarded as a quantum of "purchasing power over capital goods." Only earnings over and above the maintenance of the capital goods contributed can be regarded as income of the concern.[27] Firms which do not provide for the maintenance

---

[26]May's *Financial Accounting* (*op. cit.*, p. 49f.), goes so far as to set up a "postulate of continuity" underlying modern financial accounting practice.

[27]Questions not directly pertinent to the present study with its stress on price level changes, but important to the general problem of definition of income, relate to tax

of their inventory or their fixed capital out of earnings should be considered insolvent regardless of the magnitude of their money profits, and investors should be warned against purchasing the securities of such concerns on the capital market without adequate warning.

Estimates of the magnitude of the differences involved as between the two concepts in periods of rapid price increases have been made only roughly. Best known of these estimates at the present time is that which Professor Sumner Slichter of Harvard University presented in December 1948 to the Joint Congressional Committee on the Economic Report at its hearings on the general subject of corporate profits, (which we have abbreviated to *Profits Hearings*). Over the three-year period 1946-48 inclusive, Slichter suggests, the reported figures on corporate income alone would have been reduced by some $16.4 billion, or approximately 25 percent, had a "continuum" concept been used throughout the period.[28] The bulk of this adjustment (some $15 billion of the total) was estimated with some precision by the U. S. Department of Commerce "inventory revaluation adjustments", computed each year in connection with published national income and product statistics. These are tantamount to replacing FIFO with LIFO accounting for all business inventory, and we may take the result of LIFO on the income side (although not on the asset side) in

---

rates, interest rates, and technical progress. On these, the standard positions taken under the "continuum" concept, largely for reasons of convenience, are:

1. Income should be taken net of such taxes as are shifted forward to consumers of the firm's products or backward to suppliers of materials and labor, but gross of such taxes as are borne by the firm itself out of income or capital. (There is further dispute as to whether the corporate income and excess-profits taxes belong in the former or the latter category. In the writer's personal view, the bulk of these taxes are *not* shiftable.)

2. Interest rate changes should be ignored, and capital regarded as maintained when similar goods are repurchased, regardless of effects of interest-rate changes on their cost, their capitalized value, or their income-producing power. Compare J. R. Hicks, *Value and Capital* (Oxford. Oxford University Press, 1939), ch. 14,, sec. 3-5.

3. Technical progress, likewise, is to be ignored in defining income. Business income should be taken net of sums adequate to replace existing capital, even when the capital actually provided as replacement is improved in quality or even differs completely in form and function.

[28]*Profits Hearings*, p. 3f.

turn as equivalent to those which would follow general adoption of a "continuum" concept. The remaining $1.5 billion of Slichter's total would have resulted, according to some admittedly crude calculations, from upward adjustments of current depreciation reserves to reflect higher post-war prices. Despite tentative confirmation of Slichter's figures by studies, as yet unpublished, made under insurance company auspices by the R. W. Goldsmith Associates, these figures appear to this writer too low to follow from Slichter's own assumptions. The conservative bias appears to result from the following consideration: Slichter's figures were obtained by treating as proper depreciation charges for each of the three years 1946-48 inclusive, amounts 60 percent higher than those charged in 1940, when Slichter supposes depreciation charges to have been roughly adjusted to going prices for capital instruments. This allowance for the 60 per cent price increase which has occurred subsequently is adequate only, as Slichter himself points out, "assuming that there has been no appreciable increase in the size of the plant to be depreciated."[29] In view of the character of the intervening years' conflict and construction, this assumption certainly is ultra-conservative. This is the only modification of Slichter's procedure which seems required to apply the continuum concept in estimating business income in the sense of business contribution to net national income or product. In measuring taxable income, however, or considering wage and price changes, a further change seems to be called for. Slichter's figures allow for no additions or supplements to depreciation allowances already made during earlier years. When a machine with a 10-year life is replaced in 1949 at 1949 prices, writing up the depreciation allowance for the last year will not suffice to make the total depreciation reserve adequate for the machine's replacement. The amounts set aside in the earlier years (before substantial price increases) must likewise be supplemented out of current earnings, if the reserve is to fulfill its purpose under the continuum concept. (Slichter's computations allow for no revisions of earlier depreciation allowances already on the books.)

---

[29] *Ibid.*, p. 6.

Decision between the venture and continuum concepts of business income, like many another basic judgment in the statistical analysis of income and wealth, rests in the last analysis on subjective preferences of a quasi-esthetic character. It is hardly possible to justify any flat statement that one definition or concept is right and another wrong, or even that one is intrinsically or inherently better than another. It must suffice, when a choice is made, to present the reasons for one's individual preference in the hope of attracting general agreement and approval. Thus in the present instance, the writer is disposed to prefer the continuum over the venture concept for a number of reasons which will be mentioned below.

The continuum concept appears to coincide more closely than the venture concept with the realities of twentieth-century business practice. The typical business investment of today is in a continuously-functioning "going concern," the maintenance of whose capital should be of interest to present and potential investors. In the 16th and 17th century companies of merchant adventurers trading with Muscovy, Turkey, and the several Indies, which economic historians tell us are archetypes of the modern corporation, shares were originally not *of* stock but *in* specific Company ventures, and the venture concept did in fact apply to working capital (cargoes) if not to fixed capital (ships). Granted all this, and the consequent historical justification for the venture concept of business income, the fact remains that today's representative business, apart from exploratory "wildcatting" for oil and other mineral resources, is no longer of the venture but of the continuum type.

Adoption of the continuum concept would tend to reduce the reported figures of business income during periods of boom and inflation, increase them during periods of depression and deflation. Its major effect would be to reduce the variance of the return to equity capital. Translated from statistical to economic terms, it would lessen the risk associated with investment in equities.[30] It

---

[30]One should not exaggerate the extent to which uncertainties can be reduced by this or any other variation in accounting technique, as did Senator O'Mahoney when, commenting on the testimony of Slichter and the corroborating position of Professor William A. Paton of the University of Michigan, he characterized them as desiring "to take all of the risk out of risk capital by figuring profits on a new basis." (*Profits Hearings, op. cit.,* p. 123).

might also, insofar as tax savings were involved over the cycle, increase somewhat the expected return on these securities.[31] By lessening the risk of equity investment, adoption of the continuum concept would increase the volume of such investment and also decrease the rate of return at which it is carried on. Any such decrease in the rate of return would probably be capitalized in the form of higher prices on existing equity securities and a general upturn in the common stock indexes, with consequent capital gains for present security holders. Another possible effect, perhaps of less quantitative significance, would be to shift corporate financing somewhat away from debts and toward equities, with improved flexibility in the weathering of hard times.

Thorough-going adoption of the continuum concept, finally, would bring fixed capital accounting into consistency with the results if not the practice of the LIFO method of inventory accounting, which appears to be gaining favor in American business. If the continuum concept is not accepted, it will be difficult to justify the continued use of LIFO, and we should consider seriously the return to the standard practice of the FIFO method.

Opposition to what we have called the continuum concept has been concentrated, as we have said, among representatives of labor. This was particularly marked at the *Profits Hearings* of December 1948, when Professor Slichter's contentions, summarized above, were attacked heatedly by such men as Prof. Seymour E. Harris, leading neo-liberal economist and Slichter's colleague at Harvard University, Mr. Stanley H. Ruttenberg of the C. I. O., Mr. Donald Montgomery of the United Automobile Workers, and Mr. Russ Nixon of the United Electrical Workers.[32] The opposition could be expected in the situation then existing, since acceptance of Slichter's view would reduce by some 25 per

---

[31]Tax considerations aside, the continuum concept would almost certainly lower reported income per common share over periods of long-term price increase, which we expect to dominate the calculable future. This reduction would not, in our view, usually cause any reduction of income actually distributed as dividends per common share, but rather increase the percentage of distributable income actually paid out to stockholders rather than being added to surplus to provide for uncovered depreciation charges.

[32]The relevant testimony of Professor Harris may be found in *Profits Hearings, op. cit.,* pp. 33-36; of Mr. Ruttenberg, *ibid.,* pp. 135 f., 145-47; of Mr. Montgomery, *ibid.,* pp. 422-32; and of Mr. Nixon, *ibid.,* pp. 457-61. The intermittent comments of Senator O'Mahoney of the Joint Committee express the same position.

cent the total nest egg which the labor representatives wished to see transformed into wage increases and-or price reductions "out of profits." It could be explained on more general terms by the suspicion that business support for LIFO, for replacement depreciation, or for other implementations of the continuum concept were purely self-seeking and would disappear whenever prices should cease their upward movement.[33] Many of their objections, however, seem based on false assumptions if applied to the continuum concept applied *consistently* in intervals of falling prices as well as over the long sweep of rising prices.

1. It would *not* shift to consumers or workers the burden of financing plant expansion. It applies only to the *replacement* and not to the *accretion* of either inventory of equipment. It is irrelevant to the issue of internal vs. external sources of funds for expansion purposes, which we do not propose to discuss in this paper.[34]

2. It would *not* prejudice the issues outstanding as between "reproduction cost" and "prudent investment" as bases for public utility and allied rate regulation. Use of replacement depreciation in *measuring* business income does not require use of replacement cost in *judging its reasonableness* when so measured. The issues are sufficiently separate that no logical objections appear to exist against regulating utility income, computed by the use of replace-

---

[33]Thus Harris (*ibid.*, p. 33):

"But it is important to point out the present accounting practice has been used for generations so far as I know, and now suddenly some businessmen find it more convenient to change this accounting method. As a matter of fact, I know, and probably you know, that there is pressure being put on the accountants to change that method of accounting of business profits so that these large inflationary profits during these periods will not seem as large as they are."

And Ruttenberg (*ibid.*, p. 136):

"Again we repeat in connection with both the inventory profits and the depreciation policy that industry has devised these two arguments currently only to explain away the currently high levels of profits. If profits today were low and not being attacked for being too high, industry would not be engaged in a propaganda campaign to up depreciation allowances and deduct inventory profits."

[34]Except to point out that insofar as property and particularly dividend income is the main source of private investment funds, the statement that consumers or wage earners provide the equity capital (or "inequity capital" in Mr. Montgomery's colorful parlance) for industrial expansion is equally true or false, whether or not the funds pass through the hands of private shareholders as intermediaries between their initial receipt and their later re-investment.

ment depreciation, as a percentage of capital value in original cost or prudent investment terms. In fact, this particular combination appears to meet the *prima facie* reasonable positions of the partisans on each side, while avoiding certain of the unreasonable extremities to which each case can be carried, and it may provide some feasible compromise between the two extremist positions. But elaboration of this discussion would lead away from our primary subject.

3. It would *not* permit corporations to pocket hidden profits by charging depreciation at high prices, then postponing the actual replacements until prices were lower. It would permit *less* depreciation than the conventional method during periods of falling prices, and may even result in *negative* depreciation allowances if prices drop sufficiently rapidly, or indeed if they drop at all in the interval between the complete depreciation of some capital instrument and the time of its physical replacement.

4. It should *not* be interpreted as purporting to insulate corporations or their stockholders from changes in the purchasing power of money, which the rest of society must suffer.[35] There is in the first place no guarantee whatever that earnings will cover depreciation charges, on whatever base these latter may be computed. There is in the second place no adjustment in earnings, over and above depreciation charges, for changes in the purchasing power of money, which is not constantly utilized by other segments of the population in computing *i.e.* real wages or real farm income. Any special treatment of depreciation or inventory is not prompted by favoritism to this type of income but by the belief, expressed forcibly by Professor Hatfield, that:[36] "Profits are not determined until after allowance has been made for depreciation.

---

[35]As an example of confusion on this point, consider Senator O'Mahoney's paraphrase of what he considers to be our position (*Profits Hearings, op. cit.,* p. 96) : "Let us allow the corporation to figure its profits in a technical nonexistent dollar, while the Government and everybody else has to struggle along with the existing current dollar."

[36]Henry Rand Hatfield, *Accounting, Its Principles and Problems* (New York: Appleton-Century, 1927), p. 241 f. The same thought is expressed in journalistic fashion in a *Business Week* article read at the Profits Hearings (*op. cit.,* p. 98) by Mr. George D. Bailey, Past President of the American Institute of Accountants: "A businessman thinks of himself as a going concern. And profit isn't profit to him if he has to plow it back just to keep his plant intact."

Depreciation is not a disposition of part of the profits, but an expense without which profits can never be earned."

5. It need *not* involve any special device for computing net property income to which no analogue can be granted the recipients of wages and salaries or other forms of net labor income. A statistical concomitant of our passage from a slave to a free economy has been that labor income, derived from human capital instruments not generally salable as such, has been almost universally computed *gross* of the expenditures required for its maintenance or replacement, while income from inanimate or animal capital is taken *net* of appropriate deductions. This statistical concomitant, in the writer's view, is generally unfortunate in its effects. It results, or so it seems, in a systematic over-statement of the share of labor in the net (although not the gross) national income and product totals. Would it not be more consistent with the treatment of property income and also perhaps more realistic to deduct from gross labor income an amount, represented perhaps by a Minimum Health and Decency Budget,[37] as representing depreciation and maintenance charges on human capital, before arriving at net labor income? Some such adjustment is made, for this reason among others, in the devising of "personal exemptions" in personal income tax laws. It is made likewise, albeit for very different reasons, by research organizations in estimating the demand for consumer durable goods which seems to depend less on total income than on the "supernumerary income" remaining after purchase of necessities of life.[38]

---

[37]This particular budget has been drawn up and revised in the Bureau of Home Economics of the U. S. Department of Agriculture. Similar budgets on varying levels have been prepared by this and other agencies, both public and private, in the U. S. and in many foreign countries. For our present purposes, choice between the several minimum budgets is not a matter of great significance, inasmuch as their prices move quite closely together. Most good undergraduate textbooks on consumer economics contain sections or chapters dealing with standard budgets in the measurement of living standards. See, e.g. Warren C. Waite and Ralph Cassaday, Jr., *The Consumer and the Economic Order* (Second Edition: New York: McGraw-Hill, 1949), ch. 12.

[38]The "supernumerary income" approach is associated particularly with C. F. Roos and Victor von Szeliski's studies of automobile demand. Roos and von Szeliski, "Factors Governing Changes in Domestic Automobile Demand," in *The Dynamics of Automobile Demand* (New York: General Motors, 1939), pp. 39-42. Roos and von Szeliski, incidentally, take pains to adjust their "cost of living" deduction from total income in accordance with price changes.

131

If a Minimum Health and Decency Budget for a worker's family be taken as analogous to a depreciation allowance on fixed capital, and his net income (or supernumerary income if this cumbersome term is preferred) computed after deduction of the cost of such a budget from his gross income, the application of the continuum concept to labor as well as property income would be conceivable. The deduction required would be a variable one, depending upon the cost of the Minimum Health and Decency Budget.[39] It would yield a net (or supernumerary) income in current dollars, subject to subsequent deflation to "real" terms. Labor and investment would then be placed on the same (and in this writer's view the correct) footing. Relative shares would be more closely comparable than they are at present, net of the relevant deductions in current prices. No "double deflation" would be involved in fact for either type of income, and there would be no appearance thereof in one type not open to the other on the same terms.

It may not be practical to adjust the labor component of the net national income in the manner suggested immediately above. "Minimum health and decency" varies widely with time and place, so that the existing procedure is more objective, as well as simple and established. In dealing with taxable income, however, or in collective-bargaining negotiations, deduction of a variable "cost of subsistence" should be considered on the same footing as deduction of a variable "depreciation allowance."

Unless we can implement it in concrete terms, the continuum concept will be of little value to the practicing accountant. Such implementing this writer believes perfectly feasible. Because of the algebra involved, which is admittedly dull despite its basic simplicity, discussion of this important topic is relegated to the Appendix which follows immediately, entitled "Implementing the Continuum Concept."

---

[39]Variations in the personal exemptions for the Federal income tax with changing price levels operate very roughly along similar lines.

VI. Appendix: Implementing the Continuum Concept

We desire to modify the formulae for either the straight-line or the service-output methods of depreciation accounting[40] under conditions of price change, in such a manner that by making appropriate credits to reserve a company can accumulate a reserve sufficient but no more than sufficient to replace the equipment at the appropriate time. Let the original cost of an item of capital be C, of which a k_t th part[41] is to be set aside for depreciation in the t th year. The current convention would indicate a credit to reserve amounting to $k_t C$. If the cost of such equipment at the time of construction, which we shall call period o, was p_o and its present cost is p_t, the credit to reserve which Slichter and others would apparently advocate is

$$\frac{p_t}{p_o} k_t C \qquad \ldots\ldots\ldots (1)$$

Formula (1) is quite adequate for inventory replenishment purposes, and is in fact the modification which we advocate in place of LIFO accounting. It is also an adequate depreciation deduction in current prices for national income purposes, i.e. for estimating the business component of the national income or product and its distribution between industries. For a private business accumulating a reserve to replace existing equipment, however, it may be either too large or too small. Changes in prices affect the adequacy of *past* accumulations in reserve funds, as well

---

[40]The service-output method, perhaps somewhat less well-known than the straight-line method and less universally applicable as well, receives a sympathetic discussion in Solomon Fabricant, *Capital Consumption and Adjustment* (New York: National Bureau of Economic Research, 1938), p. 68 ff. To the economist, this method is interesting particularly in embodying certain of the ideas of "user cost" introduced formally into the literature by Lord Keynes' *General Theory* (*op. cit.*, pp. 66-73). For the sake of simplicity, particularly in the avoidance of discounting problems, we do not consider adjustments to depreciation formulae of greater complexity.

[41]In the simple straight-line method of depreciation, k_t is constant from year to year, and the subscript t is unnecessary. In the service-output method, k_t is a ratio of the output in the given year to the total output expected from the capital instrument during its working life. It is a variable, higher in prosperous than in depressed periods.

as of *current* payments into them. There is no reason for current national income statistics to be affected by any adjustments we may make in these records of bygone years, but there is every reason for the business' own income to reflect them, for tax purposes as well as reports to stockholders and the public,[42] if sufficient reserves are to be considered a charge on gross rather than net income. How can the necessary adjustments be represented algebraically?

If the company has followed the practice of adjusting current increments to its reserves to price level changes, these will have been, for periods *o, 1,....(t-1),* respectively:

$$\frac{p_0}{p_0} k_0 C, \frac{p_1}{p_0} k_1 C, \ldots, \frac{p_{t-1}}{p_0} k_{t-1} C$$

If there has been a price change since the last period *(t-1)*, these past reserves, if they are to remain adequate, must be multiplied by the proportionate price change

$$\frac{p_t - p_{t-1}}{p_0} \qquad \text{or simply} \qquad \frac{\Delta p_t}{p_0}$$

where the Greek letter Δ (delta) denotes a difference. This difference will be positive if prices are rising, negative if they are falling.

The total of reserves to be adjusted in this way is:

$$\frac{p_0}{p_0} k_0 C + \frac{p_1}{p_0} k_1 C + \ldots + \frac{p_{t-1}}{p_0} k_{t-1} C = \sum_{i=0}^{t-1} \frac{p_i}{p_0} k_i C$$

(The Greek letter Σ (sigma) is a symbol of summation used frequently in statistical work as a short-hand method of adding a number of separate items of similar form.)

---

[42] Clear-cut distinctions between a taxpayer's contribution to national income and his income for tax purposes are not new in American fiscal practice. Perhaps the outstanding case in point involves capital gains. When a taxpayer makes a capital gain (or loss) the national product is not affected in any way, but the individual taxpayer has realized an accretion to his economic power which American law considers taxable. An analogous distinction is suggested in the text.

134

The adjustment factor for all these past depreciation reserves, then, may be written:

$$\frac{\Delta p_t}{p_0} \sum_{i=0}^{t-1} \frac{p_i}{p_0} \, k_i \, C \qquad \dots (2)$$

The total depreciation adjustment is the sum of the current allowance, given by (1), and the revision of past allowances, given by (2). Addition gives a combined formula (3), which is simpler in use than in appearance.

$$\frac{p_t}{p_0} \, k_t \, C + \frac{\Delta p_t}{p_0} \sum_{i=0}^{t-1} \frac{p_i}{p_0}$$

Formula (3) has assumed the adjustment for price level changes to have been made every year, as the present discussion recommends. If in fact it is not so made, the percentage price rise, $\frac{\Delta p_t}{p_0}$, should be computed not from the previous year, but from the year when the last adjustment was made, or from p_0, the price level at the period when the equipment was constructed, if no previous adjustments at all have been made. In this last instance, formula (3) is somewhat simplified. The initial term (1) remains the same, but the past-adjustment term is modified to make the formula appear:

$$\frac{p_t}{p_0} \, k_t \, C + \frac{\Delta p_t}{p_0} \sum_{i=0}^{t-1} k_i \, C \qquad \dots (4)$$

If current credits to depreciation have taken price changes into account, as by (1) but past reserves have not been adjusted since the year o, a different modification is required in the second term of (3). This time the formula becomes slightly more complex in appearance although not in its actual computation:

135

$$\frac{p_t}{p_0} k_t\, C + \frac{(p_t-p_0)\,p_0}{p_0}\cdot\frac{}{p_0} - k_0\, C + \frac{(p_t-p_1)}{p_1}\cdot\frac{p_1}{p_0} - k_1\, C + \ldots + \frac{(p_t-p_{t-1})}{p_{t-1}}\cdot\frac{p_{t-1}}{p_0} - k_{t-1}\, C$$

$$\text{or}\qquad \frac{p_t}{p_0}\, k_t\, C + \sum_{t=0}^{t-1}\left[\frac{p_t-p_1}{p_1} - \frac{p_1}{p_0}\, k_1\, C\right]\qquad \ldots\ldots(5)$$

Other variants will undoubtedly occur to the reader who cares to experiment with these formulae. It will perhaps be more useful to the non-specialist to illustrate their use with a simple arithmetical example or two.

Let C, the cost of a machine, be $10,000. The machine was bought, let us say, in 1944 (time o), with prices in this and the next two years as given in the table below. (These are of course hypothetical figures, designed to simplify the arithmetic. It should also be noted that the relevant price figures in all computations are decimals, and not percentages or index points.) If the machine is depreciated over a ten-year period by the straight line method, each of our k_1 is simply 1/10 or 0.1. We can now compute by formula (3) and its modifications (4) and (5) the depreciation deductions appropriate to the continuum concept in year 2 (1946).

Calendar	Year Symbol (i)	Per Cent	Price Level Decimal
1944	0	100	1.00
1945	1	125	1.25
1946	2 (= t)	150	1.50

As a first step, we can determine each $k_1 C$ as 0.1 × $10,000, or $1,000, so that (1), which is the first term of (3), reduces to:

$$\frac{1.50}{1.00} \times \$1,000 \text{ or } \$1,500.$$

The second term of (3) is:

$$\frac{(1.50-1.25)}{1.00}\left[\left\{\frac{1.00}{1.00}\times\$1,000\right\} + \left\{\frac{1.25}{1.00}\times\$1,000\right\}\right] \text{ or } \$562.50$$

136

so that the total depreciation allowance, by (3) is the sum of $1,500 and $562.50, or $2,062.50, more than twice the conventional $1,000 allowance. Only the $1,500 item should be deducted for net national income and product calculations.

If a similar adjustment had been made in the previous year (1945, or 1), the total reserve would now be adequate to the requirements of capital replacement. If only the conventional $1,000 allowance had been made in the previous year, however, formula (4) would apply instead of formula (3). The first term of $1,500 would be unaffected by the change, but the second term would now read:

$$\frac{(1.50 - 1.00)}{1.00}\ (\$1,000\ +\ \$1,000) \quad \text{or } \$1,000$$

and the total depreciation allowance would be $2,500.

If the current depreciation reserve had been adjusted for price changes in year 1, but not reserves previously accumulated, formula (5) instead of either (3) or (4) would be required to bring the total reserves up to their proper level. The first term of (5) is again $1,500, but the second term is:

$$\frac{(1.50 - 1.00)}{1.00}\ (\$1,000) + \frac{(1.50 - 1.25)}{1.25}\ (\$1,250) \quad \text{or } \$750$$

for a total credit of $2,250.

Another brief arithmetical example, based on a different set of prices, will show how our formulae work out under deflation as well as inflation. Let our k_1 and C be as before, and work out depreciation allowances for year 2 ("1921") after a drastic price decline:

Year Calendar	Symbol (i)	Price Level Per Cent	Decimal
1900	0	100	1.00
1920	1	75	.75
1921	2 (= t)	50	.50

For our new year 2, while $k_t C$ is again $1,000, expression (1), which makes up the first term of formulas (3)-(5), is only $500 because of the price decline, and a $500 deduction should be made in passing from the gross to the net business contribution to national income and product. For taxable income computation, however, and for public presentation, past depreciation should also be written down when prices fall for the same reason that write-ups are recommended when prices rise. If formula (3) applies, as when all appropriate adjustments have been made in prior years, our write-down term would be:

$$\frac{(.75 - .50)}{1.00} \left[\left\{ \frac{1.00}{1.00} \times \$1,000 \right\} + \left\{ \frac{.75}{1.00} \times \$1,000 \right\} \right] \quad \text{or } \$437.50$$

for a total depreciation allowance of only ($500 — $437.50) or $62.50.

If no allowance of any kind for price changes had been made in the previous year, formula (4) would apply. Subtracted from a first term of $500, the write-down of past reserves would be:

$$\frac{(1.00 - .50)}{1.00} (\$1,000 + \$1,000) \quad \text{or } \$1,000$$

The combined depreciation allowance would be *negative* (— $500). The economic meaning of this phenomenon would be that more than enough had been set aside in two years, under the unrealistic assumption of high prices, to cover depreciation for three years at falling prices. While it is our opinion that no such precipitous price drops are to be expected in the future as this hypothetical example illustrates, it is interesting to observe the possible results of their occurrence under a continuum concept of business income.

If the current depreciation reserve had been adjusted for price changes in year 1, but not reserves previously accumulated, formula (5) instead of either (3) or (4) would again be required to place total reserves on their proper footing. The first term of (5) is again $500, but the second, or write-down term, is:

$$\frac{(1.00 - .50)}{1.00} (\$1,000) + \frac{(.75 - .50)}{.75} (\$750) \quad \text{or } \$750$$

138

and again the combined allowance becomes slightly negative (— $250).

Before we leave these examples it is perhaps worth emphasizing once more that the methods suggested, precisely because they cause such wide fluctuations in depreciation and depletion allowances, operate to reduce the fluctuations in reported business income over the business cycle, as well as to reduce it secularly during periods of predominantly rising prices. This is particularly true for business income as reported to stockholders (subject to S. E. C. approval) and for tax purposes (subject to Treasury approval), but also applies to the business contribution to the net national income and product to a lesser degree.

A problem as pressing and perplexing as the choice and computation of depreciation formulae in the implementing of our concept of business income is the choice of index numbers for computing price levels (the p's of our formulae). Let us state at the very outset that no choice of price index will be perfect for any firm or any industry. Prices do not move together, or in other words relative prices change, so that the cost of no firm's or no industry's particular collection of inventories or capital assets can be expected to follow any index number perfectly. At the same time, it should also be realized that even an imperfectly representative index is better than no index at all, which implies continuance in the bland assumption of an unchanging purchasing power of money.

A great number of index numbers have been proposed or computed for depreciation adjustments. Most of them are series already available to the public for other purposes, but some have been developed especially in connection with reducing depreciation and depletion figures to "real" terms. Carl Snyder's index number of general prices (which included wage rates, interest rates, and security prices as well as the usual commodity quotations, and which was formerly computed regularly at the Federal Reserve Bank of New York) was suggested, primarily because of its breadth and inclusiveness, by a New York accountant, Henry W. Sweeney, as the basis for a system which he called *Stabilized*

139

Accounting,[43] developed largely from his study of German accounting practices during the hyper-inflation of the early 'twenties. Professor Fabricant, for his standard study of *Capital Consumption and Adjustment*, was dissatisfied with all the published indexes and derived separate indexes of his own, largely by combination of published series.[44] Instead of striving (as did Sweeney) for a single index suitable for deflating all depreciation accounts, Fabricant followed what appears to be the more desirable method of computing separate index numbers for the prices of producers' durable goods other than building, for construction costs, and for repair and maintenance charges.

At least one business firm has gone some distance in directing its thinking along the same general lines, if we may judge by the testimony at the *Profits Hearings* of December 1948. Mr. Howard C. Greer, executive vice president of Kingan & Co., an Indianapolis meat packing house, went into great detail in preparing for the Congressional Joint Committee on the Economic Report a system of replacement depreciation using index numbers. His method may be of interest as a model, precisely because of its development by a practical business man with no acknowledged references to the scholarly literature in the field. His basic procedure bears some resemblance to Fabricant's National Bureau study. He divided depreciable items into five categories with different average lives: buildings, machinery, utensils, office equipment, and motor vehicles. Replacement depreciation was computed separately for each class; four different published index numbers were used in all, but the company made no attempt to compute indexes of its own.[45] Replacement depreciation on buildings was determined with the aid of the *Engineering News-Record's* index of industrial construction costs. On machinery

---

[43]New York: Harpers, 1936. See also Professor Paton's reference to Sweeney's work, *Profits Hearings, op. cit.*, p. 70.

[44]Fabricant, *op. cit.*, pp. 176-88. Note in particular Table 32 (p. 178 f.), in which a number of published index numbers are weighted and combined to form Fabricant's indexes of producers' durable goods prices and of construction costs.

[45]For a verbal statement of Greer's methods, see *Profits Hearings, op. cit.*, p. 402. His statistical procedures are summarized in his exhibit Table A-5, *ibid.*, p. 409 f.

and utensils, Marshall and Stevens' price index of industrial equipment was used, and on office equipment Marshall and Stevens' price index of commercial equipment. Finally, on motor vehicles, the International Harvester Company's price lists, expressed in index number form, was taken as a deflator.

Given a situation of divergent opinion as to which if any of the published price index of inventory and capital goods is applicable for deflating the accounts of any firm or industry, the writer would suggest permitting each firm to choose as it sees fit. It might, if it wished, choose some one or more of the various standard indexes public and private which are available. If it preferred, it might combine several series to form special indexes adapted to its own circumstances. In general it seems to us, in contradistinction to Mr. Sweeney, that generality of an index number is not particularly to be desired, and that accuracy, meaning specific applicability to the costs of a single industry at a particular place, is much to be preferred. If a firm's inventory, depreciation, or depletion should happen to be governed or dominated by the price of one particular commodity, price quotations for this one commodity, reduced to percentages of a base figure, might be used as they stand, without further computations of any index number whatever. There is of course some danger that complete freedom of choice might be used by particular companies for deceptive purposes through deliberate bias. To prevent such bias in either direction, the company's choice of index should be subject to scrutiny and approval in the first instance by its accountants and in the second instance by such public agencies as the S.E.C., the Treasury, or their local equivalents.

The methods we have suggested above have been developed in connection with income statements exclusively. If the income statement and the balance sheet are to be kept mutually consistent, we need hardly point out, these methods also imply periodic (annual?) write-ups and write-downs, presumably against surplus or against some specific reserve, of balance-sheet accounts for depreciable assets and for inventories. The computations them-

141

selves present no formidable problems, but the break with the accepted canons of accountancy would be severe. Furthermore, other assets, either non-depreciable tangibles such as land or intangibles such as patents and trade-marks, may also change in value as the price level moves up and down. Adjustments to their balance sheet accounts are not called for in the computation of business income, since no depreciation or depletion charges are made against them. Changes in other balance sheet items, however, may raise questions of consistency unless these are adjusted as well.

When depreciation charges increase with rising prices, as is suggested here, the book value of the underlying assets would be written up accordingly, and a capital gain would appear on the company's books. This gain, however, not being realized in a market transaction, would not be taxable under present American revenue laws. Any tax saving on the income side taken by itself would not be reduced or eliminated by the necessary balance sheet write-ups for consistency.[46] Conversely, in periods of falling prices, any additional tax liability (over the present standard procedure) would not be compensated by balance sheet write-downs.

[46]There seems to be some confusion on this point in the testimony of Russ Nixon of the United Electrical Workers, *Profits Hearings, op. cit.*, p. 460.

BUSINESS COSTS AND BUSINESS INCOME UNDER CHANGING PRICE LEVELS

THE ECONOMIST'S POINT OF VIEW

By Solomon Fabricant

BUSINESS COSTS AND BUSINESS INCOME
UNDER CHANGING PRICE LEVELS

THE ECONOMIST'S POINT OF VIEW

The nation's aggregate net income is the prime measure of the nation's economic activity. An important component of the national income is, of course, the net income of business enterprise. Now, that would be a good enough reason for economists to concern themselves with the measurement of business income. But there is another. Business income is not only important; it is also one of the more troublesome components of national income when it comes to putting together the figures and deciding what they mean. For these reasons economists have spent a good deal of time thinking of how to measure business income.

Economists have had to grapple with a number of problems. Some arise from changing price levels, some from fluctuations in the volume of production. There are difficulties caused by technological advances, and difficulties caused by alterations in consumers' tastes. Acts of God and the King's enemies also sometimes prove troublesome. In the course of analyzing and discussing these problems—a task that is by no means over—economists have established what may be called an economic point of view towards the measurement of business income, particularly in the computation of national income. This point of view can therefore best be presented to you by considering what kinds of figures on business income economists put into their calculations of the nation's aggregate income. On this occasion we shall want to limit ourselves to the way economists handle the problem of changing price levels. That is the big problem of today.

I said that economists have been worrying about the calculation of business income. I do not want to imply, however, that the business profit figures included in national income statistics are based entirely or even largely on the calculations of economists. On the contrary, the basic data on business income—and other income as well—come out of accountants' reports. What the

Reprinted by permission of The Journal of Accountancy.

economist worries about is the meaning of the accountant's figures, the coverage of these figures, and the adjustments needed to mold them to his own needs. What the economist does is to combine the figures accountants prepare for various industries, make estimates to fill in the gaps (for he wants a complete national aggregate), and introduce a relatively few—though far-reaching—adjustments to adapt the figures to his conception of the business income that is appropriate for inclusion in the national income. Even these adjustments, we shall see, are mainly applications on a larger and more consistent scale of adjustments that accountants here and there have already introduced.

The economist sometimes boasts of his advantage, over other social scientists, in possessing an objective means of measurement. The magnitude of the forces and effects with which he is concerned can be assessed with the measuring rod of money. But the economist above all is aware of the great significance of changes in the value of money. He knows that his measuring rod contracts with shrinkage in the value of money and expands with growth in its value, like the standard meter does with changes in temperature. To keep this measuring rod firm—or perhaps better expressed, to correct the observations he makes with it—the economist has developed the supplementary device of index numbers of prices. A decline in the value of money is indicated by a general price rise; a general price decline indicates a rise in the value of money. Price indexes, being essentially averages of price changes, measure these general price changes. They therefore provide an approximation to changes in the value of money. Properly used, they help to eliminate the bias that would otherwise arise were money values, such as appear in the market transactions of different times, compared as they stand.

One adjustment, then, that the economist makes of accounting figures on business income, to lessen the effect of changes in the value of money, is to multiply the dollar figures by an index of the value of money. Or—what is the same thing—he divides the dollar figures by an index of the general price level. As is commonly said, the dollar values are "deflated" or expressed in terms of "constant

144

prices." Historically, this was the first adjustment developed by economists. Usually, also, it is still one of the most important.

All are familiar with this adjustment. Few today would dream of presenting figures on wages without a correction for the increased cost of living; and indexes of the prices and incomes farmers receive are, almost by legal fiat, accompanied by indexes of the prices they pay. "Real wages" and "parity prices" are common lingo. Economists, at least, are consistent in applying similar adjustments to business income. Since everyone is acquainted with this particular adjustment, I need say no more about it, except to comment on two points.

First, while economists are thoroughly agreed that correction for changes in the general price level is necessary, there is less agreement on just how much correction is needed, in any particular case. By that I mean, simply, that there are available a number of different indexes of prices (and of course there are many more that could be computed); that these usually reveal somewhat different rates of change in prices, between any two dates; and that opinions differ as to which is most appropriate for deflating business income. For the value of money depends on what is to be done with the money: whether it is spent on consumers' goods or capital goods; whether it is spent on rich-man's goods or poor-man's goods. And, also, indexes of the prices even of the same group of goods will vary with the compiling agency. Over relatively short periods of time, however, these differences are usually not great. The area of agreement is far greater than the area of disagreement. Economists, having learned to concentrate on important issues, accept approximate measures with which they may differ in detail. National income statistics are expressed in round billions of dollars, not in dollars and cents.

My second comment is necessary to emphasize a point that is frequently misunderstood. The deflation procedure I have been discussing, namely, correction for changes in the general price level, does not remove all the biases or difficulties that arise from changes in the value of money. This correction cannot, by itself, place the business income figures for two different periods on a

145

par with one another and render them fully comparable. One important reason is that the various business costs set off against gross income, in the usual profit and loss statement, are based on "heterotemporal" prices. When I first used that word I was accused of indecently coupling Greek and Latin roots. Yet it expresses the idea succinctly. What I mean, of course, is that costs charged in, say 1940, involve prices paid not only in 1940 but also in earlier years. The ordinary deflation will not take care of this peculiarity of accounting figures. Other adjustments are needed to do that, and the economist has applied them to charges for cost of materials and charges for depreciation and depletion.

The first wrinkle in the accounting treatment of inventories and thus of cost of goods sold that bothered economists was the "lower of cost or market" valuation practice. As early as 1932, Colin Clark felt it necessary to adjust the British figures, because of it, in order to attain comparability between periods of rising prices and periods of falling prices.

Soon, however, Simon Kuznets' work on capital formation at the National Bureau of Economic Research led him to take an additional and bigger step towards adjusting the accounting figures on inventories and costs of materials. He broke down changes in the reported book values of inventories into two components. For example, when both the physical volume of inventory and the market price of the goods held in inventory rose between the beginning and end of the year, he distinguished between: (1) the value (at cost) of the increase in the number of physical units of inventory; and (2) the increase in the value of the opening physical inventory resulting from the replacement of units purchased at lower prices by units purchased at higher prices. To the economist, only the first component represents a real accretion to the country's wealth. Only the value of the physical increase in inventory is capital formation from an economic or social point of view. The second component, the increase in the value of the opening inventory, merely represents an upward revaluation of wealth already in existence, not an addition to wealth. Being such, it should not be treated as capital formation. Nor should it

146

be considered to be part of the business income appropriate for inclusion in the national income.

Put differently, the true current cost of materials consumed is not their original cost, but their replacement value. In a period of rising prices, then, and viewing the matter from the economic or social standpoint, accounting net income is too high, because accountants charge most materials consumed at original, not replacement, cost. Accounting profits include the amount by which inventories are revalued. In a period of falling prices the reverse is true. Accounting net income is then too low, in the eyes of the economist. Business income from an economic viewpoint should be determined by subtracting from sales a cost of goods sold in which the units sold are valued at current, not original, cost prices. This explains why the series prepared by the National Bureau of Economic Research to measure the nation's income includes, as a component, business income adjusted to remove inventory revaluations. The Department of Commerce has taken over the notion, and its figures on national income are similarly built up.

The economist's adjustment of inventory (or cost of goods sold) strongly resembles, of course, the "last in, first out" or the LIFO method that has come into use in some business accounts, and I therefore need not take the time to develop it in detail. Nevertheless, several comments are necessary.

It should be noted, first, that this adjustment is applied by economists to *all* (or virtually all) business income. The national income figures are thus internally consistent. The data for different industries are, in this respect, fully comparable with one another. This is not true of accounting data on business income. Lifo is used by only a fraction of all business enterprises; and in the accounts of many of those using Lifo, it is not applied to all types of inventories. The adjustment made by economists was designed precisely in order to provide complete comparability between different companies or industries and between different periods of time.

The economic adjustment is different from Lifo not only in the scope of its application but also in the way it is applied. In

147

Lifo, materials sold or consumed are charged at the cost of the most recently acquired materials. This might be the current year's price or it might be last year's price if the physical volume of inventories has been reduced from last year's level. (I am ignoring the special case of involuntary liquidation because of wartime shortages, in which the general Lifo rule is relaxed.) The economist always charges all materials sold or consumed in any year at that year's price, even when inventories are depleted during the year. The economist's method of adjustment therefore ensures that no inventory revaluation will be left in the income account to over- or under-state business income. Lifo does not. The intention, however, seems to be about the same. The purpose of Lifo, as the American Institute Committee on Accounting Procedure states, is "to relate costs to revenues more nearly on the same price level basis than would the Fifo method." The purpose of the economist's method is to relate costs to revenues on *exactly* the same—the current—price level basis.

Though the economist tries to relate costs to revenues on the same price level basis, he cannot in fact fully attain that purpose. Accounting data constitute his raw material. To adjust them, he has to know what fraction of inventories are reported on Lifo, what portion on Fifo. Of the latter, he has to know what portion is valued at the lower of cost or market, what portion on other bases. Furthermore, he has to know how replacement prices have changed in each industry. But he does not know these things very exactly. He has to estimate them. Our national income figures, therefore, are adjusted on the basis of approximations only. But, again, the economist is glad to get closer to his objective, even if he cannot reach it fully, rather than content himself with the unadjusted figures.

The adjustment is a very considerable one, when prices are changing greatly. The Department of Commerce correction has run as high as +4 billions for 1930, —3 billions for 1933, +1 billion for 1938, —3 billions for 1941, and —6 billions for 1946. (These estimates cover not only corporations but also unincorporated enterprises, except farms.) Even if these adjustments are

148

surrounded by considerable margins of error—and we may be sure they are—they are worth making.

If the objective is to relate costs to revenues on the same price level basis, there is no logical reason for stopping with the materials that come out of inventory. Charges for depreciation and depletion have to be treated in the same way. Capital assets consumed in the course of current production also should be charged at current prices rather than at original cost. If they are not, business income is—from the economist's point of view— overstated when prices are rising, understated when prices are falling.

The depreciation and depletion charges available to economists are, of course, the accountants' figures. These, therefore, also require adjustment. This adjustment, quite similar in principle to the adjustment made of inventories, is rather more difficult to make, however. Available depreciation and depletion data are pretty complicated. They combine figures relating to a great host of different dates; some are in original cost, some at cost to second owners; depreciation methods and the distinction between capital charges and maintenance charges vary among firms and even within firms; and tax-law complications, like the wartime amortization feature and the depletion methods accepted by the Treasury Department, provide stumbling blocks.

The computation of depreciation charges reminds me of a calculation reported in *Alice's Adventures in Wonderland*. Because George May once told me that it is always good form to quote from that famous authority, I won't restrain myself:

"Fourteenth of March, I *think* it was," the Mad Hatter said.

"Fifteenth," said the March hare.

"Sixteenth," said the Dormouse.

"Write that down," the King said to the jury; and the jury eagerly wrote down all three dates on their slates, and then added them up, and reduced the answers to shillings and pence.

149

I think that is how depreciation charges are calculated—with a heavy weight given to March fifteenth, in this country. Anyway, the economist has to unscramble the data that accountants provide him. And to the components he has to apply an adjustment involving a knowledge of changes in the prices of plant and equipment when the very character of this property also is modified with time, and the prices therefore are not fully comparable from time to time.

Despite all these difficulties, however, rough approximation seems possible, in my opinion, and when price changes are great, eminently worth while. It brings us closer to the truth than if we fail to make it. Such an adjustment was put into the National Bureau's calculations of national income for the period 1919-1938. The magnitude of the adjustment may be appreciated if we glance back at those figures. Take, for example, 1919, which followed the rise in prices during World War 1. Accounting measures of depreciation of business capital goods, for that year, amounted to 3.4 billion dollars. The estimate in *current* prices, however, was 5.4 billion, a difference of 2 billions. The discrepancy for 1920 was even bigger, 2.6 billion. For 1932, of course, the current price estimate was lower than the book estimate.

For 1947, I would not be surprised if current accounting calculations again understated the economic measure of depreciation by some billions. But the Department of Commerce, which provides the current statistics on national income, has not followed the lead of the National Bureau in this respect, and we therefore have no real estimate. It should be pointed out, however, that the Department agrees that revaluation of accounting depreciation charges is "indicated on conceptual grounds" (*Survey of Current Business, Supplement,* July, 1947, p. 11), and of course joins the National Bureau in excluding realized capital gains and losses from its measures of business income. Apparently the Department has not made an adjustment for the difference between book and current price estimates of depreciation because of the statistical difficulties involved. But whatever the reason for not making the adjustment, by not doing so the Department of Commerce overstates current business income in its presentation of the national accounts.

I might mention, also, that the Department further overstates business income because it adds back the tax-law deductions for depletion. These figures are, of course, almost meaningless from an economic standpoint, and therefore provide little information with which to start. But while the Department's attitude is quite understandable, its figures are none the less defective in this regard, too.

I come now to a question that has not received much consideration. Partly, I imagine, this is because it has seemed rather less important than the matters already mentioned, and it is less important during a period of great change in the general price level. Yet it is worth tossing into the forum because it will help us to see more clearly the meaning of the adjustments already described.

The basic idea of the inventory adjustment made by the economist is to keep out of business income, and thus out of national income, profits or losses—realized or unrealized—that arise out of mere changes in the prices at which the existing stock of the nation's wealth is assessed. For the nation *as a whole* is no better or worse off simply because the current value of a fixed number of units in its stock or goods has expanded or shrunk. (I pass over the exception created by international trade.) But is this true of the individual firm that owns a stock of goods the value of which has changed? The logic of the economist's inventory adjustment as now made—and the same goes for the adjustment of depreciation charges and for Lifo—implicitly states that it is true of the individual firm. It is assumed that, like the nation, the firm is no better or worse off because the current value of a fixed number of units in its stock of goods has changed.

It is clear, of course, that the individual firm is in fact not better or worse off if the unit value of its inventory has merely paralleled the general price level. But what if the two have diverged? Suppose, for example, that owing to the depletion of our resources, the unit value of the stock of copper held by nonferrous-

151

metal refiners rises more rapidly than the general price level; and that, owing to technological advances, the unit value of the stock of rayon fiber held by rayon manufacturers rises less rapidly than the general price level. Can we really say that the one group has not gained, nor the other lost, by this differential price movement? Now, if the economist is interested only in the aggregate national income, he can ignore such gains and losses, for they more or less offset one another. In that case, however, he should note explicitly that the adjusted figures he presents for an *individual* industry are exclusive of its gains or losses from differential price movements. The figures measure, in a sense, what the industry puts *into* the national product, rather than what it gets *out* of the national product.

But the economist is often interested in what an industry or firm gets out of the national product. That is, the economist is then concerned with how the purchasing power resulting from business operations is distributed among industries or firms. Then it is another matter. Whether these profits or losses are or are not included does make a difference, and in the case of a particular industry or firm may sometimes make a great deal of difference. What are the pros and cons on including them?

The gain or loss arising from differential price movements may reflect differences only in the cyclical amplitudes of prices. In that case it can be argued that the profit or loss situation is only temporary, that it will soon be succeeded by the reverse situation at the next turn of the business cycle, and that this cyclical succession need not concern us. This argument is not iron-clad. But even if it were, it does not apply to the situation in which the gain or loss arises from sustained differential price movements, that is, from trend differences, rather than cyclical differences, in price movements. Here there is no cancellation. And here there seems to be little question that to the industry or firm affected the gain or loss is real.

One may grant that such gains and losses are real yet argue against including them in the economic measure of business income on the ground that they are not part of current income, but

152

instead reflect windfall or capital gains or losses and should be treated accordingly. To this the counter-argument is, of course, that business enterprise does not take price movements to be mere disturbances of the situation in which business is done, but part and parcel thereof. Business enterprise aims at profiting, or avoiding loss, from such movements. Indeed, the exercise of foresight in this connection is a characteristic function of entrepreneurship, and active planning by business men to influence prices—whether those of goods purchased or of goods sold—rather than passively adjusting to them, is hardly unknown.

Brief mention may be made, finally, of another point. Some of the consequences of trading on a narrow equity or margin also tend to be excluded from the economic measures of business income, by the adjustments now in use. Yet the gains or losses resulting from changes in the burden of debt as price levels rise or fall influence greatly the distribution of purchasing power. For that reason these gains or losses also must find a place in a discussion of the economic measurement of business income. I will not take the time to develop these topics. Perhaps this is because I am subconsciously conforming to that professorial model of a lecture in which a third of what is said is obvious, a third is intelligible only to the brighter students, and a third is intelligible to no one. But I will admit only that I am simply trying to uncover some of the significant implications of the adjustments now used in preparing our national income figures. Only by studying these implications can we reach a real understanding of what the current economic viewpoint means, and find direction towards bettering it. In short, I am pointing to some of the unsettled problems that a study of business income must tackle.

Let me sum up the main points, on which almost all economists agree, as follows:

Accounting calculations of business income are unacceptable to economists. Current accounting reports yield figures for different companies that are not comparable with one another. Current accounting reports yield figures for a single company's operations in one year that are not comparable with figures for the

153

same company in another year. During a period of inflation, such as we are in, these incomparabilities are serious.

To obtain comparable figures that measure business income from a consistent economic point of view, economists are therefore driven to make adjustments of accounting data, or at least to attach qualifications to them. Economists follow the principle that costs should be related to revenues on the same price level basis, and that the income of one period should be compared with the income of another period on the same price level basis. In accord with this principle, economists believe that inventory revaluations should be excluded from business income, and the income estimates of the National Bureau of Economic Research and of the Department of Commerce do exclude them. Economists believe, also, that revaluations of fixed assets should be excluded from business income, and the income estimates of the National Bureau and Department of Commerce both exclude realized capital gains and losses. The estimates of the National Bureau further exclude revaluations of fixed assets arising from the charging of depreciation at original cost. The Department of Commerce also accepts the principle, but has so far implemented it only by a textual qualification of its figures. Finally, economists believe that comparisons of income over time are possible only if adjustments are made for changes in the purchasing power of money income, and all estimators of national income provide for such adjustments.

These are not small matters that we are discussing today. The accounts of business income are matters of great public concern. Cooperation among the various groups of society, so necessary to the efficient working and progressive development of our economy, is difficult to secure when there is widespread misunderstanding of how the nation's income is being distributed. To lessen—perhaps ultimately to dispel—this misunderstanding is a duty of the economists who practice social accounting. Is it not also a duty of those who practice public accounting?

154

THE VARIED IMPACT OF INFLATION ON THE CALCULATION OF BUSINESS INCOME

By SOLOMON FABRICANT

THE VARIED IMPACT OF INFLATION ON THE CALCULATION OF BUSINESS INCOME

A generation ago few people were interested in business accounts. I might add, also, that fewer still were able to find in the published income accounts and balance sheets the information they sought.

Much has happened since then to the role—and the rule—of business accounts in our economy. It will make a remarkable history when someone realizes the import of those events and sits down to describe them. The great economic and political changes of the past few decades have brought us to a situation in which the summary accounts of business are staked off as public domain, and the profits of business are viewed as matters of public concern. Business accounts are now being watched, analyzed and made use of not only by management and shareholders and regulatory commissions and competitors, but also by tax collectors, economists, statistical agencies, consumer organizations and trade unions. All these now seek vital information in these accounts.

When public policies and private strategies are influenced by business accounts, it is important that we understand what they have to tell us. This is especially necessary when inflation both sharpens interest in them and distorts the records they provide.

It is obvious that in a period of inflation the cost of living of wage earners goes up. It should be obvious, also, that the cost of replenishing inventories goes up, the cost of replacing worn-out equipment goes up, and the cost of living of stockholders goes up. Yet most accounting procedures fail to take any account, or adequate account, of these increases. Goods charged out of inventory are charged at their original cost, not at their higher replacement cost. Depreciation is charged at the original cost of the depreciating plant and equipment, not at their higher replace-

Reprinted by permission of Institute of Trade & Commerce Professions.

ment cost. As a result, inventory and plant are revalued as they are turned over. To take an example, a fixed stock of ten thousand men's shirts, worth say $20,000 in 1939, will now be valued at $40,000; and a fleet of 10 small motor trucks, worth perhaps $15,000 in 1939, will now be carried at something like $25,000, the exact amount depending on how many trucks had been replaced since 1939. Net worth will be higher by these increases in book value. Now ordinarily revaluations of assets are not allowed to get into the profit and loss account. Vigilant accountants treat them as surplus adjustments and shoo them away. But when revaluations find their way into the accounts not by deliberate reassessment of assets but by the indirect process of turnover of assets during inflation, they do get into the income account. The increase in net worth that I mentioned, the revaluation profit, will have been treated as ordinary income, indistinguishable from other income. Accountant's calculations of business profits will thus have been overstated.

Furthermore, the profits so calculated are not even corrected for changes in their purchasing power. In a nutshell, then, ordinary business accounts provide an exaggerated notion of business profits when price levels are going up.

So much, I think, is becoming recognized, though perhaps too slowly and too grudgingly. But the simple and general qualification of business accounts, to which this recognition leads, is not enough to avoid misinterpretation. We must realize, also, that the accounts of different industries and different enterprises are affected by inflation in different ways and in different degrees. Even stabilization of prices, if and when it comes, will not mean the end of inflation's effects on the calculated profits of each and every industry.

Why may the impact of inflation be greater on the business accounts of one industry than on those of another? There are a number of factors. These are: (1) variation, among industries, in the importance of physical assets in business operations; (2) variation in the rate of turnover of physical assets; (3) variation in the average age—or year of acquisition—of capital assets;

156

(4) variation in the rate of rise in prices paid for physical assets; and (5) variation in the accounting procedures followed.

A brief comment on each of these will be sufficient to indicate its significance.

In an industry in which physical assets—plant and equipment and inventories—are of minor importance in the balance sheet, costs of materials and depreciation changes will usually be of minor importance in the income account. Even serious errors in the calculation of these costs will not appreciably distort calculated net income. When plant and equipment and inventories are important, however, and prices are rising, differences between original and replacement costs will bulk large compared with profits. Inclusion in net income of "revaluation profits" will seriously overstate net income.

The rate of turnover of assets also is relevant. Other things being equal, the more rapid the rate of turnover, the quicker does a rise in prices cause upward revaluations to materialize. The quicker, therefore, are calculated profits affected. Correspondingly, the slower the rate of turnover, the slower is the impact on profits. (I am, of course, discussing this factor with reference to the inflation that began only a few years ago. Should prices continue to march up indefinitely, differences in rates of turnover would eventually cease to play a significant role.) The interesting point here is that the effects of inflation on calculated business profits may appear even after—sometimes, long after—price levels have become stabilized. Thus, the public utilities, which hold long-lived assets, might be understating depreciation charges and over-stating profits for some time after the end of an inflationary movement. Indeed, they might be doing so even after deflation had begun and been reflected by downward inventory revaluations in other industries.

The effects of variation in average age of assets and in rate of price rise are obvious. Firms that were set up and in full operation in 1939 will be carrying their capital assets at values far below those of firms that sprang up or expanded greatly in recent years. Depreciation charges of the former group will understate

157

replacement costs more seriously than depreciation charges of the latter group.

As for price changes, variation among them is more considerable than most people suppose. It is one of the reasons why a single or general price index for putting original costs onto a replacement cost basis cannot be wholly applicable to all types of industries.

The final factor is a variation in accounting procedure. Firms already using the last-in, first-out, method of charging costs of materials—LIFO—are to that extent already correcting their accounts for the effects of inflation. Similarly, firms using "accelerated" depreciation or other devices for increasing depreciation charges above original-cost levels are recognizing and to that extent correcting for the effects of inflation. Naturally, also, when firms use maintenance rather than depreciation accounting, the impact of inflation on calculated profits is lessened. But not all firms do use these devices. Nor do those using them use them to the same extent. For this reason the accounts of different firms and industries are not comparable. Some reported profits are seriously, others are less seriously, affected by rising prices.

In principle, the net result of these several factors is measured by the sum of an inventory-revaluation adjustment and an adjustment for the difference between depreciation calculated at original cost and at replacement cost. I wish I could tell you how much these sums are, for various industries, and how their proportion to calculated profits varies from one industry to another. Unfortunately, only the inventory adjustment has been computed for each industrial group.

For all corporations, and for 1947, upward inventory revaluations accounted for 5 billion dollars of the 18 billion of corporate profits after tax, or 28 percent, according to the Department of Commerce. For wholesale trade, however, the percentage was 78, and for tobacco manufactures, 70. In contrast, for public utilities it was 15 percent and for textile mills, 12 percent, while the probable percentage for real estate and a few other like industries was too small even to be worth calculating. In the case of rubber manufactures, the inventory revaluation was downward, rather than upward as in all other industries, and as a consequence calculated profits of rubber corporations were *lower* than they would otherwise have been.

In 1948 total inventory revaluations were lower than in 1947. They amounted to 3,300 billions or 16 per cent of income after taxes, and I imagine that, unlike 1947, *downward* revaluations tended to depress calculated profits in more than one industry. The proportion of such downward revaluations may turn out to be even greater in 1949.

But revaluations that arise out of charging depreciation at original cost will continue to be positive for years to come, in most industries. The revaluations will, of course, diminish in size should levels become stabilized.

After World War I, to cite some calculations made in 1938, it took twenty years or more before the prices underlying depreciation charges caught up with current reproduction costs. In 1919 depreciation charges were about 30 percent below the amount they would have been had they been figured at the level of reproduction costs. The drop in prices after 1920 naturally reduced the gap. But since the price level in the 1920's was still well above that of 1913, the gap remained, diminishing as time went on. It was 20 percent in 1923, and still about 10 percent in 1929. Not until another drop occurred in prices, during the early 1930's, did the prices underlying depreciation charges come to equal—and then to exceed—reproduction costs. These estimates relate to business as a whole. I am sure that if we had them, the data for individual industries would show great variation in amount and timing.

I have said enough, I think, to demonstrate that the impact of rising prices on calculations of business profits varies among industries and firms. For the sound use of business accounts we need to know what that impact is. The individual reader of an income account is in no position to make the calculation himself. I think it is up to the accountants.

MONETARY THEORY AND THE PRICE LEVEL TREND IN THE FUTURE

---

by CLARK WARBURTON

CONTENTS

MONETARY THEORY AND THE PRICE
LEVEL TREND IN THE FUTURE

Nearly one-third of Mr. Bronfenbrenner's monograph, *Business Income Concepts in the Light of Monetary Theory,* is devoted to support of the proposition: "the weight of both authority and evidence seems to indicate a long-term trend of general prices rising erratically into the indefinite future".[1] The rest of the monograph, except for an introductory section on the scope of monetary theory, deals with the effects of the assumed upward price trend on the problem of determining business income.

The evidence cited by Mr. Bronfenbrenner in support of his forecast of a rising price trend is to me unconvincing. Further, price level theory and factual studies have progressed sufficiently so that we know the nature of the force which brought about many of the long periods of rising prices and of falling prices in the past, and can reasonably assume that the same kind of force was operating in other cases. Still further, this force is now under the control of existing governmental agencies. That is to say, we now have both the knowledge and the power to push the price level, as a matter of deliberate national policy, in either direction or to maintain a reasonable degree of stability.

We know also that maintenance of stability in the price level will provide very real tangible benefits to all the major groups in the population. Consequently, it is a reasonable proposition to assume that when this knowledge is widely disseminated the leaders of business, farm, and labor organizations will find it to their advantage to attempt to achieve a stable price level for an indefinite period in the future. We can also be confident that if a concerted support of this objective by such groups is made, Congress will impose on the governmental agencies holding monetary power the responsibility of using that power to attain the objective.

---

[1] Martin Bronfenbrenner, *Business Income Concepts in the Light of Monetary Theory* (Business Income Study Group, American Institute of Accountants, 1950) (pp. 97-142 of this volume).

The possibility of attaining, by deliberate action, a long period of price stability in the future is obviously of great interest to the Business Income Study Group. The disturbing questions regarding business income measurement with which the group is concerned relate to problems associated with a falling or rising price level. There may be a substantial difference between the procedures which should be developed if the problem is viewed as one which will continue indefinitely in the future and those which are appropriate if the problem is confined to the making of adjustments to price level changes which have already occurred.

Scope and Content of Monetary Theory

The difference between my view of the future price level and that of Mr. Bronfenbrenner rests largely on a difference in our understanding of the content, findings, and status of monetary theory. It is therefore appropriate to begin this paper, as Mr. Bronfenbrenner begins his monograph, with some comments on the meaning and scope of monetary theory.

Elucidation of the difference between our concepts of the scope and character of monetary theory can appropriately begin with the difference in our reactions toward one of the most interesting changes in economic thought in recent decades. What Mr. Bronfenbrenner describes as the "emancipation" of monetary theory from primary concern with price level movement and determination, would, I believe, be described more accurately as an illogical ejection of the vital core of monetary theory. Monetary theory, as I understand it, may be defined as the theory of the value of money and of the consequences of changes in the quantity of money which affect its value. Correa Walsh's book of nearly a half century ago, *The Fundamental Problem in Monetary Science*, which was devoted to the problem of what group of prices should be used as the basis for maintaining a stable value of money, was appropriately and correctly entitled.

This ejected segment of theory was oriented toward the same phase of economic life as present-day "monetary" theory. Mone-

162

tary theory throughout the nineteenth century and in the early part of the twentieth, when it emphasized the movement and determination of the price level, dealt just as fully as modern theory, though with fewer quantitative measurements because fewer quantitative data were available, with "aggregative economics" or "macro-economics," "the theory of income and employment," the national income and product, and the total volume of output and employment. That is to say, traditional monetary theory, for nearly two centuries before its "emancipation," was primarily concerned with the maintenance of effective demand and full employment.

Mr. Bronfenbrenner, after commenting on the boundaries between monetary and economic theory, and assigning such over-all aspects of the economy as employment and national income to the former and problems of relative prices and income distribution to the latter, comments: "The two main branches of economics have not yet been integrated in any completely satisfactory manner". This lack of integration was not a characteristic of nineteenth and early twentieth century economic theory, though some economists gave primary attention to one branch of theory while others looked at another branch and the integrating connections still needed considerable polishing and fitting.

The pre-depression body of theory regarding the value of money, which dealt not only with the measurement and determination of the price level but also with the benefits of "stable money," was an important segment of traditional theory. It was, in fact, a concomitant of the classical theory of equilibrium which might have been designated, appropriately, the theory of disequilibrium, or theory of monetary disequilibrium. There is good evidence that this theory of disequilibrium was understood and accepted by those who developed and emphasized the theory of equilibrium. It appears to have been undue attention to Ricardo's cryptic remark that changes in the quantity of money affect only prices, and neglect of Marshall's comment on Ricardo's carelessness with respect to time, that have led present day economists to forget that their predecessors of the nineteenth century had a theory of disequilibrium as well as a theory of equilibrium.[2]

The basic content and logic of the theory of monetary disequilibrium are simple, though its details have many ramifications. It consists essentially of two parts. One part is a simple application to money of the pervading economic principle of supply and demand. If the supply of money increases more rapidly than the rate of progress in producing economic goods the value of money relative to goods will tend to fall, that is, the level of prices will rise. If the quantity of circulating medium is contracted, or does not grow when increases in population and productivity are enlarging productive capacity, the value of the unit of circulating medium will rise, that is, the price level will fall.

The second and much the larger part of the theory of monetary disequilibrium is a description of the process by which the value of money becomes adjusted to changes in its quantity (relative to productive capacity), and of the disturbances to business and employment and the injustices in the distribution of the national income and product which result from the character of this process.

The reason for the lack of integration in contemporary theory to which Mr. Bronfenbrenner refers is the simple fact that by neglecting the applicability of the principle of supply and demand to money and the concomitant theory of the process of price level determination, modern theorists have thrown away the connecting link which was in their hands. That this link was not thrown away and rejected because it had been found faulty can, I think, be readily demonstrated. There has been no examination of the factual record of changes in the quantity of circulating medium, the price level, and the course of business, in the light of the theory of monetary disequilibrium, by theorists associated with

---

[2]Ricardo recognized that money is subject to variation in value, as are other things, but asserted that variation in the value of money affects all prices and makes no difference in the rate of profit. (David Ricardo, *Principles of Political Economy* (1817), pp. 29-32.) In this discussion Ricardo did not specify whether he referred to immediate or ultimate effects—a case of his carelessness with regard to the element of time to which Alfred Marshall called attention (*Principles of Economics*, 8th edition, 1920, p. 82).

164

what is called "Keynesian economics," nor by those associated with business cycle research projects.

The link from traditional economic theory which has been thrown away by contemporary economists is precisely that part of economic theory which is most pertinent to the permanent solution of the problem for which the Business Income Study Group was established. However, before picking up the link to examine it in more detail, it appears to be desirable to examine the evidence cited by Mr. Bronfenbrenner to support his belief that we can forecast an upward movement of the price level for an indefinite period of time.

The Trend of Prices

Mr. Bronfenbrenner supports his prediction of a probable rising price trend in the future with two types of evidence. One of these is the historical situation; the other the existing pressure for maintenance of full employment and acknowledgment by governments of their responsibility for preventing severe lapses from full employment.

The historical evidence submitted by Mr. Bronfenbrenner is not convincing as a basis for forecasting the trend over the next generation or two. His remark that the century and a quarter following the Napoleonic wars was perhaps the longest period in history without marked upward trend of prices in the leading commercial nations seems to be at variance with the reports of economists who have given special attention to price history. Thorpe and Taylor, for example, cite five previous cases of periods nearly or more than a century in length without significant upward trend of prices, and three of these were a century and a half or longer. All were in regions with civilizations properly classified as commercial. The periods and places are as follows: Western Europe from 1660 to 1745, and also from 1375 to 1475; the Roman Empire during the first 180 years of the Christian era; Greece from about 400 B. C. to about 150 B. C.; and Babylonia for nearly three centuries subsequent to about 2570 B. C. The same authors cite the same number of periods of approximately a century or

165

more with rising price trends, and an additional period of two-thirds of a century. The six periods are: Western Europe 1745-1815, 1475-1660, and 1150-1375; the Roman Empire 180-400 A. D.; Greece 600 to 400 B. C.; and Babylonia, for a prolonged period subsequent to the three centuries of stability.

Further, Mr. Bronfenbrenner's choice of 1940 as the terminal date of the period beginning with the close of the Napoleonic wars is unsatisfactory. The year 1815 was the end of a 70-year period of rising prices; 1940 was in the midst of another long period of rising prices. The 135 years since 1815 should be broken into at least two periods. For about 80 years, 1815 to 1895, the trend of prices in both Europe and America was downward, with an interruption of about two decades in the middle of the period. During the 55 years since 1895 prices have been rising, with a sharp interruption of a few years during the great depression. If we were to argue from historical analogy, using approximately the historical period selected by Mr. Bronfenbrenner, it would be far more logical to conclude that we are likely to face another decade or two of rising prices, and then to have three-fourths of a century of falling prices.

Mr. Bronfenbrenner is undoubtedly correct in believing that the periods of rising prices during the past thousand years have carried the price level upward to a greater extent than the periods of falling prices have carried it downward. However, the existence of numerous periods of widely varying lengths in which prices were falling as well as numerous periods in which prices were rising means that the historical record by itself is not at all a suitable basis for predicting the trend during the next few decades. If historical evidence is to be used for this problem it is the circumstances under which rising prices and falling prices, respectively, have occurred that must be utilized.

Within the various long periods of rising or falling prices there have been notable interruptions to the trends—interruptions which lasted from half a decade to a quarter of a century. Some of these interruptions were associated with wars; and we know that in these cases the change in the quantity of circulating medium

166

resulting from monetary policies associated with war financing constituted the force which produced sharply rising prices. It is also universally recognized that the periods of sharply declining prices in the United States following the Revolutionary and Civil wars were associated with monetary policies designed to contract the circulating medium in order to resume convertibility of the currency into metallic coin. Other interruptions to the trends, such as the period of rising prices around the eighteen-fifties, are clearly associated with changes in the supply of monetary metals. Also, the various long periods of rising prices in Greece, the Roman Empire, and western Europe mentioned by Thorpe and Taylor, as they point out, were periods when the supply of monetary metals was greatly increased. Similarly, the long periods of falling prices were those when production of monetary metals was small.

Recognition by price historians of the relationship of rising and falling prices to variations in the rate of production of monetary metals and to variations in other types of circulating medium, such as government paper, constitutes as acknowledgment of the applicability to money of the general principle of supply and demand. It is, therefore, a strange episode in the development of economic thought, that many contemporary theorists assume, either explicitly or implicitly, that the principle of supply and demand does not really function in respect to money under present circumstances.

Mr. Bronfenbrenner's argument from the strength of the philosophy of full employment and the impact of organized pressure groups is also not convincing. I would agree that those forces are now sufficiently strong so that the recurrence of another period of deflation and unemployment as severe as that of the early nineteen-thirties is unlikely. However, the experience of the past two years suggests that these forces are not strong enough to prevent a decline of prices of 2 or 3 percent per year. The nation's tolerance of unemployment of the magnitude associated with such a rate of price decline seems to have been demonstrated.[3] In addition, as Mr. Bronfenbrenner points out, we are developing devices such as guaranteed annual wages, severance pay plans, and unemployment insurance which expand the limits of tolerance.

Nor does it follow from the increased power of farm and labor organizations that the pressures exerted by these groups will inevitably be exerted in a way to produce a long-run upward trend of prices. The American Farm Bureau Federation is on record as favoring governmental policies which will produce a stable price level. With the increasing emphasis placed on pension funds, trade union leaders will be increasingly aware of the unfavorable aspects of a continuous rise in prices. As trade unions become stronger and their members better informed regarding the ultimate effect of the policies for which they may stand it seems likely that they will also stress the desirability of stability in the level of prices.[4] If price level stability is a practical objective of governmental policy, there seem to be good reasons for assuming that pressure groups will add their weight to attempts at its achievement.

Underlying Factors in Rising and Falling Price Trends

The long upward trend of prices prior to 1815—which constitutes Mr. Bronfenbrenner's historical support of a forecast of an upward trend in the future—occurred at a time when metals served as the principal circulating medium. The nineteenth century and the first third of the twentieth was a period of transition from a circulating medium consisting primarily of metals, first to a circulating medium consisting largely of bank credit convertible into metals, and then to a circulating medium consisting primarily of bank credit divorced, as a practical matter, from its nominal metallic base.

---

[3]From September 1948 to February 1950, the consumers' price index of the Department of Labor declined at the rate of 3.2 percent per year.

[4]This conclusion has been reached by Professor W. A. Morton in a recent study, "Trade Unionism, Full Employment, and Inflation," *American Economic Review*, Vol. XL (March 1950), pp. 13-39.

The major force which for several centuries prior to the nineteenth produced a predominantly rising price trend—but occasionally produced a falling trend—was the rate of production of monetary metals. If we neglect wartime interludes with a circulating medium consisting of or directly based on government credit and war financing processes, the periods of rising or falling trends in prices during the transitional century and a third were also associated with changing rates of production of the monetary metals. This force is no longer operative. It would seem, therefore, that the historical experience on which Mr. Bronfenbrenner relies has little or no bearing on the probable price trend in the future. At least the question must be raised—what does historical experience offer regarding the behavior of price trends under a bank credit type of circulating medium which is not closely tied to a metallic base?

The offhand answer which would, I am sure, be given to this question by nearly all economists, whether they specialize in monetary theory or not, is that the price trend under this circumstance is even more likely to be upward than in the case of a metallic currency or of a convertible bank credit currency. Certainly the nature of banks, simply because their own obligations are an accepted means of payment, is such that they have an inherent tendency to carry forward at a rapid rate the process of expansion of circulating medium, regardless of the need of the economy for increasing supplies of circulating medium. It is, of course, this characteristic of banks which underlay the strength of the tradition that, if banks are to provide circulating medium, that medium must be convertible into a metallic currency. But the basis and strength of this tradition does not answer the question: what is the historical evidence about bank credit systems where this tradition has been discarded or effectively weakened?

This is a question which has never been thoroughly examined, but the answer seems to be that the inherent expansionary tendency of such a system is so strong that one of two things occurs: the system expands and prices rise so rapidly that faith in the currency is obliterated and through one process or another the

169

excessive growth of the banks leads to their destruction, *or* the system is or comes to be controlled or dominantly influenced by a group of persons who, by tradition or statute or some other form of governmental influence, base their primary decisions on what is regarded as good policy for society. In the latter case, price level stability may become an objective. There are, of course, many cases where a government controlled bank or a profit-making banking system under the dominance of a central bank has followed policies which produced an upward trend of prices, and some cases where falling prices resulted. Taken all together, these episodes mean—or at least suggest—that a bank credit type of circulating medium can be governed so as to produce rising, falling, or stable prices.

If we look also at wartime periods and other occasions when Governments have issued fiat money or irredeemable Treasury obligations for use as circulating medium, we find that the greater number of cases resulted in rising prices. But this is by no means universal. Governments have sometimes reversed the process, as in the United States during the decade following 1865, and falling prices have been produced.

In summary, we see in the past four general types of monetary systems, which may be distinguished by the dominant form of circulating medium: metallic coins; Government credit or fiat paper; bank credit convertible into metallic currency; and inconvertible bank credit. Under all of these the price trend may be either upward or downward, or neither, for periods ranging in length from say, half a decade, to scores or even hundreds of years.

When a person with the scientific point of view looks at a variety of situations such as this, he assumes that there must be some underlying force which operates through the various circumstances to produce the common result. He then formulates a hypothesis on the basis of common observations, a theoretical principle, or special scrutiny of a few cases; and proceeds to investigate as many cases as possible on the basis of the hypothesis. Frequently, the hypothesis will need many refinements in order to be found a valid general explanation of the phenomena under study; and sometimes, of course, it will have to be abandoned and a new one selected for investigation.

In the case of price trends, an obvious hypothesis is the traditional quantity theory of the value of money, representing—as has been said above—an application to the circulating medium of the general economic principle of supply and demand. Mr. Bronfenbrenner acknowledges the relevancy of this hypothesis to the nineteenth century type of monetary system of bank credit on a gold standard basis. He fails, however, to make use of the hypothesis in dealing with the existing monetary system: inconvertible bank credit held in restraint by a powerful central banking system. This hypothesis, to reiterate a point made in the introduction to this paper, is one of the two important phases of the vital core of monetary theory which most contemporary theorists, presumably including Mr. Bronfenbrenner, have ejected from their thinking.

The Process of a Changing Price Level

If an exhaustive study of price level changes in the past were to be undertaken in the light of the quantity theory hypothesis, a very simple form of that hypothesis might be used as a starting point. We might, for example, assume that the price level is directly proportional to the quantity of circulating medium. That this is not the case is, of course, readily seen. We might next take into account the need for a varying quantity of circulating medium associated with a changing volume of goods and services produced or going through the marketing process. When this is done, we might find a general relationship between changes in the quantity of money, adjusted for changes in the quantity of production or of goods offered in the markets, and changes in the price level. But we would quickly find two types of discrepancy. First, when we look at short period changes, that is, for periods shorter than those designated "cycles" in studies of business fluctuations, we are likely to find substantial divergences from the hypothesis. Second, if we compare data for periods with a substantial number of intervening years (say two or three decades

171

or more) but in similar stages of the "business cycle" we are likely to find that the price level has not risen as much, or has fallen more, than we would expect on the basis of the hypothesis.

At this point we might discard the hypothesis—and that is what most contemporary theorists have done. But the nineteenth century predecessors of today's theorists had developed important further refinements of the quantity theory. The most important aspects of these refinements were those which I have mentioned in speaking of their theory of the process of changes in the price level—the second phase of the vital core of monetary theory which has been discarded by contemporary economists. It may be worth-while to look at this process as it was described by some of the eighteenth and nineteenth century theorists.

David Hume, two hundred years ago, commented on the process of price level changes as follows:

> "A nation whose money decreases, is actually at that time, much weaker and more miserable than another nation who possesses no more money, but is on the encreasing hand. This will be easily accounted for, if we consider that the alterations in the quantity of money, either on the one side or the other, are not immediately attended with proportionable alterations in the price of commodities. There is always an interval before matters be adjusted to their new situation; and this interval is as pernicious to industry, when gold and silver are diminishing, as it is advantageous when these metals are encreasing."[5]

Erick Bollman, writing in the United States in 1811 commented as follows:

> "But in *what manner* prices advance, when the quantity of circulating medium increases, is a question not equally well understood.
>
> The effect on prices which an increased quantity of circulating medium produces, must, obviously, depend much on the mode in which such increase takes place, and on the concomitant circumstances.
>
> If we suppose for instance, that the exact measure of the increase were at once generally known, and practically

[5]David Hume, "Essay on Money," *Political Discourses* (1752).

172

felt by nearly every individual of the nation, the probability is, that the prices of all commodities would advance at once in the same ratio . . .

But this is not the way, in which the augmentation of the circulating medium of any country has ever been effected. The additional supplies of it are generally ushered into circulation by slow degrees, mostly without the knowledge of the public, and frequently, even of the parties into whose hands they pass in the first instance; so that the augmentation is seldom thought of, until it becomes perceptible, by the gradual, and we may say, involuntary change in the state of the markets.

Most of the articles, therefore, the value of which was in some measure fixed and steady, before the augmentation of the circulating medium took place, and principally those of which the supply and consumption are nearly regular, will, for a long time, preserve their accustomed prices . . . But, *when an extraordinary demand, or a deficient supply, causes a relative or real scarcity of any one of them, then the price begins to rise, and becomes an object of contention between the holders and the purchasers . . .*"[6]

Thomas Attwood, a contemporary of Ricardo in England, wrote as follows in 1817:

"If prices were to fall suddenly, and generally, and equally, in all things, *and if it was well understood, that the amount of debts and obligations were to fall in the same proportion, at the same time,* it is possible that such a fall might take place without arresting consumption and production, and in that case it would neither be injurious or beneficial in any great degree, but when a fall of this kind takes place in an obscure and unknown way, first upon one article and then upon another, without any correspondent fall taking place upon debts and obligations, it has the effect of destroying all confidence in property, and all inducements to its production, or to the employment of labourers in any way.

"But whenever these terms or relations [an established price structure] are broken up, a general want of confi-

---

[6](Erick Bollmann), "A Letter to Alexander Baring, Esq., on the Present State of the Currency of Great Britain," *American Review of History and Politics,* II (1811), 250-251.

173

dence is occasioned, and a general demand takes place upon property, each individual seeking to lessen those credits and engagements which are likely to involve him in losses or ruin, and to exchange his stocks for money, in order that he may become possessed of greater stocks by repurchasing at some future time, or at least be enabled to meet securely those monied engagements which all men are more or less exposed to . . .

"At the same time the stocks are thus forced upon the markets, the consumption of the markets is reduced, by the impoverishment and diminished expenditure of individuals, who are obliged to contract their expences within their reduced means, and it takes a considerable period before the general reduction of all prices will enable those reduced means to consume their former amount of commodities."[7]

With this view of the process of the changing price level, change in the price level tends to lag behind the quantity of circulating medium. Consequently, changes in the price level proportional to changes in the quantity of circulating medium will not be shown by a direct comparison of the two statistical series.

Another element in the process of adjustment of prices to changes in the quantity of circulating medium was also referred to by various nineteenth century writers. The report of the United States Monetary Commission of 1876 contained the following comment on the situation when the quantity of money is increasing or decreasing:

"Whenever it becomes apparent that prices are rising and money falling in value in consequence of an increase in its volume, the greatest activity takes place in exchanges and productive enterprises. Everyone becomes anxious to share in the advantages of rising markets. The inducement to hoard money is taken away, and consequently the disposition to hoard it ceases. Its circulation becomes exceedingly active, and for the very plain reason that there could be no motive for holding or hoarding money when it is falling in value, while there would be the strongest pos-

[7]Thomas Attwood, *Prosperity Restored* (1817), pp. 36-37 and 79.

174

sible motive for exchanging it for property, or for the labor which creates property, when prices are rising."

"While the volume of money is decreasing, even although very slowly, the value of each unit of money is increasing in corresponding ratio, and property is falling in price. . . Exchanges become sluggish, because those who have money will not part with it for either property or services, beyond the requirements of actual current necessities, for the obvious reason that money alone is increasing in value, while everything else is declining in price. This results in the withdrawal of money from the channels of circulation, and its deposit in great hoards, where it can exert no influence on prices. This hoarding of money from the nature of things must continue and increase not only until the shrinkage of its volume has actually ceased, but until capitalists are entirely satisfied that money lying idle on special deposit will no longer afford them revenue, and that the lowest level of prices has been reached. It is this hoarding of money, when its volume shrinks, which causes a fall in prices greater than would be caused by the direct effect of a decrease in the stock of money."[8]

Alfred Marshall referred to the same phenomenon as follows:

"For when prices are likely to rise, people rush to borrow money and buy goods, and thus help prices to rise; business is inflated, and is managed recklessly and wastefully; those working on borrowed capital pay back less real value than they borrowed, and enrich themselves at the expense of the community. When afterwards credit is shaken and prices begin to fall, everyone wants to get rid of commodities and get hold of money which is rapidly rising in value; this makes prices fall all the faster, and the further fall makes credit shrink even more, and thus for a long time prices fall because prices have fallen."[9]

Much earlier, Erick Bollman had referred to the tendency of prices to vary with more amplitude than the circulating medium,

---

[8]*Report* of the United States Monetary Commission (1877), pp. 49 and 53.
[9]Alfred Marshall, *Principles of Economics* (London: Macmillan and Co., 1890; eighth edition, 1920), pp. 594-95.

175

without mentioning the accompanying change in monetary velocity.

> "It is also to be observed, that prices once in motion, never rise and fall, in exact proportion with the cause giving them the first impulse, but *advance,* as it were, *with a momentum of elasticity,* which they inevitably derive from the very constitution of the human mind, and which always occasions them to *vibrate beyond the point in which they finally settle.*"[10]

Thus a changing quantity of circulating medium, according to nineteenth century theory, results in price level changes which first lag behind and then become more than proportional to the change in the quantity of circulating medium relative to the available goods and services.

There is an additional element in the relationship of variations in the quantity of circulating medium to variations in the price level which was rarely mentioned by nineteenth century economists but also needs recognition. This is a tendency for the people of a country, as they grow more prosperous, or for other socio-economic reasons, to hold relatively larger amounts of circulating medium or cash balances as a reserve for use in times of emergency or for special purposes. Changes in complicated inter-relationships of business enterprises may also cause business concerns taken as a whole to hold more cash balances relative to the value of the output of the economy.[11]

That is to say, in examining factual data with respect to the quantity of money and the price level we must take into account at least four collateral factors: the need for a growth in the circulating medium to match expanding production of the economy, the tendency of prices to lag, the tendency for them to move more violently than variation in the quantity of circulating medium, and the tendency of the population as time passes to hold relatively

---

[10]*Op. cit.,* p. 252.

[11]Statistical data bearing on this aspect of the problem, for the century and a half since 1800, together with a discussion of the principal factors which appear to have been operative, are given in my article, "The Secular Trend in Monetary Velocity," *The Quarterly Journal of Economics,* February 1949, pp. 68-91.

larger cash balances. When appropriate allowance is made for these factors, the factual data for recent years supports the application of the principle of supply and demand to the value of money.

Theory of Business Depression

The vital core of nineteenth century monetary theory which has been rejected by most contemporary economists was not only a theory of the value of money, or determination of the price level, but also a theory of the origin of business depression. Consequently, since I do not agree with my contemporaries in rejecting the theory of monetary disequilibrium, I can be more bold than Mr. Bronfenbrenner in commenting on the probability of business depressions in the future. He comments on business cycle theory as follows: "We shall not venture on the disputatious terrain of business cycle theory, except for a statement, to which most economists and business men will agree, that these downward movements will continue at irregular intervals in the future for some time. (We have not learned to eliminate them, although we can perhaps lessen their amplitudes and mitigate their effects.)"[12]

The painful character of the process of downward price adjustment when that is made necessary by monetary contraction, except possibly when it occurs very slowly and only in moderate degree, was recognized as clearly by nineteenth century economists as by Mr. Bronfenbrenner. It was also recognized that the reverse situation, that is, the process of a rising price level as a consequence of excessive monetary expansion, produces great disturbances but is not so painful. Perhaps this is analogous to other aspects of human affairs, such as human growth. The child grows rapidly to an adult and an adult shrinks a little as he ages without great pain or disturbance, but a severe reduction in a man's height occurs only under conditions such that the results are catastrophic. This sort of analogy was hinted at by one of the

---

[12]Bronfenbrenner, *op. cit.,* p. 106.

177

nineteenth century economists. S. Dana Horton, speaking to the International Monetary Conference, Paris, in 1881, commented as follows:

"Here, then, are the two controlling facts, a certain quantity of money in existence and the need of an annual increase in this quantity.

You may say, with Ricardo, that if this base were half what it is . . . money would render the same service to humanity as before. Gentlemen, this is absolutely true. . . . But, gentlemen, this saying of Ricardo's is true in the same sense as it is true that if it had pleased the destiny, which rules these matters, to make us all a foot shorter than we are, men would still be men. The thing is conceivable, gentlemen, but it is not practicable. . . .

. . . it is not the result, it is the means of arriving at it that is important. Of course, I can say, if I wish to, that I should be perfectly content if I were to lose a foot of my height. But how are you to arrive at a height of five instead of six feet?"[13]

In the same talk Mr. Horton went on to describe the impact of the change in the value of money upon business expectations and business men's decisions:

"The world of business, the world of men of enterprise, the world in the midst of which men of force and capacity act, is an organism; and the motive which urges these men to the production of wealth is the hope of receiving a little more than they give; it is the difference between the cost of production and the price at which sale is made afterwards which makes the organism move. When all the prices at which sales are made are falling, when the force of gravitation which rules the world slackens, there is less movement, there is less production, less consumption, less success in business; there is embarrassment, there is a prolonged crisis, or, what we call in English, hard times. When prices rise, on the contrary, there is always an encouragement to production."[14]

---

[13]S. Dana Horton, address May 19, 1881, *Proceedings of the International Monetary Conference,* Paris (Cincinnati: Robert Clarke and Co., 1881), pp. 311-12.
[14]*Ibid.,* p. 312.

Alfred Marshall, whom we might describe as the dean of the equilibrium theorists, referred as follows to the boom and depression impact of changes in the value of money:

"Thus the want of a proper standard of purchasing power is the chief cause of the survival of the monstrous fallacy that there can be too much produced of everything. The fluctuations in the value of what we use as our standard are ever either flurrying up business activity into unwholesome fever, or else closing factories and workshops by the thousand in businesses that have nothing radically wrong with them, but in which whoever buys raw material and hires labour is likely to sell when general prices have further fallen. Perhaps the bad habits of mind and temper engendered by the periods of business fever do more real harm than the periods of idleness; but it is less conspicuous and less easily traced. In times of stagnation he who runs may read in waste and gaunt faces a degradation of physique and a weakening of energy which often tells its tale throughout the whole of the rest of the lives of the men, women, and children who have suffered from it."[15]

Many of the economists and government officials who held these views believed that it is possible to provide the nation with a quantity of circulating medium that will increase at a reasonable rate of growth and will therefore maintain a reasonable stability in the value of money. The United States Monetary Commission of 1876 stated:

"It is in a volume of money keeping even pace with advancing population and commerce, and in the resulting steadiness of prices, that the wholesome nutriment of a healthy vitality is to be found. The highest moral, intellectual, and material development of nations is promoted by the use of money unchanging in its value. That kind of money, instead of being the oppressor, is one of the great instrumentalities of commerce and industry . . . It is only under steady prices that the production of wealth can reach

---

[15]Alfred Marshall, "Remedies for Fluctuation of General Prices," *The Contemporary Review*, LI, pp. 358-59.

its permanent maximum, and that its equitable distribution is possible." [16]

Mr. Horton, at the International Monetary Conference a few years later, said:

"To sum up the matter, gentlemen, I hope that all will admit that the great problem of monetary legislation is, and also will be, to maintain the stability of the international and national purchasing power of money. Here is the ideal, stability." [17]

The recommendations of the United States Monetary Commission of 1876 and of the American delegates at the International Monetary Conference of 1881 were based upon an understanding of the circumstances which had been responsible for the deficiency of circulating medium in that period of falling prices. They pointed out that in the 1850's new gold mines in California and Australia had added unusually large amounts to the world's monetary base and that this had been the generating factor in the rising price trend of that decade; and that in the years 1864-66 the paper money issues of the United States and Italy had further augmented what Mr. Horton called "the money base". During the succeeding years these sources of addition to the world's money base had not provided sufficient growth. Further, Germany and the United States had accumulated large stocks of gold in the 1870's—Germany for the purpose of replacing silver in her monetary system, and the United States in preparing for resumption of specie payments in gold. These accumulations had come for the most part out of England's gold stock. This had produced a worldwide monetary deficiency, and falling prices in all countries with monetary systems linked with gold or sterling. Under these circumstances it was thoroughly appropriate that the remedy suggested was an agreement among all the leading nations of the world to retain or to adopt a bimetallic monetary base.

---

[16]*Report* of the United States Monetary Commission (1877), pp. 51-52.
[17]S. Dana Horton, address cited, p. 312.

With respect to the more technical question of how much growth of circulating medium, and therefore how much expansion in the money base of the world, or of the United States, was needed to secure a stable price level, the nineteenth century economists had an adequate theoretical answer, namely, "a volume of money keeping even pace with advancing population and commerce." However, in practice they were not able to implement this answer with precision because of inadequate factual data. The character of the discussion of the needs of commerce indicates that the idea which that word represented was the quantity of goods coming into marketing channels. Increase in commerce during most of the nineteenth century was more rapid than in the volume of production, because of a decline in the proportion of output utilized in direct home consumption and because of changes in market organization as the shipping and sale of commodities was extended to larger and more distant areas. No measure was available, either for the quantity of output nor for the other elements in "advancing" commerce.

Central Bank Theory and Monetary Disequilibrium

Representatives of England at the International Monetary Conference would not agree with those who were urging adoption of a bimetallic monetary standard by the leading nations. The movement for international bimetallism collapsed, and the conditions described by the American representatives continued for another decade and a half. The falling price trend was not reversed until gold discoveries in Alaska and the Yukon, toward the end of the century, again provided a rapid rate of enlargement of the world's monetary base.

Lack of growth in the monetary base was not the only factor preventing an increase in the circulating medium in accordance with the needs of commerce. This was especially true in the United States, where there were four disturbing factors which were recognized: the particular conditions of issue of circulating medium in the form of hand-to-hand currency; the Independent Treasury System; an inadequate mobility and inappropriate sea-

181

sonal variations in bank credit; and use by banks in the money centers of correspondent reserve balances for call loans in the securities market. Economists, bankers, and others who studied these problems looked at the operations of central banks in various European countries which had aided in adjusting the supply of circulating medium to "the needs of trade." There was, in consequence, a growing body of central banking theory based on the principle that such an institution, with appropriate powers, could substantially modify, without abandoning the gold standard, the features of the monetary system which produced undesirable fluctuations in the quantity of circulating medium. To illustrate the character of this theory and the potential accomplishments of central banks, as seen by economists in the first three decades of the twentieth century, it is sufficient to refer to statements by Henry Parker Willis and Gustav Cassel.

Henry Parker Willis, who is understood to have had more influence on the monetary theory underlying the Federal Reserve Act than any other economist, remarked that "the function of the central bank is undoubtedly that of regulating or controlling price levels, since its work is that of controlling the production and rate of consumption of commodities," and declared that the essential function of the central bank is the stabilization of credit.[18]

The belief that a central bank can and should influence the quantity of circulating medium and thereby appropriately adjust that quantity to the needs of the nation is in essence a belief that a nation's monetary system should be deliberately managed, and that such management can produce better results than was accomplished by the gold standard system as it developed in the latter part of the nineteenth century and the early part of the twentieth. As studies progressed of the operations of central banking systems in various countries, particularly of the Bank of England at the time when England dominated the world's foreign commerce and sterling was the circulating medium not only of Eng-

[18]Henry Parker Willis, *The Theory and Practice of Central Banking* (New York: Harper and Bros., 1936), p. 35; and my notes on his lectures in banking at Columbia University, 1928-29.

land but also of the world with respect to international transactions, it began to be realized that the gold standard itself had not been an unmanaged automatic system. Gustav Cassel in 1934 wrote as follows:

"It is a common notion that the present-day controversies regarding monetary policy can ultimately be reduced to the question: managed currency or not? What the other alternative might be has never been clearly seen. People have been brought up in the belief that the gold standard was a kind of automatic currency which did not require any definite monetary policy. And to this very day there are numbers of folks who suppose that any deliberate regulation of the purchasing power of money would be superfluous if only the gold standard were universally restored.

The view that the gold standard works automatically is based on an antiquated idea of the gold currency as a monetary system in which the circulating medium consists of gold. This view, however, becomes untenable according as the note-issuing central bank assumes the character of an institution which largely determines the amount of money in circulation. . . .

The purchasing power of a currency will therefore always depend on the way in which the central bank regulates the monetary supply. In this respect the gold standard is no exception. It can be maintained only if the purchasing power of the currency relatively to goods is constantly regulated so as to correspond to that of gold. This regulation is effected by the central bank's discount policy, or, more generally expressed, its entire credit policy. The fact that many central banks have succeeded for decades in maintaining the gold standard is proof positive that the central bank, by its credit policy, possesses effective control over the purchasing power of the currency, and thus that a deliberate regulation of that purchasing power is possible. Those who, in the heat of present-day controversies, maintain the opposite should carefully ponder this incontrovertible testimony of experience."[19]

[19]Gustav Cassel, *Quarterly Report* of the Skandinaviska Kreditaktiebolaget for January, 1934. Quoted by Norman Lombard in *Monetary Statemanship* (New York: Harper and Brothers, 1934), pp. 78-79. For a recent statement of similar import see William Adams Brown, Jr., "Gold as a Monetary Standard, 1914-1949," *The Journal of Economic History,* Supplement IX-1949, pp. 39-49.

Under today's circumstances central banks are not under the limited restraints of the gold standard operating simultaneously in a number of countries. Consequently, their power, particularly in a leading nation like the United States, is even more potent than is indicated by the historical experience to which Cassel referred.

The theory of how the central banking system operates is quite simple. It starts with the assumption that banks, as a matter of practice, tend to carry the expansion of their credit to the limit permitted by the laws and circumstances under which they operate. In the United States the dominant limitation is the percentage reserve requirement which is imposed upon them, and the record shows that they do, except in very unusual circumstances, keep their assets and deposits close to the limit permitted by their reserves. In the case of banks that are members of the Federal Reserve system, which hold about 70 percent of all the bank deposits of the nation (excluding inter-bank accounts), the legal reserve consists solely of balances in the Federal Reserve banks.

Member bank balances in Federal Reserve banks are a major portion of the liabilities of those banks. Variations in the aggregate amount of member bank reserve balances are dominated by variations in the assets of the Federal Reserve banks, since the reserve accounts are the residual or variable portion of Federal Reserve bank liabilities. This result of variations in the assets of Federal Reserve banks remains dominant, even though variations may occur in other types of liabilities in the Federal Reserve banks, or changes may be made in the percentage reserve requirements, or deposits may shift from a bank or category having one percentage reserve requirement to a bank or category with another percentage reserve requirement. The volume of assets of the Federal Reserve bank is determined by the asset-acquisition and relinquishment policies established by the Federal Reserve authorities. By adjustments in these policies, which consist largely of adjustments of the terms on which assets are acquired or relinquished, the Federal Reserve authorities can cause the quantity of bank reserves to move in such a way as to offset other influences on the amount or effectiveness of reserves, and can also cause the effective amount of reserves to be enlarged or contracted within a very wide range.[20]

Under unusual circumstances forces other than the amount of bank reserves may limit the expansion of commercial banks, and under normal circumstances the rate of such expansion is somewhat dependent upon the inter-relationships of banks through the check-clearing process. Banks which expand too rapidly relative to other banks tend to lose reserves so that when, for example, bank reserves are rapidly increased in one group of banks, it is not until the increase has been distributed through the system that its full expansionary effect is felt.

This theory of the role of changing bank reserves in originating business depression was developed prior to establishment of the Federal Reserve System. The difference in the situation resulting from the Federal Reserve Act is in the nature of the forces which dominantly influence the quantity of bank reserves. If the theory is correct, we should find upon examination of the factual evidence that each of the business depressions in the United States since the establishment of the Federal Reserve system has been preceded by Federal Reserve actions which impinged upon bank reserves and caused them to contract, either absolutely or relative to a reasonable rate of growth. Further, if the theory is correct, the handling of the asset-acquisition and relinquishment policies of the Federal Reserve bank with more skill and finesse would have prevented those depressions from occurring or at least would have confined them to extreme mildness. Still further, if this central banking theory and the underlying theory of monetary disequilibrium are correct, appropriate skill in handling the asset-acquisition and relinquishment policies of the Federal Reserve Banks would have resulted in an appropriate rate of growth in the

---

[20]The only significant exception to this power of the central banking system is the case when the assets of the Federal Reserve banks consist almost solely of gold and, as is the case, they cannot offer it freely for sale. This circumstance was of practical importance only in a few years during the latter half of the decade of the 1930's.

reserves of commercial banks and hence in a rate of growth in the circulating medium of the nation which would have avoided either an upward or downward trend in the price level.

Factual Data and the Theory of Disequilibrium

For several years my chief task has been a study of the relation of banking to business fluctuations. In connection with this study quarterly statistical series have been prepared, covering the past thirty years, of the circulating medium or money, *i. e.*, bank deposits and currency, held by business and individuals, of the rate of use of money for purchase of final products of the economy, and of the amount of bank reserves adjusted for technical factors bearing on their effectiveness. These series make it possible to compare the sequence of events at business cycle turning points and during the intervening periods of downswing and upswing with the assumptions of the theory of monetary disequilibrium. The series have been published and their results described elsewhere.[21] It is therefore sufficient here to call attention to the most significant results.

Between the World Wars there were five business downturns of sufficient seriousness to become known as depressions in the study of business cycles; and an equal number of upswings from the troughs of depression. In all five cases the point of transition between prosperity and stable or rising prices, on the one hand, and declining prices, employment, and output, on the other, followed turning points in the effective volume of bank reserves relative to the estimated needed rate of growth. Likewise, the

---

[21]"Quantity and Frequency of Use of Money in the United States, 1919-45," *Journal of Political Economy*, LIV (October 1946), pp. 436-50; "Bank Reserves and Business Fluctuations," *Journal of the American Statistical Association*, 43 (December 1948), pp. 547-58; and "Index Numbers of the Elements of the Equation of Exchange," presented at a joint meeting of the Econometric Society and the American Statistical Association, December 28, 1948 (mimeographed—copy available on request to the author, McLean, Va.). See also the following articles, in which the results are compared with business cycle turning points: "Banks and Business Fluctuations," *Estadística*, March 1950; and "Theory of Turning Points in Business Fluctuations," *Quarterly Journal of Economics* (forthcoming issue).

recoveries followed low points in reserves.[22] For each of the ten turning points the publications of the Federal Reserve system show what changes occurred in the conditions on which assets were acquired or relinquished by the Federal Reserve banks.

This correspondence between the sequence of events in the record and the sequence involved in the theory of monetary disequilibrium is not confined to the turning points. The duration and depth of each of the downswings and upswings was closely related to the rate and degree of deviation in the amount of effective bank reserves from the estimated normal rate of growth.

The 6-year period, 1923-28, is the longest period, during the third of a century that the Federal Reserve System has been in existence, when the rate of growth in effective bank reserves—though varying from year to year—was close to the estimated rate needed for stability of prices of output and sale of the full output of the economy at such prices. That period was a time of general prosperity, with a closer approach to full employment and price stability than at any other time since establishment of the Federal Reserve system. Within this 6-year period there were two brief depressions, in 1924 and 1927. Both were preceded by actions of the Federal Reserve authorities which impinged upon bank reserves and caused them to grow at a rate which was less than normal; and in both cases the recoveries were preceded by turnabouts in central bank policy which were made quickly after the downswing became evident.

The experience of the interwar period is now being repeated. Effective member bank reserves, relative to trend, turned downward at the beginning of 1948. Peaks in prices and business came in the autumn. In May 1949 a series of reductions in percentage reserve requirements was begun, resulting in a trough in effective reserves in the second quarter of the year. A few months later business seemed ready to pick up, but in the latter part of 1949 and the early months of 1950 asset-relinquishment policies of the Federal Reserve banks offset the reductions in percentage reserve

---

[22]In a very small number of cases the turning points occurred in the same month.

187

requirements.[23] The present prospect is that the recession will continue until bank reserves begin to grow again.

A Guide for Central Bank Operations

The experience of the past third of a century in the United States, as indicated by study of the data, supports the observation of Ralph G. Hawtrey some years ago: "Once the monetary authorities of the world can bring themselves to refrain from *causing* depressions, their task will become relatively easy."[24] The same experience supports with equal force the proposition that when central banks also stop indulging in the policies which permit price inflation the battle for economic stability, full employment, and stable prices will have been won.

It is only in comparatively recent years that sufficient data have been available to provide a reasonably good measure of the rate of growth in the circulating medium, and hence in effective bank reserves, which is needed for stability of the level of prices. Consequently the standards for central bank operations previously used in attempts to adjust the quantity of circulating medium to the needs of the economy have been based on the principle of correcting errors in monetary policy after the effects of those errors had became visible. Such guides for central bank action, as developed by theorists in the nineteenth century or the early part of the twentieth, were of three sorts: (1) gold movements and the state of the foreign exchange market; (2) an index of prices; and (3) the state of employment, profits and unused capacity.

The first of the three guides to central bank policy was proved by historical experience to have some advantages but to be inadequate for maintaining economic stability in all countries or even in one country. When one country with a central bank started to correct its own position a disturbance was created in other countries. Gold movements and foreign exchange rates resulting from

---

[23]At the end of March 1950, effective bank reserves were about 3.5 percent higher than on the corresponding date in 1949. That is to say, they were lower relative to trend than a year earlier, when the series of reductions in percentage reserve requirements was begun.

[24]Ralph G. Hawtrey, *A Century of Bank Rate* (London: Longmans, Green and Co., 1938), p. 273.

188

a good harvest in one part of the world and a poor harvest in another might induce central bank action which intensified the disturbance in its own country. Advocates of the maintenance of stable prices as a required objective of central bank policy argued that reversal of central bank policy whenever an index of prices started downward or upward should keep fluctuations in the level of prices within a relatively narrow range. The practice of looking at the state of business as indicated by information regarding unemployment, business profits, and changes in the volume of output was another application of the principle of correcting past errors before their effects became significantly large. It was this kind of objective which was used by the authorities of the Federal Reserve system during the period 1923-28 when a group of successive changes in policy resulted in a fair degree of stability and reasonably full employment.

Monetary theorists, however, recognized that under the gold standard operative in several nations the range of action by the central bank of any one country, and therefore the power to maintain a given price level indefinitely, was limited. The situation was described by John Maynard Keynes in 1931 as follows:

"... credit control is used to describe a system in which the central banking authorities deliberately determine, sometimes in anticipation of gold movements and sometimes in disregard of them, both the quantity and the price of credit with a view to the achievement of certain economic objectives, such as price stability or stability of employment and output or stock exchange stability. Although it is admitted that a country under a gold standard cannot persist indefinitely in a policy which disregards gold movements, experience has shown that a financially strong country or one with large gold reserves can ignore their effects for a considerable time."

"A central bank, which is free to govern the volume of cash and reserve money in its monetary system by the joint use of bank rate policy and open market operations, is master of the situation and is in a position to control not merely the volume of credit but the rate of investment, the level of prices and in the long run the level of incomes, provided that the objectives it sets before itself are compatible with its legal obligations . . ."[25]

In the *General Theory* there is an ambiguous passage which suggests that as a result of the great depression Keynes modified the opinion expressed above or that he thought the powers of the Federal Reserve authorities were limited by "legal obligations" which he did not specify. "Nevertheless, the most enlightened monetary control might find itself in difficulties, faced with a boom of the 1929 type in America, and armed with no other weapons than those possessed at that time by the Federal Reserve System; and none of the alternatives within its power might make much difference to the result."[26] However, the factual record is in conformity with the earlier statement and does not support the passage in the *General Theory*. Study of the pertinent data shows that the depression was led by a substantial deviation in effective bank reserves below the reasonable rate of growth, that the beginning of this deviation in 1928 and 1929 was the direct result of Federal Reserve policies (the nature of which is described in the Annual Reports of the Federal Reserve Board), that its accentuation in the succeeding years would have been avoided by acquisition through open market operations or otherwise of a suitable volume of assets by the Federal Reserve banks, and that the legal powers of the System were fully ample to permit such acquisition.

There seems to me to be no escape from the conclusion that the cause of the banking debacle and therefore of the great depression was the fact that the Federal Reserve authorities dropped completely, as guides for action, the maintenance of stability of prices of output or of employment and business activity, and substituted the false goal of checking speculation. Study of the factual data shows that at the time of action by the Federal Reserve authorities the level of stock prices was not unduly high,

[25]J. M. Keynes, "Credit Control," *Encyclopaedia of the Social Sciences*, Vol. IV (New York: Macmillan Company, 1931), pp. 550-51 and 552.

[26]*The General Theory of Employment, Interest, and Money* (New York: Harcourt, Brace and Company, 1936), p. 327.

as measured by the level of such prices in a year such as 1922 and subsequent developments with respect to corporation earnings, the proportion of those earnings retained by stockholders after income taxes, and the rate of interest. Keynes was right, in another passage in the *General Theory,* when he said: "In the United States employment was very satisfactory in 1928-29 on normal standards; but I have seen no evidence of a shortage of labor, except, perhaps, in the case of a few groups of highly specialized workers. Some 'bottle-necks' were reached, but output as a whole was still capable of further expansion. . . . It would be absurd to assert of the United States in 1929 the existence of over-investment in the strict sense." He was also right when he said: "Thus an increase in the rate of interest, as a remedy for the state of affairs arising out of a prolonged period of abnormally heavy new investment, belongs to the species of remedy which cures the disease by killing the patient."[27] But he failed to realize that in the case of the United States in 1929 the disease existed only in the unsupported imagination of the monetary authorities and other persons who had no understanding of the theory of property values in a normally functioning expanding economy.

Under the present situation, the restraints of the gold standard are no longer operative. Also, sufficient factual data are now available to permit measurement, within a reasonable margin of error, of the factors which create the need for growth in the money supply. The factors which require consideration are the trends in population, in productivity, and in the rate of use or circuit velocity of money. The data for these trends, when combined, indicate that in the United States the needed rate of growth in the money supply and therefore in effective bank reserves is about 5 per cent per year. The deviations in effective bank reserves from this rate of growth during the past thirty years, which have been associated with business downswings and upswings, have been of the order of magnitude of two to forty percent per year. That is to say, the experience of this period suggests that a deviation from the 5 percent per year line of

---

[27]*Ibid.,* pp. 322 and 323.

growth of less than 2 percent in a year may be tolerable, because it is not likely to produce a serious price inflation, on the one hand, nor a deep depression on the other. However, a persistent deviation of this magnitude in one direction would result in a substantial change in the level of prices in the course of a generation or even a decade.

Trends in population, productivity, and monetary velocity may change as time goes by and monetary authorities should be alert to the detection of such changes as soon as possible. Because of the difficulty of ascertaining changes in secular trends promptly a comprehensive index of prices of final products of the economy should be regarded as the ultimate test of the adequacy of monetary policy. That is to say, if the chosen rate of growth in effective bank reserves, computed from the best available data, when used for monetary policy results in a declining or rising price trend, a moderate adjustment in policy will be needed to correct the error.

The criterion of a reasonable rate of growth in the amount of effective bank reserves does not mean a completely rigid adherence to this trend. Some variation to meet particular needs, at least for seasonal purposes, may be desirable. However, the central bank authorities should be instructed to provide for such variation only when the need has been demonstrated. The need for a reasonable rate of growth in the money supply and the disastrous results of wide departures therefrom have been so thoroughly demonstrated that adherence to a reasonable rate of growth should be accepted as the proper objective for monetary policy.

Problem of Business Income Determination
Under a Stable Price Level

My disagreement with Mr. Bronfenbrenner's forecast of a rising price level in the future does not extend to problems of business income determination in the event of such a trend. Most of his comments on this problem are relevant and acceptable. Neither would I disagree with the point of view regarding the problem of business income determination under changing price levels which has been expressed by Mr. Fabricant and in the monographs

192

previously published by the Study Group.[28] Consequently, the only comments on the specific problem of the Study Group, that of business income measurement, which I would like to make here are a few remarks on the adjustment of business accounts to a price level chosen for maintenance in the future.

The proposal for the use of central bank policy to provide a stable price level in the future involves—as a means of knowing whether or not this is accomplished—the construction of a more comprehensive index of prices of the final products of the economy than is now available. When such an index is constructed, it should be carried backward for a substantial number of years. This would make it possible for business concerns to make approximations of the difference between the current and probable future replacement cost of their plant, equipment, and inventories, and the amounts shown for these items on their books. The same sort of comparison could be made with respect to depreciation allowances.[29] On the basis of these approximations business concerns could adjust their accounts for previous changes in the price level.

When stabilization of the price level becomes a matter of public policy, or is discussed by Congressional banking and currency committees, it probably would be desirable for business groups to seek legislation authorizing the Bureau of Internal Revenue to recognize without subjection to income tax such adjustments in accounts and allowances as are needed to bring them into appropriate relationship with the price level which is to be maintained. The details of such adjustments lie in the field of accounting rather than in that of monetary theory.

---

[28]Solomon Fabricant, "Business Costs and Business Income under Changing Price Levels," pp. 143-154 of this volume; Arthur H. Dean, "An Inquiry into the Nature of Business Income under Present Price Levels" (1949); and George O. May, "Business Income and Price Levels, An Accounting Study" (1949).

[29] Such comparisons would not of course take into account differences in the prices of capital goods as a group, nor prices of the particular items in the assets of any one firm, relative to prices of final products as a whole.

STUDY GROUP ON BUSINESS INCOME

DISCUSSION OF MONOGRAPHS

May 13, 1950

Present at the May 13, 1950, meeting of the Study Group on Business Income were the following members and invited guests:

SIDNEY S. ALEXANDER

CHESTER I. BARNARD

CARMAN G. BLOUGH

S. J. BROAD

PERCIVAL F. BRUNDAGE

MORRIS A. COPELAND

WILLIAM W. CUMBERLAND

ARTHUR H. DEAN

JAMES L. DOHR

SOLOMON FABRICANT

RAYMOND W. GOLDSMITH

JOHN H. HASKELL

STANLEY HOLME
    representing PHILIP D. REED

GEORGE O. MAY

HIRAM T. SCOVILL

CHARLES W. SMITH

CLARK WARBURTON

EDWARD B. WILCOX

SATURDAY MORNING SESSION
May 13, 1950

The meeting was called to order at 10 a.m. by Mr. Brundage, who after some preliminaries invited Mr. Fabricant to open the discussion.

MR. FABRICANT: I could say a few words which would get Mr. Alexander started off.

This document that we have circulated contains a number of discussions by economists of business income, particularly in a regime of rising price levels. The one by Mr. Alexander, which starts it off and which he will, of course, discuss himself, makes the point very nicely that in a static type of society you could get along with essentially a single and simple type of concept of business income. It is only in a dynamic economy in which you have rising or changing prices, technological changes of various kinds and other things of the sort which cause uncertainty to arise in a situation, that various concepts of income will compete with one another for one's attention.

Mr. Alexander goes into some of the criteria and things of interest, in choosing particular concepts for particular purposes.

Mr. Bronfenbrenner continues the discussion mainly by picking out two main groups of concepts, the "venture" and "continuum" concepts, as he calls them, for continuing discussion in the light of the several problems that confront the economy today, and spends also a fair amount of time in—I should not say demonstrating, because Mr. Warburton is here—but arguing that it is very likely on historical and other grounds that we may be in for a series of rises of prices.

The document circulated then goes on to include two very small statements by myself in which the emphasis is placed primarily on a national income point of view, which the economist frequently takes in measuring business income.

195

It then concludes with Mr. Warburton's statement that there is nothing inevitable about a rising price trend, and that if you wish it not to be so it will not be so.

MR. BRUNDAGE: That is a very concise summary.

How would you like to deal with this now? Shall we ask Mr. Alexander to introduce it, or would you like to start with asking him questions? And how do you feel about it?

MR. ALEXANDER: I am willing either way.

MR. BRUNDAGE: Have you any general comments you would like to make?

MR. ALEXANDER: I think that Mr. Fabricant has put his finger on the very heart of what I have done, when he pointed out that the dynamic situation introduces a lot of problems into the measurement of income, that can be fairly simply solved in a static situation but have no unique solution in a dynamic situation, which is defined simply by changes in prices and changes in business prospects.

Those are the two most important types of changes that render difficult the measurement of income and they introduce the problem of what you do when a price changes because the value of money, your standard of account, changes, and what you do when prospects change, which means that your assets do not really have the value that they had at time of purchase.

If your prospects improve, your assets—by which I mean the total assets of the corporation, including going value, of course—increase.

I think the fundamental problems of income measurement in a dynamic economy are raised by the great variety of different concepts of income that can then be derived by taking originally slightly different points of view as to what it is you mean by income. As you all know, a slight difference of points of view at the beginning can lead you to a great diversion of results at the end.

The principal point then that I did make was that no single one of these income concepts has any absolute claim to being

196

the true concept. In measuring income we are doing it usually for a particular purpose, but not always for the same purpose.

In a static situation, almost all of these purposes would be satisfied by essentially the same measure. In a dynamic situation, you will find that the same measure will not do for all of these purposes, and consequently you must choose from among the different results you can get, according to what it is you want to use the income concepts for.

In particular, with respect to the topic that has received perhaps the most recent attention in the fundamental question of measurement of income, the question of depreciation on the basis of cost or replacement, you can make a good case for either one, each from its own point of view.

Like any good argument, any argument that is really good, it is founded on two differences in basic viewpoint.

To summarize very succinctly what these differences are: If income is to be measured in such a manner as to say that a man's income or an artificial person's income is to be the amount that the person can dispose of over the period considered and be as well off at the end of the period as at the beginning, all we need to do to justify a depreciation based on replacement is to say that by "as well off" we mean as well off in real terms.

Whatever changes of money value occur, we will have to try somehow or other to eliminate them and keep the measure in real terms.

If that is what we are after, then it is depreciation by replacement value.

On the other hand, if we say that this real measure is not what we are after, we use money in almost all the other business affairs as a standard of value; when you borrow a dollar, you have to repay a dollar; nobody forces you to pay back more dollars if the value of the dollar goes down. So we can easily concede for many purposes a money measure is appropriate; then a valuation of the depreciation allowance on a cost basis is proper.

That begins to illustrate the sort of criterion you must use at every point.

197

I will stop there for any questions or discussion, since that does illustrate the general tenor of the argument, although I have developed the argument, I think, to apply to a lot of other rather fundamental questions in the determination of profit.

MR. BRUNDAGE: May I ask: When you are discussing income under "certainty", is that of any value in our particular study, except perhaps as an introduction to what you are going to say afterwards?

There is no certainty in business.

MR. ALEXANDER: That depends upon what it is you are studying.

I was given this topic as The Measurement of Income Under Price Changes from the point of view of the economist. I very early came to the conclusion that the economists and the accountants were not talking about the same thing very much. I had thought of starting, you see, as most of the discussion I have come across does start, with the idea that the accountant is measuring the income in terms of the differences between revenues and costs, and the fundamental problem of accounting is how to assign these costs to a given period.

With that fundamental problem I have nothing to do. I just assume that as solved some way or other. Whichever way it is solved I am willing to accept.

The point where I do find the divergence begins—and that is why I had to start so very early in the income concept—is that the accountant does regard income as the difference between revenues and costs, while the economist regards income as the difference between net worth at the two periods.

Mr. May will say that I malign the accountants. He has some very respectable sources to show that even the accountants go back to what I had called the economic concept. But that is a going back. If you look at these older and very respected sources, it is true you find it. But if you look at the practical handbooks— and in this connection I have used the *Accountants' Handbook* liberally, not because I regard that as the highest authority necessarily, but because I find it the best concrete expression of the

198

things I want to comment on—then you find that the questions are not solved by a recourse back to this fundamental concept of change of net worth, but they are always solved in terms of matching costs and revenues.

Matching costs and revenues is fine in a static condition; but in a dynamic condition the trouble with matching costs and revenues is that there are accretions and losses which do not come in via revenues and costs.

It is, then, because a very fundamental difference does exist between the income concept, starting off from a change in net worth, and the income concept, starting off from matching costs and revenues, that I found it necessary to go back to the very fundamentals of the income concept.

There are such problems as variation of income, which is impossible under a strict economic definition of income. The easiest example I can give where the accountant recognizes the impossibility of variation is of an appreciation bond, let us say a Series "E" Bond. I have used this example before. You buy it for $75 and ten years later it is worth $100.

No accountant says, I believe, that the income of that bond is zero for nine years and three hundred and sixty-four days of its life, and $25 on the last day of the tenth year.

There, because the situation is regarded as fairly certain, the income is accrued.

In a business, you do not do that. If you had a business that, somehow or other, the way you measure costs and the way you measure revenues, has over nine years costs just equal to revenue and over the tenth year has a revenue $25 greater than the cost, you then say that is the income of the tenth year.

What I am trying to illustrate here is that here is a whole body of divergences from the theoretical income concepts which are necessitated by the practical operations of accounting, and because of those divergencies it was very difficult just to come in at a very late stage, as many have done—many have come in at the very late stage of where you are taking it for granted that you are measuring income by costs and revenues, and they say that you

199

had better put the income on the basis of the measure of net worth as between two periods.

I went through the testimony before the Joint Committee, and many distinguished men testified to this extent, and none went beyond the point of saying that it is unreasonable to use dollars of different purchasing power; they did not get into the fundamental of income far enough to say why in their view you should use dollars of the same purchasing power.

I merely say that for some purposes you would want to use dollars of the same purchasing power, and for other purposes you might want to use dollars of different purchasing power.

In order to distinguish among those purposes, you have to distinguish more fundamentally what it is you are trying to get at when you are measuring income. That was the justification of this rather difficult and highly theoretical early discussion, which occupies a very large proportion of the manuscript. It was trying to get to a position regarding the economist's concept in his theory—now I must distinguish between the economist's concept in his theory and the economist's concept in the measurement of national income.

I think Mr. Fabricant will bear me out that in the measurement of national income the economist has been willing to leave his theoretical basis, and, partly because of the information which has been furnished by accountants and partly because the purpose in hand requires a concept different from the purely theoretical concept of income, the economist in measuring national income has started from a point much closer to the matching of costs and revenues than is consistent with the theoretical concept of income.

In particular, in the measurement of the national income, for example, no account is taken of the fact that the national income should be (as you can prove, in theory, income should be) that amount which can be consumed this year with the expectation that an equal amount can be consumed throughout the future. In the case of national income, with increasing productivity, that would mean that under present measures of national income we should be consuming our capital, because you are expecting

200

productivity to increase. That is, if you maintain the same amount of capital over the future with increased productivity, you expect that the amount you can produce will increase from year to year. Right?

Therefore, if you are defining income as the amount that you can consume, and just consume as much every year in the future, you could plan to have a constantly diminishing amount of capital from year to year, because each year your capital will support more consumption.

That is sort of a sophisticated point I bring in, but I bring it in just to emphasize the fact that the economist in his actual measurement of national income does not follow the strict theoretical definition of income, and usually for a good reason, the reason being that the purpose he has in mind is not quite the same as the purpose you have in mind when you define income basically —I am taking it for granted we will agree—as the economic definition of income, namely, the amount that can be consumed in any period, leaving you as well off at the end of the period as at the beginning.

It can very easily be proved that income becomes equivalent then to the amount you can consume in any period with the expectation that you can have an equal consumption in all subsequent periods.

MR. BRUNDAGE: We ought to have a comment from the economists on that.

MR. COPELAND: If I understand what you mean by a pure theoretical definition of income, it is a definition on which a certain group of economists, at any rate, can agree in the abstract, but which has no specific concrete meanings, no way of putting it into figures.

MR. ALEXANDER: I would say there are a lot of ways of putting it into figures.

MR. COPELAND: In a dynamic society—and I don't think there was ever one which wasn't—it means the concept is an ambiguous concept, and it is a subjective concept because it depends on someone's expectations.

201

I would not think that you would get very far forward in a factual study of economics if you are proceeding on a purely subjective basis.

MR. ALEXANDER: I grant the point Mr. Copeland has made. In fact, that is the basis of my presentation.

You say that the definition is ambiguous, and it is exactly the very ambiguities that I have been attempting to trace.

This is my whole point: that even if you agree on the terms and definition that you are going to use, you still can give those terms a somewhat different meaning, and for each particular meaning you give them you get a different rule for how to calculate income.

MR. COPELAND: What you are saying is that you can get a group of economists to agree on a formula of words but not on the meaning of the words.

MR. ALEXANDER: I would say that is a very common occurrence in social life: that words mean different things for different people and in different activities, and for that reason I bring my principal point, which is that you cannot then go back to this agreed definition and say categorically that this agreed definition supports this measure of income and not that one.

It is precisely because of the ambiguity that you have indicated that we have different measures of income, and because that ambiguity is highly fundamental and because there is that subjective element—that is not all, but one, of the important facts—we will get different measures of income.

I would also like to point out—and this is not a direct meeting of the point you have made, but something suggested by what you have said—that for many of the most important uses of income by a private business, these subjective elements are governed by certain considerations, that, whatever the books show, if you believe that the future of this company is to be such that it can distribute dividends of, let us say, a thousand dollars a year and you figure the interest rate at five percent, you would be foolish to think this company worth only two thousand dollars if the books show it is worth about two thousand dollars.

I say that for many purposes the final criterion that is wanted is a subjective measure based upon your estimate of future earning power, and that is something that you cannot get away from.

On the other hand, you cannot get away from the fact that what is wanted in accounting are objective measures, and therefore some way or other the gap must be bridged between the objective measure, which most accountants will agree is what the accountant should limit himself to, and the subjective measure, which is really the final desire.

In many ways I suggest that accountants must direct their attention to so presenting their objective measures as to give the best basis to the man we call the business man to make his subjective projection, which is the real and final measure of capital and income, the real and final measure of capital being what it is worth to somebody; whatever the books show is merely perhaps an aid in someone's forming a judgment of what it is worth to him.

MR. BRUNDAGE: You mean that the income of Corporation A may be different whether it is considered by the president, by the board of directors, by one of the employees, or by the controller.

MR. ALEXANDER: Definitely.

MR. COPELAND: Yes.

MR. ALEXANDER: I would definitely say that a present judgment of income—I question whether a "the income" exists—is the basis for action of each person concerned with the corporation.

Let us take rather a stockholder and a prospective stockholder, one who is going to buy and one who is going to sell. They are vitally interested in what the income is.

I say that the relevant income to each of those is the income based in the case of each one upon his own subjective statement of future earning power, and that for them the most useful accounting measure is that one which gives them that information on which such a subjective estimate can best be based.

I think it is completely agreed—and I am not trying to argue that the accountant should perform the subjective function—I am arguing that for this particular purpose of income (one of the

203

most important, namely, judging how to manage your portfolio) the income concept that is best is the best expectation of the future, and the man who guesses that best is the one that is going to be the best off.

MR. WARBURTON: I would like to raise the same question that Mr. Copeland raised in just a little different form.

I refer to page 33 which contains Mr. Alexander's reference to there being a difference in the practice between measuring national income and what he has called the economic concept.

I have written this question in the margin: Isn't this saying that the economist has more than one definition of income, and wouldn't it be better to avoid the phrase "the economic income concept" and to substitute some other phrase?

Then, continuing over on page 38 where we have three classifications of income, entitled respectively economic income, tangible income and accountant's income: I wonder whether it wouldn't be better to give those titles, or give them a nomenclature that is more descriptive of the contents.

In the first one, perhaps it would be better to avoid the word "economic" and call it perhaps the "capitalization" concept of income.

The second one, the "tangible income concept"; the third, probably—I am not sure—might be called the "historical cost concept".

MR. BRUNDAGE: On what page is that?

MR. WARBURTON: 38. That is, instead of contesting the definition of "economic income" which is only one definition used by economists, we might give these different concepts labels which have some significance with respect to the content of the concept.

I would say that it would be quite an improvement to do so. It would remove some of the objections in the matter.

MR. MAY: And substitute the indefinite article for the definite article. Substitute "an economic" and "a tangible".

What seems to me interesting about this proposition is that your definition comes down to something like this: An interest

204

rate on capital plus or minus differences in successive expectations, appraisals of expectations.

MR. ALEXANDER: That is right.

MR. MAY: You have simplified it by calling it an interest rate, but when you define interest rates you say an interest rate means a set of rules which isn't an interest rate but is a group of varying assumptions of expectations applied to different dates in the future, so that it is even more complex than you have put it today. But in so far as the accepted interest rates are concerned, income becomes determined mainly by your deciding the proper interest rate to apply.

That is one of the great defects to my mind of the depletion method that is now employed.

I think, to carry that along, Mr. Copeland has stated my objection. In fact, I think he stated it rather clearly when he said that Hicks has rejected this economic concept as being useless even for economic analyses, and I would suggest, as our purpose is to try to evolve some concept of income that is capable of implementation by accounting methods, and Mr. Hicks has rejected it for his purpose, *a fortiori*, it is no good to us as a practical proposition.

I think that is what you have proved. There is an economic concept held by a very respectable body of opinion that is of no practical use to this particular group. So far, that is one thing we have demonstrated that I think is valuable and we can go on from there. That is my feeling. We can get back to the concepts that are used for national income, which I think are much closer to our point of view for our own determination, rather than your remote one.

MR. ALEXANDER: I am perfectly willing to agree that it is not a concept which can be applied by an accountant, but I will not agree that it therefore has no use in considering the methods of accounting for this reason:

This set of rules, which I call the rate of interest, is a very important consideration for any man who really cares about income. To the income recipient it makes a great deal of difference, for any decision that I am going to make, whether or not I would just as soon have a dollar a hundred years from now or whether I very strongly prefer the dollar now.

Those are the sorts of considerations that are implicit in the rate of interest, and it does make a difference which way I have the preference. And according to whether I have the preference or do not have the preference, I would say that income A is greater than income B, or vice versa, and therefore you cannot get away from it. Merely because you cannot measure something does not mean that you can get away from the importance of it.

The question of the way in which future payments are to be stacked up against present payments and future receipts against present receipts is an important element of business decisions.

MR. MAY: Yes, but business income must be essentially a record of the past.

MR. ALEXANDER: I would say that a record must be of the past.

MR. MAY: Yes.

MR. ALEXANDER: But that business income must be a record of the past for all uses I would absolutely deny. I would say that a record of the past can be presented to help formulate a concept of income.

MR. MAY: But I am talking about the accounting concept of income. Accounting is a recording profession to begin with, and it must be statistical. The first thing that is necessary is to have a synthesis of underlying postulates. One of the underlying postulates is that you continue in business, that you continue the operations. That would not be a part of your postulates. Therefore, the fluctuations in the value of the assets that you have to have to continue in business are immaterial as long as you continue in business.

There is a whole big batch of considerations.

MR. ALEXANDER: No, sir. It is not a postulate of accounting, I would say, that you continue in business at exactly the same level. I would say it is one of the most important business judgments to decide at what level you do continue in business. You can assume continuity without considering perfect stability.

As long as you can vary, as long as you can buy at one time and sell at another, have more inventory in a year when you expect prices to rise and less when you expect prices to fall, then it is important to take——

MR. MAY: You say capital assets?

MR. ALEXANDER: Capital assets are just like an inventory that lasts a lot longer.

MR. MAY: No, because by hypothesis you cannot sell them today, because you intend to stay in business. You can cut down your inventory or enlarge your inventory, but your main business investment has to stay all the time, or else you haven't the wherewithall to conduct business.

You cannot go in and out of capital assets as you go in and out of inventory.

MR. FABRICANT: The difference is merely of degree. You cannot get rid of all of your inventory, either.

MR. MAY: A difference in degree is ultimately a difference in kind. Thomas Adams used to say that the difference between a fifty per cent. tax and a five per cent. tax was more than a matter of degree.

MR. FABRICANT: You say an accountant's conception of income must be a record of the past. Included in the record of the past are your business expectations. You haven't got around to the problem of what you are going to do with your expectations.

MR. MAY: That, of course, is one of the most difficult things, to fix that within a narrow limit.

MR. FABRICANT: I agree with that.

MR. MAY: There are so many elements in this problem that you have to cast aside a whole lot of non-essentials and concentrate on the major elements. That is what we have to do all the time.

Accounting, to begin with, is a process of classification according to major points of resemblance while ignoring minor points of difference. That runs throughout accounting. I think we have to start with that. As I said, I think our object is to get a concept of income that is capable of being implemented by accounting methods.

We have to do a lot of that discarding and concentrate on essentials, and say that changes in degree might be so great as to involve changes in character.

We have to have that agreement, I think, if we are going to get started towards practical results.

MR. GOLDSMITH: The basic income concept which Mr. Alexander worked with—and I think he has usefully demonstrated what it means—has come into economics in the last ten or fifteen years, really starting with Hicks.

I am not sure whether from an economic point of view it has turned out to be an improvement. I am not so much worried as an economist, maybe, that accountants could not follow it, but I am worried that it is not an operative definition; I mean in the wide sense. It is not a concept where you can show the steps by which it can be reduced to quantities.

I think generally that we should try as little as possible, or not at all, to work with concepts that are not operative, because if we try to do it, then of course we get back to the point that we cannot exclude the future completely from the measurement of income. That I think is clear.

I would not go as far as Mr. Alexander, at least in working this out consistently, went whole-hog the other way and really made the measurement of today's income mostly a problem of the future.

Where I think the whole problem comes up in national income calculations is in the means of keeping capital intact. But that I think is really, as you said, the only essential point where it comes in.

Probably the important approach to get an approximation of bringing together the economist's and accountants' concepts is to try to define whatever flows from this concept in the annual income statement, in such a way that it meets the economist's standards.

208

Of course, Mr. Alexander emphasized those two problems: how you treat inventory and how you treat depreciation.

For practical work I doubt that the difference is so great, but I am not sure that even strictly as economists we have to proceed on this Hicksian concept, which is based on the equivalence of welfare at the beginning and end of the period.

That implies another difficulty· with which I do not remember if Mr. Alexander dealt. That comes from a point which Mr. May stressed.

After all, such an income concept should be valid for the individual, and as a matter of fact that is where Hicks developed it in his book.

The important thing is to measure the individual's income, not so much a corporation's income. That was entirely secondary.

Of course, the moment you have the individual's income in the sense of economic welfare, it immediately ties in with expected length of life. In the individual's case, obviously the income of a man of ninety years of age, everything else being the same, is different from that of a man of thirty, because in order to be equally well off for the rest of his life quite different things are required in the case of a man of ninety and a man of thirty.

Then you are caught between business income calculations and individual income calculations, because, as Mr. May says, a business has to regard its life as infinite, whereas the individual cannot do that (unless you go so far as to regard the income of your children, grandchildren and so forth, as of the same importance as your own, which leads to very different conceptual problems).

While I think this is extremely important as demonstrating the problems of the Hicksian concept—let us call it that; I do not want to start an argument about it—by following that out and showing what it means, I am not sure whether the actual problem we are facing is not one of getting back to trying to solve the specific economic problems which arise from this link to the future in the annual income accounts, which is given as the problem of keeping capital intact.

MR. CUMBERLAND: My difficulty in examining this material seems to focus on what seems to be the effort to measure two things by a single standard. One, of course, is money flow, and the other is the flow of goods and services.

Mr. Alexander meets it in an ingenious way by taking two concepts and following them out. That is all right, but as has already been said, if the work of the committee is to be fruitful, it seems to me it must be available for operating use.

My experience and interest, aside from theory, is in corporate activity and in security markets. Very well. It seems to me that it would be somewhat difficult to apply some of these principles in either of those fields.

For example, let us take the securities market at the present time. I think Mr. Haskell will bear me out that the ordinary prospective buyer and seller of equities at the present time, and perhaps of obligations, too, is not influenced by what is going to be the flow of goods over the next few years, but what is going to be the course in the value of money.

It is a guessing contest as to what money is going to do. It seems to me that the treatment of money in the studies has been somewhat weak. I am not suggesting that the group should address itself to the problem of money and monetary stabilization and that sort of thing. Needless to say, it is a very difficult subject. But I suspect that in some of the papers that have been presented, on fluctuations in value of money and historically, it is true that virtually all fluctuations are one way, and that is down: a decline in the unit value of money.

That is historically true, so far as I can recall, for every single country. As long as that is true, let us not confuse it with dynamism. A decline in the value of money is not necessarily dynamic.

So, Mr. Chairman, it seems to me that it might be of some value to discuss whether in trying to measure money on the one side and the flow of goods and services on the other, and to do it by the same vehicle, we may have involved ourselves in an

210

impossible thing. We may have recognized that the two things have to be measured and handled in different terms.

MR. BRUNDAGE: Mr. Warburton, do you want to comment on that suggestion?

MR. WARBURTON: I do not think I have anything to add to what I said in my paper. I assume you people have read it, and I hope my point of view is stated clearly.

MR. FABRICANT: I would like to supplement the remarks of the previous speaker by giving the impression I have after reading Mr. Warburton's statement.

It reminded me of a doctor—I think it was during the Great Depression—who gave up medicine because he felt much more could be done for the sick by raising the level of national income than by practicing medicine, and he became a Communist. I am wondering whether Mr. Warburton isn't really suggesting that we stop practicing medicine and try to reorganize the economic system in such a way that we get price stability and thus solve the problem.

I think we have to accept the situation in a certain sense as one in which we probably will have rising prices, and then we do have this problem still with us, as to how to measure national income in such a situation.

MR. BRUNDAGE: Before you answer, I would like to come back to Mr. Cumberland's suggestion.

Would you be willing to write up something for this group on that subject?

MR. CUMBERLAND: I can make the effort. I cannot do it in the next two or three months because I am pretty well engaged.

MR. BRUNDAGE: Is there anyone else whom you can think of who would be able to make a contribution in that direction?

MR. CUMBERLAND: Yes. There are two people with whom I have discussed it at considerable length. I don't know whether either one is available. One is Rufus Tucker, economist of General Motors, and the other is Bradford Smith, economist at United States Steel.

MR. BROAD: I am not an economist. Mr. Alexander has spoken about the expectation of the future as of a subjective

211

nature, and it seems to me that that subjective nature is entitled to an estimation of an income flow. He has to determine what an income flow is. He fixes interest rates for the next ten years or the next year and so on, but he is getting down to the question of the value of income, it seems to me.

To get estimates of the subjective value of the future, you need something to start with. You get back to the accountant. He starts with a series of income statements which are made use of in measuring the earning power of the future. I think they should be presented in a method that would enable a man to make a reasonable judgment, or an informed judgment, as to the future course of events.

If, however, we bring a lot of highly subjective, almost entirely theoretical concepts into the determination of the basic data on which he is going to make those judgments, we are multiplying subjective judgments by subjective judgment and theory by theory. We apply subjective judgments to the statement of the past, and another man puts his judgment on top of that one, and I think we get so far from reality that it is quite impractical.

There may be some methods by which he can judge the past which are based on, let us say, acceptable data, not entirely subjective judgments, and it seems to me that the suggestion we make from an accounting standpoint, if we are to go usefully in that direction, is to take those values which we know are very much off the beam and apply some sort of a formula to them and try to put a measure based on a certain amount of objective fact, I will call it.

A lot of people do not like that term. I will call it objective fact and apply it to what has happened in the past, measured not by my judgment but something which a group like this would agree is a proper basis for judging these figures.

I do not think we can consider his thinking however. He is going to have something to start on and make his own judgment. We cannot help him make his own judgment. I think the only thing would be to limit it to that past period.

MR. FARBICANT: The problem of the economist is to provide the data.

MR. BROAD: He has to explain what the income of the past was, not the future judgment.

MR. ALEXANDER: May I reply to that, Mr. Brundage.

I am in perfect agreement with everything you have said up to the very last point, which was something to the effect that this does not help make the judgment. It does help make the judgment, of course, and this goes back to the point Mr. May raised, that the accountant deals with recorded events. I say that is fine; the accountant deals with recorded events. That is all he can be expected to deal with, and I agree with you, Mr. Broad, when you say that for the accountant to insert his judgment at this point would be much more harmful than beneficial, because each person using it would much prefer some different judgment.

On the other hand, where judgments are sufficiently widespread and common throughout the economy (such as in the case of obsolescence, we will say, although that is a delicate point), you may then take some subjective elements into account. That is a matter of degree, in that case; the general principle still stands.

The accountant deals only with recorded events, or if he does, in a few points, bring in elements which depend on the future, he does take these elements in a generally accepted way, so that the really controversial parts of the subjective evaluation of the future are, in my opinion, quite properly avoided by the accountant.

I have no quarrel with that, and the accountant then does stick to recorded events. But I then do have this statement to make: an accountant does a little more than record events; he manipulates them a little; he adds and subtracts and then sub-totals and gives names to the sub-totals, and there is one to which he gives the name "income". My whole point is that that income is not a measure of the difference by which the corporation is better off, or the equity of the corporation is better off, at the end of the period than at the beginning. And it isn't because, in order to form that judgment—this point was argued before—you have to make some of the subjective judgments of the future. This income statement is at best the amount the corporation or the

213

owners of the corporation are better off, subject to certain assumptions; and these particular assumptions are stability of the price level, and that historical costs, adjusted for those portions of cost so far charged to expenses, do measure the value of assets at the present time.

Subject to those two assumptions, you see, what the accountant gets out of the recorded past will be what I have been calling economic income, and you may wish to call it something else. I do not care, but I want to say that the result of that series of recorded operations, a perfectly legitimate result, still is not income from the starting point which I took.

You may say that that is an irrelevant starting point. I would argue that it is a relevant starting point to a lot of decisions.

So the two points I choose to make are these: that this concept of income, the amount that can be disposed of, leaving the person, real or artificial, as well off at the end of a period as he is at the beginning, is a useful concept of income; that the result of the traditional manipulation of recorded costs and revenues by the accountant will be an approximation to this concept which I have taken only under special circumstances, which are the circumstances of a static state or stability; and that the divergence may help serve as a guide.

This is the concrete contribution I have tried to make. This is the reason for going all through this discussion: that the divergence may help serve as a guide when the instability has been so great as to lead you to feel that perhaps some qualification, in footnote, perhaps,—I do not care where the qualification comes— some qualification must be made to the result of the record.

The record is done in the money of account. If you really follow this record completely, you will not record depreciation, perhaps, because depreciation is something you impute; you are not recording an event; you are recording your imputation of the event.

But I will agree with Mr. Broad that when the imputation is made, it is acceptable throughout in spite of the subjective measurement of depreciation. You cannot measure depreciation in any

214

way. You have to say that you expect in a business period of time this amount of value will have disappeared, and you therefore assign it through a rather arbitrary method to various periods. But everybody says, all right, that is reasonable.

MR. BROAD: You mentioned two assumptions there, Mr. Alexander. One is with relation to the changing level of the currency or value of money.

MR. ALEXANDER: That is right.

MR. BROAD: In your assumption you are speaking there of what has happened in the past rather than the future. You would not ask an accountant what will happen in the future.

MR. ALEXANDER: Yes, primarily.

MR. BROAD: Another assumption you make is in relation to depreciation, the assumed future life.

MR. ALEXANDER: Not future life. Future earning power.

MR. BRUNDAGE: Useful life.

MR. ALEXANDER: It is not just life. It is earning power. The two concepts come together only when——

MR. BROAD: That is where your subjective judgment comes in very heavily.

MR. ALEXANDER: That is right. And I say the two concepts come into agreement only when the value of any asset—and I measure value now, in this case, by what it will in fact earn over the future, brought to the present by some suitable rate of interest system—that when that value over the future is equal to the value of the asset, minus that proportion of it hitherto charged to annual costs, than under those conditions, the two income concepts come together, so that the divergence is introduced by the variation of the value of money and of future prospects.

MR. MAY: I do not agree with that at all.

MR. ALEXANDER: All right. Let us get to the basis of it.

MR. MAY: I take exception to the word "traditional". The present concept is not traditional.

MR. ALEXANDER: Neo-traditional, I will make it.

MR. MAY: The traditional field of accounting has been business accounting as distinguished from the big utilities. It started,

215

I would say, about 1920, this difference in the value of the assets at the beginning and at the end of the year. That is, from the balance sheet point of view.

I think probably it was the decision of the Supreme Court in the income tax cases and the changes in the price level during the First World War that brought about a reconsideration of that attitude. It is perfectly obvious that the increase in money value of capital assets that occurred in the First World War was not income in the real sense, because the assets could not be realized except at the expense of discontinuing the business, and that ran up against the postulate of continuity and permanance which is vital in all accounting.

But the other feature of that is, that the value of particular assets is immaterial from your standpoint. It is the collective value, and that is something with which the accountant cannot be concerned. That has no relation to the depreciation of particular assets at all. That is fundamental difference. It is one of the main points where I think your point of view may be very interesting, but it does not lead to any practical concept.

Of course, I think that a great study could be made, something entirely different, in the nature of a study of margins of error in concepts of the measurement of income on the present basis. That would be much more illuminating for the investor than anything else.

I think we are not sufficiently conscious of the margins of error that there are in existing accounts.

There is only one other point I would like to mention at this time: that the use of accounts as a method for appraisal by the investor is only one of about ten uses which accounts are expected to serve. It cannot serve them all well, and we should not therefore devote any part of our efforts to try to make accounts exact; we should concentrate, rather, on trying to do something to make them better than they are.

Today, for instance, the proportion of fruits of industry that go to labor and capital respectively, things like that, are more important from the broad standpoint than from the point of view that you are concerned with, in the subjective appraisal of the value of future income agreements.

I think we have to keep all of the eight or ten objectives of accounting clearly in mind, and all of them, I think, except this one perhaps, lay stress on practicability and the necessity of avoiding variations as far as possible.

I think, talking as a pragmatist, those are the points that seem to interest me.

MR. FABRICANT: I just want to add this, Mr. May:

Your suggestion about a study of margins of error in accounts seems to me extraordinarily interesting. I am wondering if you would not want to expand a little bit more on that, either now or later, as to what you have in mind. How would one go about doing the job?

MR. MAY: I should think it would be quite easy to do it by taking, and restating, your accounts on a different set of assumptions that might be adopted. The difference of the aggregate results might not be so large, but the difference in distribution between years might be colossal. I mean, differences of the utilities using the sinking fund basis, as compared with those that used the depreciation basis of the Federal Power Commission and split up in very small units, might be studied. People would be amazed to find the difference that it makes. I think it would be an extremely useful study.

MR. WILCOX: Part of the study would have to take into consideration the things that Mr. Smith mentioned in his paper.

MR. MAY: Surely.

MR. ALEXANDER: I should like to return to the points you have mentioned.

One very fundamental point which I would like to question— you have made it several times—is that because of the continunity assumption, a change in the value of assets (especially fixed assets, I presume), is irrelevant because they cannot be realized. I disagree. I say that the very nature of the continuity assumption means that these assets will be realized some time.

217

The reason the assets are more valuable is that presumably their services will receive higher recompense. That is on one concept.

I agree with your eight or ten objectives, that for each of these objectives there may be differences; but I say that for a lot of these differences a capital gain is quite relevant, and it is quite relevant when it is accrued. For other concepts, capital gain is quite irrelevant.

When you say "realized" you mean, changed into dollars. I say that is not such an important form of realization. It is what it is worth to you that really counts for many, many uses.

Therefore, it should be taken into account.

MR. MAY: That is only what it is worth as a part of whole. It is like saying what a bolt of a machine is worth, which is irrelevant.

MR. ALEXANDER: The individual assets do not matter. It is the earning power of the assembly as a whole.

But if you do want to use the concept of the earning power of the assembly as a whole—as I thought we might—as a guide as to what it is best to do (and that is what I thought the whole study is: to use such considerations as a guide as to how to record the elements which accountants record), then I say it can be used as a guide to depreciation. Under the assumption that the prospects do not change, then, how would you want to measure depreciation?

In other words, putting it into accountant's terminology, where it can legitimately be assumed that the going value will not change: then, since you have a value for the whole, since you have now assumed that the going value will be maintained if only, let us say, the value of this company's assets is maintained, you get a guide to depreciation.

That, I think, is one of the best justifications from a theoretical standpoint of the preoccupation with maintaining capital intact, when you measure capital in a partial sense, such as tanglible capital.

Some people have gone so far as to say, "That is ridiculous, because everybody recognizes obsolescence." But you would not say that a company that has maintained buggies in good shape has maintained its capital intact.

What I would call for many purposes the accountant's fundamental assumption, when he labels the result of his recorded computations as income, is that if the changes which I have recorded are taken into account we can in many cases assume that the unrecorded factors have not changed significantly, and therefore what I present is a good measure of the total change.

For many purposes that is so, and that then brings in the importance of saying, "Yes, but then what happens when the external change, the change in the value of money or in prospects, is so great as to make untenable this position which is the foundation, I think, of the accountant's position, namely, that he can safely ignore changes in going value or changes in the value of money, as he usually can do?"

MR. MAY: May I continue?

From an accounting sense, I think what it would mean is to bring in what you would call economic obsolescence of the enterprise as a factor in depreciation, which is the one thing which is now excluded. Depreciation, as it is computed today, is based on the explicit assumption that the enterprise is going to be continued during the whole life of the unit employed as a unit. You are bringing in the fact that it is not.

MR. ALEXANDER: For certain uses, yes.

MR. MAY: And using it to affect further a provision that is made. You bring in that new element and you would change the method of treating the other one.

MR. BRUNDAGE: Suppose a company is manufacturing penicillin, that it has tanks, everything, equipment and so on, and some new mold is discovered which cannot be processed in the same way at all, which completely destroys the demand for penicillin. What is your interpretation of that situation?

MR. ALEXANDER: I think that from what I have called the economic concept—and I grant there are other concepts—the company has sustained a tremendous loss. Here was a company

219

which, up to this time—unless, of course, this is something which was expected—had an expectation of earning a great deal for some time in the future, and henceforth the company is worth zero.

MR. FABRICANT: Would you allocate the loss to the year in which it occurs?

MR. ALEXANDER: That is another question. That is a question which I take up quite separately. That is the principal distinction, I would say, between a capital gain or loss and any other type of gain or loss.

Capital gains and losses and ordinary gains and losses can usually easily be distinguished until we get to the point where we think they are separate. But any clever person who wants to fool with the terms can always construct cases on the margin where it is difficult to say whether this is a capital gain or an ordinary gain.

In principle the things come close together. In practice they lie far enough apart; except that the timing of a capital gain is important. By "capital gain" I shall mean essentially what I term "unexpected" gain. There are two types of capital gain, so called: One is the sort that is very similar to the appreciation of an income bond, and I would agree that such a capital gain, which is essentially an appreciation in lieu of other payment, can clearly be associated with other forms of income. The other type of capital gain is recognized when an asset is realized to be worth a different amount from what it had previously been considered to be worth. This is "unexpected" capital gain.

The confusing thing about a capital gain is that as of the point of recognition it is not income. I will grant that. It is a revision of your wealth estimate. You made a mistake in saying how well off you were; so at that point a capital gain does not look at all like income, as I had previously defined it: namely, an accretion to your wealth. You had something; you still have it; now you realize it is worth more than it was before. This potential was in it, but it was unrecognized.

It does claim to be considered like income when we think of the time you acquired this asset, perhaps. When you acquired this asset, you acquired it for what you thought it was worth. You now think it is worth something different. Somewhere in between you became wealthier, because you parted with, let us say $100 for the asset; you now have an asset of which you clearly recognize the worth to be $1000; so that somewhere in this process some income is to be recognized.

The way you assign it to the time period within that, I say, is an arbitrary choice that can be made as you like. I would say that there would be some technical advantage in saying that you earned that income at the time you bought that asset, but that is pretty arbitrary. And it would lead for practical purposes to a lot of difficulties in assigning it to so fine a period, and then you have to be practical, as accountants and tax collectors have been, and give rules of thumb which are practical in their operation.

MR. BROAD: May I raise a different point? I am sorry if I seem to be criticizing your monograph.

MR. ALEXANDER: No. You are bringing out points which I am glad to see brought out.

MR. BROAD: Assuming one had divine powers; assuming an interest rate of five percent and assume one made a perfect guess at the value. Is income thereafter exactly five percent of the value?

MR. ALEXANDER: Plus whatever you leave in.

MR. BROAD: That does not happen very often. Assuming that it did happen, it would be very nice.

As we go along, we find that it is not a perfect guess, and there are errors in it. You have unexpected gains and unexpected losses to take into account.

Isn't that measurement of income a measurement of past errors, rather than a measurement of income?

MR. ALEXANDER: No.

MR. BROAD: I am wondering if it is a useful concept.

MR. ALEXANDER: You measure the expected gain.

MR. BROAD: That is an error.

221

MR. ALEXANDER: In its role of error, it is not income. It is income only if the unexpected gain is on something which you previously acquired for less than you now believe it to be worth.

In other words, what I am trying to point out is that a mere revaluation of your wealth clearly is not income. That answers your question of measuring, but it indicates that at some previous time, unless you have had this forever—you might say, if it is your own working ability, then you would never count a capital gain on it. That is done in practice, but we do not, for human beings generally, capitalize future earnings. This becomes relevant only through an asset like that of a corporation.

Take the case of a corporation. You buy something for $100, and you and everybody else realizes at the end of five years that this is worth $1,000. I maintain that for most of the purposes for which income is used—and I will still grant that you can find purposes for which it is not so—but for most of the purposes for which income is used, it is useful to say that some time between the time you bought it for $100 and now it is worth or became worth $1,000, and here is where the economist will differ from the accountant.

You recognize it to be worth $1,000. You can appropriately say to yourself that for most of the purposes for which income is used there has been an income of $900 from this transaction.

MR. BROAD: I think under your particular theory, if you had pre-vision——

MR. ALEXANDER: You could not have bought it for $100 if everybody had pre-vision. You made your gain then. You bought it for $100. You had the pre-vision then.

MR. BROAD: The profit is made in purchasing it on an incorrect valuation.

MR. ALEXANDER: You may assign it to the valuation. I say that this becomes an arbitrary revision of what you are after, what your objective is. But I would say my general principle is that for a whole broad group of objectives, it would seem more desirable to recognize the case where an asset is obtained for a certain value and later recognized to be worth more, then as a

222

result of that sequence of circumstances to presume that the person who acquired the asset for less than it is worth gained an income out of the sequence of actions, and that it then becomes another question to decide how you are going to assign that.

MR. MAY: How would you then define worth for that purpose?

MR. ALEXANDER: You define worth in accordance with the objective for which you are measuring the worth. You then begin to get different measures of worth, depending upon what your objective is. You cannot get away from that. That is the nature of worth.

MR. MAY: That is what I am trying to get to. That is my whole argument. It isn't necessarily what you can realize for it if you sell it.

MR. ALEXANDER: That is a lower limit.

MR. MAY: No, it isn't.

MR. ALEXANDER: If you can sell it, and you value it at less than that, you are well advised to sell it.

MR. MAY: But if it is an indispensable part of a whole?

MR. ALEXANDER: Then it is worth more to you than you can sell it for.

MR. MAY: Not necessarily.

MR. ALEXANDER: Oh yes. If it is indispensable, that is what I call infinite value.

You know, when something is indispensable, that is pretty valuable.

MR. MAY: Not indispensable, but useful where it is.

MR. ALEXANDER: What do you lose if you sell it?

MR. MAY: You have to replace it with something that costs more, that will not give you any more worth.

MR. ALEXANDER: If you have a good market, the limits come close together.

MR. MAY: No, they do not. One of the points of your thinking is that you assume a value determined by sale and demand, by demand and supply; and you are dealing, when you talk about capital assets, in the commodities for which there is no market, there is no demand, there is no supply, because there is nobody wanting to buy machinery where and as it is.

So you have an imaginary market; you have an imaginary value, and you get about the fifth degree of imagination into your concepts.

MR. ALEXANDER: For concepts that is what happens. Whenever you get to a philosophic concept, the imagination has to work overtime.

MR. MAY: That brings me to the conclusion that your excursion has been valuable to us, because it shows we must go to another road.

MR. BRUNDAGE: Mr. Barnard, have you comments?

MR. BARNARD: I do not know if I can get close enough to the technical points. The first thing that occurs to me is that it is inevitable that there would be more than one theoretical concept. There is the economic concept defined as political economy; for instance, national assets, from the long-haul point of view of a society as a whole. I do not think you could make that very quantitative, but it is the language which is talked all the time, and talked more and more. It is the economics of a socialized business system as a whole, in which frequently what is one business's loss is another business's gain, and there is no change in the income.

Then there is the economics of a private individual, which must be enormously varied. Any purpose of action, any goal is a valuation. I think you have to take that into account.

It seems to me that in an attempt to get economic concepts tied into accounting concepts, what your accountant has to do is take some mean, a point of view, both as to the period of time and as to the social scope of the interest.

There is certainly an ordinary or business accounting for corporations. The interest is not that confined exclusively to the particular corporation. The accounting is made for the interest of others. It is made with respect to a particular kind of community, and there has to be some practical averaging or taking of a mean, by convention, and that will involve a great many subjective elements.

Mr. May talks about a fundamental postulate of a continuity of business; if anything is subjective I don't know how it could be more subjective than that postulate. What is useful in the system of accounting must be relevant to the system of business transactions.

The only other comment I have relates to a particular detail. When you say that you buy a thing for $1,000 and that you assume it is worth that at the time, I think that is a fundamental contradiction from the point of view of business. When you buy a thing for $1,000, you buy it on the expectation that it is worth more than that. Whether you are right or not is determined by subsequent events. You may lose or you may gain. But always you take that into account.

Furthermore, when you are dealing with this thing as an aggregate, it is the constant employment of business judgment to say that this detail in the present aggregate is either better or worse than it could be if you substitute something else, so you get a constant valuation of a detail which operates as an organic whole.

I do not know if I have said anything that makes sense, but these are points that come out in the discussion.

MR. ALEXANDER: I think it makes a great deal of sense. You have said in concrete terms what I hoped I was saying in a lot of abstract terms.

First of all, when you say you buy something and hope it is worth more, I would certainly agree; and if you prove to be right, I would certainly say there should be some income involved in that operation.

MR. BARNARD: As I read your paper, I did not find myself in disagreement, but I found a great deal of difficulty in tying a conventional accounting system to the theoretical considerations involved, from an accounting point of view.

It is not an economic concept. It is a collection of concepts that economists have to deal with.

That makes a great deal of difficulty for the economists, it seems to me, when you try to tie the two things together. I believe the tie-up is to approach some middle consideration, which will be of practical usefulness to the present state of society.

I do not know that accounting will be the same thing one hundred years from now.

MR. BRUNDAGE: I hope not.

MR. DEAN: I read Mr. Alexander's paper with a great deal of interest, and I was fascinated by it.

In the first place, I am not enough of an economist to be able to criticize it, but isn't the problem of this committee (rather than to say whether this is, or is not, correct from an economist's standpoint), to try to get something which we can utilize in everyday business life, which from a business man's standpoint or an accountant's standpoint is something which he can measure?

I think that one of the reasons for these accounting conventions is because greater experience has shown us that something which looked to be an increase in value subsequently does not prove to be so.

One of your biggest problems as a lawyer in working with people on the issue of securities is the fact that you have somebody who bought a manufacturing plant at the bottom of the depression, when it was operating at fifteen or twenty percent of capacity. Then it goes up to a hundred percent of capacity, and then he has some very substantial earnings, and then he wants to go out and hire an appraisal company and use some capitalizing factor and project his earnings, not at the past ratio, but the current ratio, and take the appreciation up on the books.

It may be unrealized appreciation; but he may be back to where he was in 1932.

So you have this accounting convention, that you do not have income until it is changed into dollars.

Mr. May was talking about the indispensable. Take the pipeline companies that were organized about twenty years or so ago, to go out and get a number of gas leases. Their great cry is that they have to value those at original cost. Some of them got them in connection with oil wells, so that they have no book value cost. They cannot earn at all. Therefore, they say, "Let's go out and sell the leases."

They sell them to an independent company, and it is said they have tremendous realized gains. If gas is indispensable, then they are dependent upon their ability to go out and contract on the current market for sufficient natural gas to try to take care of the pipe-line.

They may be able to contract for the gas, but they don't know. Therefore, they don't really know when those natural gas leases are sold today, whether that is real gain today, or whether they have deprived the enterprise of what ought to have been a fixed asset; you cannot really project with any degree of certainty the future income.

In every problem of research there are dozens of things that fascinate and interest you. But in every-day practice you have to cast those things out of your mind and come back and say "Well, to what extent will it be useful to this particular project, and to what extent can the ordinary person keeping accounts in a business, or an accountant, measure this, so that he will have some form of utilization?" You can (a) measure what the costs are, and (b) measure what the costs are in relation to other people's, in the same line of business; (c) for tax purposes; (d) for public utility income, profit sharing and pension costs.

Despite the fact that all the Supreme Court judges have used the phrase "purposiveness", actually it may be calculated on a different basis. You have to have some kind of a central core or theory of reporting of income for business, or for the purpose of investors or for the people who are going to use it, or it becomes somewhat useless. I agree with you: there is a terrific amount of subjective thought in the interpretation of income.

Take your illustration of a manufacturing chemist. I have been discussing that problem for the last three or four months, but I do not regard those assets as useless, because they have gained a tremendous amount of know-how in connection with the manufacture of one drug. While the physical assets are com-

227

pletely useless in connection with the manufacture of the new drug, we have decided on a program of costing out the remaining cost of our old assets because of their utilization to us in connection with the development of the new drug.

Theoretically, perhaps, we are not using those old assets at all, but it does seem to us perfectly fair as a part of the cost for the development of the drug that we first go into the old proposition; and that is certainly a subjective determination as to whether we are going to wipe them all off or charge them to depreciation reserve or cost them out over some period.

I am wondering whether the problem of this committee is not to try to narrow our economist's concept of income down into something which the accountant and the business man can utilize in every-day daily practice.

MR. BRUNDAGE: I do not think Mr. Broad was saying there was no subjective determination of income in the accountant's mind. We want to get away from it as much as possible and have other checks besides our own guess on the useful life of a machine.

MR. DEAN: Before we get through today, I would like to ask Mr. Cumberland, if he has the time, what is the fundamental weakness running through the paper so far.

MR. BRUNDAGE: I think this is a good time, if you want to do that.

MR. CUMBERLAND: That is rather a hard assignment you have given me. Once more, let me go back and elaborate just a little more on money versus goods.

If I have a fundamental criticism, it will focus on that point.

It seems to me that the way the treatment has developed in the course of the studies, it has been based almost altogether on monetary treatment. It would be very, very difficult in my judgment as an economist to avoid that, because we live in a pecuniary economy; money is the basis of corporate thinking, individual thinking, investment thinking, and yet to my mind it leaves a great deal to be desired.

You do not get wealthy and you do not raise the standard of income by having more counters. You raise it by having more goods and services.

Perhaps I am a bit allergic to that fact, because I have lived in countries that have, may I say, enjoyed great inflations. I have seen responsible, thrifty people wiped out and economies pretty well disrupted. Yet your accounts in monetary terms could be in perfect order.

Hence, when this study group was organized, I was very glad to join, and I proceeded to get sick, and couldn't take much part in it, which was my loss. But I had hoped that those two things could be measured in some way, that the method could be found, both by the individual and the corporation, to combine what is the basic standard of living, on the one hand, as compared with the vehicle by which it more or less has to be reported and accounted for: in money.

Let me go back to money just a moment. Here I quote Robert Warren, who has just died, whom I regard as the greatest authority and one of the most incisive students on money in the United States in recent years.

He phrased it like this. We first started with money and goods being equal. But money was a physical concept. It was not so many counters, but so much grain, so much this or that. Finally we learned that it took the most convenient form as one of the precious metals.

Very well. The next concept was that money, when it could be left on deposit in the form of precious metals by Lilliputian bankers, if you will—it was found that people who left it on deposit did not want it in the immediate future, and the bankers could safely lend it.

Actually the money was still in the warehouse. It was still a physical asset. But against that physical asset was issued some kind of promise to pay.

It did not take governments very long to create the concept or establish the concept of the promise to pay, and that promise to pay is behind money that cannot be monetized.

The Government has a claim against all the assets and income of the entire population; therefore a government promise to pay, whether it be in the form of government bonds or in the form

229

of a piece of paper currency, is based on the assets and income of the entire population.

But you will see that the original concept of money has been completely reversed. From having money as an asset, a physical asset, money is now a promise to pay. It is a liability. That has happened in virtually all countries.

I was completely in discord with Mr. Warburton's original remarks that we have it in our knowledge and power to have such price levels as we want, whether up or down or stable. He says that another monograph is unconvincing to him, while this is doubly unconvincing to me, on the basis of the record; that money value goes one way and that is down, historically.

Now we come to the application. At least as I see it, it is a rather difficult task. I agree with you completely. It has to be something which can be applied or it isn't of much help.

Some corporations even like to be conscientious. They would like to have some method by which they can keep some kind of a continuous economic concept. There are others—I could name many—that purposely and consciously borrowed money over recent years, because they say there is no question that they will be able to repay that money in cheaper dollars. To my mind, that is just as untrue as these other concepts.

Take the corporations who wish to be conscientious. Some of them have even asked how they go about applying that desire to be good citizens. Frankly, I do not know how. I cannot tell them how. I do not think an accountant or economist has yet been able to give the answer.

To answer your question, I do not think the committee has yet found the answer. That does not say that the committee has not been hard working and ingenious and all that. It simply means that, to my mind, it is an exceptionally hard problem to which it has addressed itself.

MR. BRUNDAGE: Does anyone else wish to comment? How about you, Mr. Blough.

MR. BLOUGH: I do not think I have very much to add that has not already been said.

I was thinking along the lines of Mr. Bronfenbrenner. I do not know of what value it is to have any common concept of business income developed. It cannot be practically applied generally, and it seems to me the economist should seek to get away from any concept of income which cannot be applied generally.

What is the use of developing fine-spun theories if they cannot be made of any use?

I think accountants have a lot of things from which they may have to get loose, but I think the economists have a good many too, which they will have to get rid of if there is going to be a getting together on these things.

The idea of attempting to measure income from year to year in terms of accretion of future earning power, taking into consideration all of the assets of a company seems to me pretty far-fetched, because there are so many things that prevent any practical application of that.

I was thinking, for example, of a company that has very large interests in copper deposits, let us say. The value of those copper deposits depends on what the future price of copper is going to be. Comes a time when some discovery is made of other sources of copper which are thought to be pretty lush, and immediately the value of the copper deposits goes down. The next year it is discovered that those new deposits were not anywhere near what they were expected to be, and immediately the value of the copper deposits goes up.

Those things are happening all the time. In one period of three or four years, copper miners had the feeling that many of their deposits were practically valueless because the cost of getting out the copper was so great that it was impossible to do it profitably. A few years later they had discovered methods of treating the ore which made it possible to anticipate substantial profits.

How we can ever hope to give effect to the future earning power of the assets we have in that copper mine, from year to year, with any practical usefulness is something which I find very difficult to imagine.

MR. ALEXANDER: May I reply to that?

231

MR. BRUNDAGE: Yes.

MR. ALEXANDER: I would very strongly agree with you, and perhaps you are just rephrasing what Mr. May said concerning the fact that the line you have to take of practical application would obviously not follow the line of the economic measure.

I would agree. In fact, my principal concern was, and I thought that was what had been laid out for me to do, to go into the concept; and one of the things that occurred everywhere was when we had a difference between the concept I first defined and the actual operation of accountants in measuring income. Does this difference arise because the accountants have a different concept, or does it arise because practical considerations prevent their using this concept, which they would be only too happy to use if there was a good objective measure of the quantity involved; but they refrain from using a poor measure of it, feeling that— and quite justifiably—it would be worse than none.

In short, for those who would look to anything I have tried to do, and say, "Well, this doesn't tell me how to measure income in practice," I would say that is not what I attempted to do. There is a difference between refining a concept and suggesting changes in practice.

This is the answer to those who say, "But then there is no use in refining a concept if it is so fancy that nobody can apply it." I say, "But look at the ones that you can apply. You get difficult questions concerning which variation you can apply." You get difficult questions concerning which variation of two methods you should use. Whenever a situation such as that comes up, it is very nice to have a fundamental body of inapplicable concepts to go to and say, as between these two possibilities one may be somewhat more in accord with my fundamental concept.

The only trouble with this situation is that even here, because of the many purposes of income which Mr. Dean lists, and which others of us had in mind, there isn't even a single body of concepts, a single concept to which you can refer whenever these practical differences come up. That was the stage to which I had hoped to bring the discussion: to the point that it is very nice to get a concept, because a concept can help you make practical decisions, even if you cannot apply the concept in its full purity to practical cases.

If you are in the unfortunate situation where you have several fundamental concepts, and these differ among themselves according to the purpose for which you are making the measurement, you then will find that you will have only one decision to make: Either you measure income this way or that way; if you measure it this way, it is in accord with concept A, and if you measure it that way it is in accord with concept B.

You haven't gotten very far, except that you have the beginning of wisdom. You have then the knowledge that you cannot justify depreciation by method A. That is true; anything else is error.

You can say, measuring depreciation by method A is perfectly consistent with this concept of income. Method B is perfectly consistent with the other concept.

If you have some other thing in mind, for example, tax policy, you can reduce this question of depreciation by cost versus depreciation by replacement. Do you want to make this position comparable to the position of the man who has held cash all the time, or comparable to the position of a man who has held an asset against the moving of a price level? Then you have a clear indication of what you should do in the measure of depreciation.

Vice versa, any measure you use for depreciation then makes an implicit choice between these two fundamental concepts. That is all you are going to do.

All I had hoped to do was to bring out the fact that these different choices of practices do imply different concepts; or, vice versa, these different concepts do imply different choices.

I am the first to recognize that it would be absolutely impossible to try to bring into the recorded accounts changing expectations of future movements. However, it is by no means impossible to carry in the back of your head the fact that this is the purpose which serves very well many of the uses to which income should be put. So that the recorded facts which help illuminate this type of event are especially valuable.

233

That is the argument that I have tried to make.

MR. BARNARD: I think it is important to recognize that no matter how practically perfected a useful system of accounting will be, you are continuously going to be up against economic concepts of accounting on the part of the various people in the population. You are going to be constantly up against defending yourselves for the practical concept which you are using. So it isn't irrelevant to have this kind of study and discussion at all.

You are just at the beginning of a long period of this kind of thing. I want to say, because I am somewhat involved in supporting it, that it seems to me that you can come out with what you call a neutral or negative result, but it is a very useful thing, if it is only a long step in the process of philosophy, of social management, of economic enterprise, that you have just got to go through with it.

The courts are going to be in it; the business men are going to be in it; the individuals and investors are going to be in it. So this isn't beside the point at all. It is revelant in my opinion. I quite agree with Mr. Alexander in that.

I would like to throw something into this which I do not think is sufficiently taken into account. I believe that capital gain is a much more important consideration in business operations than is generally recognized, and accounting systems tend to minimize it.

There is an enormous amount of business done where the fellow who does it hopes he can get a current operating profit to keep going, because he thinks the outcome, in the last analysis, that makes it worth while to take the risks depends upon the prospects of getting capital gain.

I do not know if it is true or not, but I knew about it twenty-five years or so ago: The Gulf Oil Company used to buy filling station outfits and buy large plots, in places where they thought the increase in value of the land was the real ultimate thing which they would win. They expected also to make a current profit, but there is risk in that. If you can combine the two prospects in one, it seems to me that minimizes the risk.

234

I believe that is very much neglected. I fought with Samuel Cousins about that in one of the first statements by the National Economic Bureau.

I am dead sure that capital gain prospect is a very fundamental part of business operations, and it has to be taken into account in both the economic and accounting thinking about it.

My third comment, entirely disassociated from this; referring to Mr. May's remarks, it seems to me that what you are up to here, in the long run, as a practical proposition is to get the subjective elements, the assumptions, the postulates outside the conventional system you adopt, so that after you adopt it you can operate with the least possible subjectivism, estimate and so forth.

That is a counsel of perfecting the system, but unless people recognize the difference between a postulate external to the adoption of a system and a whole series of them, that you operate within the system—if it is the second, you haven't got much system; you haven't anything you can rely upon. If you can get the subjective in the postulate on the outside, I think you have made great progress, because you have a chance for agreement among people for interpretation in what has taken place.

MR. DEAN: I think Mr. Alexander's paper is of tremendous importance in relation with, say, the Securities and Exchange Commission, with regard to the last paper that Mr. King sent out. They said they would not regard anything as in accordance with sound accounting principles unless you could point to something which is generally accepted, unless you can point to some body of opinion or document which supports it.

I went down to the Commission and said I felt in a sense it was desirable, but in a sense it was undesirable, because it sort of closed the door to thinking.

It seems to me that if accountants and lawyers have any real value to society other than ordinary humdrum work, it is to try to be thinking forward, trying to think of problems that are going to be posed. If you were confronted with an extraordinarily different problem, you ought to be able to think up some method for it in order to see that the presentation of income account, for instance, was a more true presentation, even though nobody had been able to think of it before.

I pointed out to them a problem that they had before: One of the large lumber companies which many years ago spent money for land and put in pine and spruce and hemlock trees. Thirty years ago there wasn't anybody who would not say that that timber growth had increased the value of the land before they began to measure it.

A lumber company cannot value any timber that they are going to utilize thirty-five or forty or fifty years from now, because it has no value in present earnings, but you certainly ought to be able to take that growth onto your books in some form or other.

I think we must get these various concepts of income so that we could say, Well, even though it isn't a generally accepted accounting practice or a generally accepted accounting convention, there is this recognized body of thinking that in this particular problem you can meet it in this particular way. If we do not, I am afraid that we and the economists are all going to tend to become stereotyped in our thinking, and we are not going to recognize that society and our economic problems have changed, while we are still going along the same road.

MR. BLOUGH: Mr. Dean, that is one of the things I had in mind. We have again to try and adapt our practice to thoughts of loss of physical assets and obsolescence, but we have not given attention, I think, to the recognition of these changes in value upwards. I have the feeling that to be realistic in our accounting, we have to recognize in some way or other a method by which those values may be given effect within the accounts, to make the accounts more realistic in line with the earning power and capacity of the assets themselves.

MR. BROAD: There has been quite a lot of accounting discussion on that point in the last two or three years, and several articles written on that subject: the realistic nature of cost in some respects.

I was very much interested in what Mr. Barnard had to say about capital gains. I think if we did nothing more in this group

236

than to try to make that definition more real, we would have gone a long way and made a lot of progress.

To my mind, the difference between LIFO and FIFO is largely the result of a capital gain item. That is not theoretically perfect, but it is in the right direction.

In the same way, about the money problem; if you regard it as a measure of capital gain in the income account, it may simplify things. If we could segregate those things in accounting and try to measure them, we might make quite a contribution to the understanding of statements.

There is no doubt in my mind that a man looking for investments, particularly one who has a lot of money to invest, is looking for capital gains more than income. He wants the twenty-five percent tax rate.

It is a very real thing in business. People are investing more with relation to capital gains, particularly the big investors, than they are with regard to current income. I say "more." I mean, perhaps, equally.

I do not think accounting has emphasized that factor, particularly during the period in which it has been more important, when we have had this decrease in the value of money. If you say you consider it by money rather than by value—I think Mr. Cumberland brought that problem out—if you are going to measure it by money, you have a capital gain.

There are two kinds of capital gain, as I see them, and we might very well isolate the two of them. If we isolate the idea of capital gain, we have done a lot.

MR. MAY: I think there is a good deal to be done in that way. I think there is quite a good deal in the point that Mr. Dean made too.

I would just like to mention something that strikes me as one of the best illustrations of improved methods, which brings in the name of Thornton, a great contributor.

In the moving picture industry they used to say that all returns are returns of capital until we have our money back, and then it is all profit. Thornton went about it in a scientific way,

237

and he made a curve of earnings of several hundred films, and he found there was an extraordinary uniformity in the curves in the ordinary type of program—not the special things like these big films.

On that basis he developed a method of writing off the cost of the films against the revenues on the basis of those curves. That has become absolutely universal now. There was a lot of opposition, because it was theoretical, but I think accounting has to be a great deal more theoretical and less practical in the sense of Disraeli, who defined a practical man as a man who practiced the theories of his forefathers.

MR. DOHR: I do not think I have anything to say that has not already been said. I approached the monograph like a number of other people: Accountants are doing something; what should we do differently as a result of this monograph?

While I am stimulated to great pleasure in reading it, I cannot put my finger on anything that we are doing differently.

MR. SCOVILL: I think listening to all this has been of interest. I did not have the opportunity to read Mr. Alexander's work or Mr. Warburton's manual; therefore I am not in a position to offer comments.

I am interested in Mr. Alexander's approach to teaching accounting by calling for the single income method of accounting and calling attention to the fact that if accountants are to be consistent, the accounts of profit over a period of twenty years ought to be the same under the single method or the double method, which seems to me to indicate that a complete single income statement ought to be in vogue. That means some of our results over a twenty-year period would be the same under the orthodox method as under the single method, which I think we might call the economic approach.

Of course, that does not mean that there are no drawbacks. I cannot help wondering how we would give effect to withdrawals that are made from time to time, and their real value, because under the economic or the single income approach to profits in a given period, we take the net worth of the present time and add

238

back the withdrawals during the period, and the difference between that result and the net worth at the beginning is our profit.

It seems to me if we are going to give some effect to the value of the dollar from time to time as these withdrawals are made— I have not studied that carefully enough to say what effect it would have.

Another thought that comes to me in connection with the application of what I have heard in Mr. Alexander's suggestion is in the livestock business, and in farms in general. Thinking in terms of livestock or in terms of orchards which are being developed, I often try to think of what application it may have for profits determined in livestock. Do you start with the date of conception, or do you start with some later date, to increase the value of your livestock and get the profit?

The problem comes in evaluating a lot of chickens or something of that sort. Would we value the rooster in terms of his future productivity, or just how would we value him? Those are things which come in under that point of view. I think, as had been said here, that the accountants must make a contribution to this problem, and I am very glad of this opportunity to sit in and listen and try to help the thinking.

I am pretty sure that we can contribute something to it in the future.

MR. BRUNDAGE: Mr. Smith.

MR. SMITH: It seems to me we are discussing two basic although different concepts. One is a concept concerning the standard currency of the realm, the standard in which contracts and money agreements and so forth are constantly being made; and the other one is a flow of goods or services or satisfactions.

I think the economist will have to have more definiteness in his thinking in the latter case; better means of measurement and improvement in his methods before they can be used in accounting without causing confusion.

The time may arise when it can be done. I do not think it is here by quite some distance and at this date.

MR. HASKELL: I feel like Mr. Scovill. I have not been able to read the monographs, but I would very much like to say that I am glad of the opportunity to listen in.

There are a couple of points I could make about what Mr. Broad said in the emphasis on capital gains. I think what he said is true. I do not think we should overlook the fact that there is occurring in this country a much wider distribution not only of Government Savings Bonds but of corporate stocks; and in that category of the smaller and widespread investor, the employee who is entitled under these growing plans of stock ownership to become a stockholder, emphasis seems to me to be on the income side, and dividend returns, as in comparison with the return of other forms of property.

What Mr. Dean said about the SEC is terribly discouraging. We see in the stock exchange the dead hand of the ICC in regard to accounting methods, and I think the accounting profession, if I can speak for them, ought to throw up their hands at some of these restrictions.

It seems to me to be a great threat to progress that the SEC should get into the philosophy that the ICC has in its rigid adherence to what is today, without flexibility to permit improvements in the future.

That brings me to the final thing: We hear a lot about the fact that moral principles in education are not keeping up with scientific progress. That is true, it seems to me. It also seems to me that technological advances in business and science and research together are going ahead faster than the ability of thoughtful leaders in accounting and of economists to keep up with the added needs thrown upon them.

Just as it is true that moral leadership has not kept up with the scientific, so in fairness we should admit that we are not abreast of the problem.

More and more annual records, audit reports, reports to employees that we see coming across the stock desk in the Exchange have been of much more help in explaining the problem and the

240

differences shown in trend of economic value as compared with the old system.

It is something reports have to do, because now there is a better understanding on the part of the securities holder, labor and the general public of the efforts of companies like Steel and General Motors to support these huge profits, to try to give a clear understanding of what they actually represent.

Maybe it is impossible to achieve any result that would bring more homogeneity and usefulness into the reports that should envisage a fear of inflation, such as Dr. Cumberland and many of us have experienced abroad, but I do not think we can overlook the great possibility that we might have some substantial and continued inflation; to the extent that we do, this lack of a method is going to become more severe and result in an undermining of the profit system in this country.

Perhaps the problem is so vast that there can be no agreement on a complete solution, but it might be helpful if the membership of this group would come out with reasonably unanimous agreement on certain simple partial steps toward a better understanding which can be used to combat the dangerous things that are retrogressive in the field.

If, for example, the group could agree as to the extent of the margin of error in accounts, or, as Mr. Dean mentioned, the need to be flexible, and be able to progress on some of these other fundamentals. Even if they cannot offer a solution, such agreement would seem to have a tremendous influence on leaders of thought, government, industry, and in universities which would help to a better understanding of corporate accounting; which certainly will be necessary if we are going to have a greatly enlarged number of people owning corporate securities in this country.

I do not think that is very constructive, but at least it is reporting some things that have been seen from the companies' side, as we see it in the Stock Exchange.

MR. BROAD: Mr. Chairman, I think Mr. Haskell misunderstood me when I spoke of capital gains.

I was not talking about capital gains in the securities markets, but in the form that Mr. Barnard mentioned: An oil company buying a service station or an oil company buying reserves which it may not use for twenty or twenty-five years. If you invest in New York City real estate, if you invest on Sixth Avenue in a big way, not in the hope of an immediate substantial gain but with the expectation that Sixth Avenue may be one of the leading centers of New York, that is the line in which we were following the discussion.

MR. HASKELL: I stand corrected. I really did jump to a conclusion. I was thinking of the securities market.

MR. BRUNDAGE: I think the biggest capital gain of all is in the case of a small business man who is devoting all of his energies to it, not for what he hopes to get in a year, but what he hopes to build it up to.

MR. FABRICANT: The best example of that is the United States. The pushing forward of farmers who were intent on the capital gain in land values.

MR. ALEXANDER: It was that sort of thing I had in mind when I said that national income is usually understated. We do not calculate certain of these benefits in our income, and I do not believe that accountants take into consideration this corresponding development of a business that is getting itself on a firm foundation.

MR. BRUNDAGE: Nor should they.

MR. ALEXANDER: I say that the company that has done this is better off than the company which has not done it, and for certain circumstances that should be taken into account.

MR. CUMBERLAND: Mr. Chairman, could I ask whether Mr. Dean or Mr. Barnard think that there can be satisfactory accounts and accounting procedures—I am talking now about corporate accounts—so long as there are large changes in the value of money?

MR. BARNARD: I would not think so, to answer for myself. It is a question of speed.

MR. CUMBERLAND: This matter of growth which you have mentioned, and I think very pertinently—I agree with you—is very interesting. I do not see any way to handle the problem of violent fluctuations in the value of money.

MR. BARNARD: Everything else is made unstable when the value of money changes rapidly. Your whole concept of life is upset. That is why I feel quite sure you cannot adapt your subsidiary system to the condition.

MR. DEAN: Mr. May and I were down in Houston, speaking before the controllers of oil companies, and one of them asked me a question from the floor: If money was considered in terms of a dollar and you got paid back the same dollar that the Government borrowed, and you had to state your accounts in dollars, it was impossible to have any concept of a fluctuating dollar.

I said: President Truman said he is going to increase the national income, which is roughly $226,000,000,000 or $240,000,-000,000 to $300,000,000,000. Suppose he does that by further inflation, so that the purchasing power of the dollar decreases? Suppose you are an oil company and measure your production in terms of barrels. Your company's reported production was six million barrels. Suppose tomorrow the Bureau of Standards halves the size of the barrel. Does that mean your production is twelve million barrels? He said, certainly not.

MR. GOLDSMITH: One of the problems Mr. Alexander brings out in connection with the going value: I think that economists and accountants always try to keep some close connection between the income account and the balance sheet. If you begin defining income that way, then of course the item called goodwill is not very important but can become quite a dominant item on the balance sheet, and changes in it are crucial.

You are faced with the problem of really splitting the change in the going concern value into such changes as reflect changes in the value of money and changes in the expectations that are separate from that.

On the one hand, following that out, you find income accounts are much more susceptible to changes in money.

We do not have a change in the value of most fixed assets. As the value of money changes, you would get an additional problem, which is always very difficult, and has been alluded to here: You cannot resolve the total value of the business into the value of its components.

You get the change in the going value. Do you want to record that simply as a change in an unclassified item in the balance sheet, whatever you call it, or are you then trying, particularly over a period of considerably fluctuating prices, to assign part of the change to individual assets and only keep the remainder, which is more specifically the effect of the change in the expectations, or rather the unexpected change? I guess following this out—and it is very interesting—you get into a problem which should be explored: The question of how this affects the balance sheet. It concerns itself with the question of the balance sheet and income, but you would then get nearer the problem where you do have to keep two types of balance sheet: one which is strictly in the currency of the realm and which would become more fluctuating than it is now, which to a large extent ignores changes in the fluctuations of money, and another one which would reflect changes in the purchasing power of money.

Apparently the feeling seems to be that the differences now are not too great. If the tendency of increasing prices keeps up the differences will become even larger, so that real thought will have to be given as to how for you can go in that direction.

In some countries which have tremendous inflations, from our point of view we can say, unfortunately the inflations did not last long enough, because when they really got to think those things out, in Germany, say, in 1922, then the inflation was stopped.

We never had an industrial economy in the position where they had to answer the question which would come up only where there is a very substantial rise in prices which goes on continuously, of the character which sooner or later has to be undone by a devaluation of the currency.

I don't think anyone expects that what we face is one of the high inflations such as we had in Europe and which we are having now in South American countries, which is a different thing from the situation when a price level goes up five percent a year for a generation.

There is the question of what you do now; but there is the question we have to consider, whether it is possible and feasible, in addition to a system of income accounting and the balance sheet, which is expressed purely in the currency of the realm, to go farther and to take into account changes such as Mr. Alexander's study would indicate.

MR. HASKELL: Mr. Brundage, could I ask a question?

Do Mr. Dean and Mr. Barnard feel that it is hopeless to work toward some way of minimizing the impact of money changes?

I assume that was one of the fundamental end products of this study of income, and on which this group has made no conclusions.

MR. BRUNDAGE: I think we have been approaching it from different points of view as professionals with the hope that perhaps after this meeting we would get to work on trying to combine and integrate them to come to some conclusions.

I do not think that Mr. Barnard and Mr. Dean meant that because statements were unreliable, they could not be improved. They can be clarified, perhaps.

MR. DEAN: I think that there has been too great an emphasis on the illustrations in annual reports rather than on the thoughts in annual reports. I think if somebody were to come along and have some kind of a public award dinner for the thinking that has gone into the annual reports rather than the pictures in the annual reports, you would get a lot better and clearer presentation to your stockholders.

I would say most of those who got the rewards have given the most misleading reports that are issued.

MR. HASKELL: I would not take issue, but I must say that the Exchange has not given any of those awards. The only awards which were given were the Junior Achievement Awards.

MR. DEAN: I saw in one of these reports a picture of change in assets as against the condition of a year before, completely

245

ignoring a $5,000,000 bank loan. Here are the current assets of a year before, and here (indicating higher) are the current assets of today.

MR. HOLME: Mr. Chairman, I apologize for arriving a little late.

I did have time to read this monograph and I was greatly impressed with the very careful thinking that has gone into it.

I am very much interested in what comes after lunch: A discussion of the action to be taken by the group. It occurs to me that we might perhaps after lunch think along these lines, that we are in somewhat of a dilemma. There is this question of the constantly changing value of money; but at the same time I think this group, at least, and many others too, feel that it is important to develop further these economic concepts of measurement that are becoming increasingly important to us, not only from the national point of view, but from the business point of view. Therefore, perhaps, one solution, one way out of the dilemma, might be to do as the gentleman over here suggested, that is, make a few relatively simple suggestions, and perhaps we might also consider, if it seemed wise, joining with those other groups who are advocating measures which will bring a return to a sounder currency.

Here we are. At the present time we laugh at our French friends because they do not pay taxes, but what are we doing in this country? We are running a deficit that amounts to the same thing in an indirect way.

I happen to be mixed up with a group of business men who are giving a lot of their time to this whole question of bringing a better balance in world trade.

One of the most fundamental things that we are trying to find is a way of urging our friends in foreign countries—and we have to turn attention to it in our own affairs here too—to bring about reforms of one kind or another which will bring about a sounder currency, so you can put them on a convertible basis.

Mr. Chairman, I just throw that out by way of suggestion. Perhaps that might be a path along which we might move; because

246

if the dollar were kept reasonably constant, if, as you say, you receive a dollar and you get the same dollar back again later on, we have to find a way, it seems to me, of bringing that into the picture, and perhaps we can combine these two things together in some way.

Mr. Brundage: Thank you.

Mr. Wlicox has been quiet this morning.

Mr. Wilcox: I am glad to have that virtue recognized.

I think one of the things that has come up this morning as a further study in carrying out the degrees of subjectivity and objectivity that enter into the concept of income is that there seems to be a fairly clear consensus that the degree of such activity that should enter into the determination of published income should be kept fairly well down, so that we do not compound one man's subjectivity with another man's subjectivity and reach a high-level abstraction away from what a semanticist would call a non-verbal level.

If we could keep our conception of income fairly close to the non-verbal income, it would be very useful and it seems to me that is what has been fairly well agreed on this morning. Where the optimum point is, I don't know.

When Mr. Broad spoke about it, he said it had to have some subjective judgments, and we might include in them such concepts as the LIFO inventory judgments and the methods of depreciation.

It might be that we will draw the line just below those and leave them out.

It may be that we will arrive at a concept of reported income which would reflect a dollar income geared to the currency unit, with the idea that the optimum point of subjective judgment was finally determined to be at that level, and that the thing for which then we should aim is narrowing areas of inconsistency in reporting and producing more uniform figures, such as one of the monographs we had here—I've forgotten which one—complained about.

So that we could, for purposes of economic income, apply adjustments more uniformly and for purposes of financial analysis

247

have clearer, widespread understanding of what the income figures we are using do mean, even though they may be limited in their significance, leaving to the degree of subjective evaluation a little bit more than we might have if we set the point somewhere else and tried to do part of the subjective work first.

The possibility that this discussion seems to me to open up, and the one that appeals to me, is that idea that in the increasingly complex situations that we have in income determination, perhaps our leaning ought to be toward a submission to the public, and for general purposes, of a highly consistent and highly objective income determination, even though it is admittedly or relatively reduced significance, so that the significance which people want to attach to it for various purposes can be achieved with considerable knowledge of what figures they are talking about and using when they take the material that they have.

That sounds like defeatism to some people, and I am sure that it meets with a good deal of disapproval, but it appeals to me, and it appeals to me more this morning, after listening to some of this conversation about these subjects.

MR. DEAN: Mr. Wilcox, doesn't a tremendous amount of subjectivity go into it anyhow?

I sat in a board meeting last week and they were saying, "We've done sufficient work with this pilot plant so that we can build a production plant." The chief engineer said, "Oh no. Let's build another pilot plant, because we can charge it up to expenses, and if we build a production plant we will have to capitalize it."

Another one said, "If we take $10,000,000 out and build a production plant, we will have to show debentures, whereas if we are going to lease it, we will have a lease that will go over two years. If we have a lease we will be able to charge our lease out on the basis of the current dollar."

There are fundamental items entering into your income account that make it tremendously subjective.

MR. SMITH: They do make the income account suggestive. It leads you to certain considerations that are reflected in your income account.

248

Mr. Dean: That is true. But where you are comparing income account of Company A with that of Company B, the operating results may be very different.

Take one large mail-order house which has consistently entered into leases through a subsidiary; a subsidiary borrows money; they enter into a lease which is very carefully calculated to pay the operating expenses, the taxes, the amortization and the interest on the loan, and the subsidiary is dissolved—there isn't a dime of funded debt on the balance for that particular company.

If you look at that company and compare it with another one that follows the opposite theory—I have seen any number of investment analyses submitted to a finance committee, saying, "Let's not buy Company A, because it's got loads of funded debt; whereas let's buy Company B because it has no funded debt."

Actually Company B has ten times the funded debt of Company A.

Mr. Smith: I think that is one of the things that should be discussed a bit.

Mr. Haskell: There is a great deal of thinking among corporate executives along the lines of two mail-order companies listed on the Exchange, following diametrically opposite methods. One buys by purchase agreement, and the other finances them out of their own funds.

I agree that it would be very useful at this point, in view of this new development, to discuss this.

Mr. May: I said the other day in connection with this that the combination of inflation and high income taxes and artificially lower interest rates was having an effect upon our accounting like that of Prohibition on our drinking habits.

Results have been sought by artificial means that are not allowed to be reached by natural means. You have to look below the surface of the contractual agreements and try to find out what the realities are.

Whether that is objective or subjective thinking I don't know.

Mr. Brundage: Mr. Warburton, you haven't had any real opportunity to present your comments on the previous papers

249

that we have discussed, and also on your own. Would you like to have the floor?

MR. WARBURTON: I do not think I have anything to add to the comments on the other papers. I might just clarify one or two small points with respect to mine, and the relation of it to the points of view expressed by other people.

I would agree, of course, that looking at the future from the point of view of probability, the rising price trend is more probable than the falling price trend, but I do think that in the paper on which I commented, as to which my aim was directed, the probability of a rising price trend for the next quarter or half century was overstated, and consequently the probability of a falling price trend was understated.

Then, just a comment that goes back to one or two of Mr. Fabricant's remarks, and one or two other things that have been said here about the relationship of this group to other groups.

I would not subscribe to the view that we can expect to follow the middle course between the rising and falling price trends by just wishing. It will take more active work than that. I do think that some of us might well divert our energies to an attempt to organize public opinion in favor of the monetary policy that is aimed at that middle course.

I would not assume, however, that such an effort is at all the function of this group as the Business Income Study Group.

MR. BROAD: Do you not think that one thing that could be done toward emphasizing the desirability of a stable currency is to show the effects of an unstable one?

MR. WARBURTON: To be sure. It would be very helpful.

MR. BRUNDAGE: One suggestion came out here from Mr. May's comments and that was about a study of the inaccuracies, errors of presentation.

Do you want to go ahead with something of that sort?

MR. FABRICANT: I was wondering, Mr. May, if your idea is not one of comparing alternative methods rather than errors.

MR. MAY: How they can be reduced.

MR. ALEXANDER: What is the correct line from which you are going to measure them?

MR. MAY: For instance, you have two alternative methods now, like the sinking fund method of depreciation or the diminishing balance.

MR. ALEXANDER: These are differences between alternative methods.

MR. MAY: Yes. One would show that the railroads were making money and the other would show that on the aggregate they are losing money.

Of course, the biggest problem is the postulate of continuity which underlies all the accounting today, with the implicit assumption that the enterprise will go on indefinitely.

I believe that is implied by what is called the going-concern principle.

The question arises: What do you do when it becomes evident that the postulate is no longer valid, which happened to the street railway companies many years ago and is happening to a great many of the railroads today? How do you figure income there? At the time of abandonment?

There is a major question which has never been tackled.

MR. DEAN: Take your bituminous coals. The pension has gone from six cents a ton to thirty cents a ton, and that will be roughly about $150,000,000 a year based on calculations of production.

The decline in the consumption of bituminous coal has been accompanied by a tremendous turn to natural gas, and there is a movement on foot to curtail the importation of oil.

What is putting these miners out of work is the rise in the cost of bituminous coal with respect to other competitive fuels. Lewis says, "That is very simple. You increase the take per ton in order to be able to insure that the miners get what they need. You have to up the take to keep pace with the rise in the cost of living." So that sooner or later the bituminous coal industry will disappear.

MR. MAY: Take the utilities. I mentioned that today the greater return which is allowed is in part not a rise in the rate of return but a recognition that the profits are not wholly real. The

251

problem of what the utilities should be allowed to earn in gross revenues is what they are facing, and the governing bodies are compensating by allowing them something under the guise of a return on which income tax has to be paid.

We are getting a good deal of confusion in the computation of the profit of utilities in just that way.

MR. HOLME: I certainly feel that due to all these regulations we have it is extremely difficult to know where you come out. I think in the case of utilities it may be a little clearer. It is a little more difficult to see than in the case of the railroads, but I often wonder what would happen if the Interstate Commerce Commission overnight had its regulatory powers removed. I would be very curious to know what the railroads would actually do. I think you would get wholesale abandonment of many lines which are now not on an economic basis.

I am inclined to believe that on some of their longhaul stuff you would not find that they could, as the politicians say, gouge the public. They would be quick to find they could not do it. I think we would have a much more real situation in our transportation if that were done.

MR. MAY: I always watch the railroads, because I think what happens in the railroad happens next in the utilities and next in the heavy industries and all the way up to nationalization. So I would watch the history of the railroads with great care.

MR. HOLME: I think this is a very good bell-wether, if that is the right word.

MR. WILCOX: Mr. Chairman, you raised a question a minute ago with reference to this possible study of the margins of error and that is before us, I take it.

I just want to offer a comment on that with fear and trembling. I get in trouble by trying to guess what I think other people mean, and perhaps I am doing that now, but I will offer a preview of an objection that I would expect to make to the results of the study.

If the study does not bring in this point that I think Mr. Smith brought to attention so well, with respect to the effect on earnings of the changes in technology and the efficiency of existing units of

252

equipment as compared with units that may be purchased on the current price level: If that factor is not brought into the problem of the margins of error, I will be very much inclined, I think, to write off the conclusions.

MR. MAY: You have two problems. One of them is measuring the quantum of the property exhaustion and then to distribute it over a period; another problem, of expressing it in money.

You could show the effect of the variations, assuming the quantum has been determined initially.

What difference does it make in your results the way you deal with your other two factors? That would entirely eliminate your question of the effect of technological progress, because that would be a factor in determining the quantum in the first place.

MR. WILCOX: If I understand you correctly, you mean you would bring it into the determination of the quantum?

MR. MAY: No. You are figuring what variations there would be, purely in the method of accounting, assuming the same physical facts. That would be an interesting study. It is not at all limited to the industries where depreciation would be very, very important.

MR. FABRICANT: You will run up against some people who are going to object because some of the alternatives deal obviously with nonsensical results.

I remember—I think it was 1934—that I wrote one of these little papers for the National Bureau. I took the aggregate income of all corporations from 1929 to 1932, presented the profit figures shown there and said, "What would happen to the net result of that income if you were to use alternative methods of calculation and then presented that result"?

One of the directors of the National Bureau wrote back saying that no matter what I did with those figures he could not believe that corporations were making money in 1932.

MR. BRUNDAGE: Unless you have some further comments——

MR. FABRICANT: I was wondering whether we were going to aim a few comments at Mr. Bronfenbrenner's statement apart from those that Mr. Warburton has raised.

MR. BRUNDAGE: Have you any comments?

MR. FABRICANT: There are one or two things that bothered me. When I made my initial statement here, I assumed that was not the time to make these comments, but Mr. Bronfenbrenner seemed to me to show a misunderstanding in the function of depreciation reserve, for example, in his argument that the calculation of net income in a given year should take into account not only the difference between current prices and original cost prices on the depreciation charges for that year, but also the difference between the current prices, say, in the preceeding years which were used for calculating depreciation charges and the current charges, including a correction for the depreciation reserve itself.

It seems to me that was a misconception.

MR. MAY: Mr. J. R. N. Stone argued the same point with me in England last year.

MR. ALEXANDER: It would be correct if depreciation reserves were accumulated in cash, but only with that presumption.

MR. GOLDSMITH: Wasn't Mr. Bronfenbrenner tending possibly in the direction of the point which was raised by Mr. Alexander, in taking into account the entire change of the going concern's net worth? I mean, not only the change of net worth which is brought about by net retained income, as it has been defined, but including the change in the value, expressed in monetary terms, of the whole remaining assets.

Otherwise, unless he had that in mind, you are certainly right, but I am trying to put an interpretation on it which would make some sense.

MR. ALEXANDER: Even if he had that in mind, even if this other characteristic is absent—and I would say, isn't generally absent—it would not be true that if an equal amount is held in cash, then the correction for the past reserve is wrong; because the correction is based on the idea that, the value of money having changed, you have not put aside enough.

If the form in which you put aside depreciation reserve is used, or whatever comes into your firm any way, you can then say it is in real assets, and you do not have to correct for a change in the value of money. Whatever definition you take, it will come out the same.

MR. FABRICANT: I think Mr. Bronfenbrenner had something of that sort in mind, but certainly the method proposed would not take care of it.

MR. BLOUGH: Presumably you have an offset from the balance-sheet side of it, and if you have a deficiency in the reserve due to the change, which you do not recognize, it is offset by an unrecognized item on the assets side.

MR. ALEXANDER: Unless the offset is in cash.

MR. BLOUGH: It would not be in the case of depreciation.

MR. ALEXANDER: You also have to take account of the cash liabilities.

MR. FABRICANT: He presents us with the idea of the maintenance costs of a man, as a basis for getting at net income of workers for comparison with net income of corporations. As he mentions, of course, the idea is recognized in such things as income exemptions. It seemed to me, however, that there is an enormous difference, a difference of degree of the sort that becomes a difference of kind, in calculating what is the maintenance cost for a business enterprise and what is the maintenance cost of a man. In the case of a man, it seems to me you have all kinds of variations depending on the standard of living. This minimum of decency is often quoted, and it has an interesting upward trend. That would not be true of corporations, I am sure.

I just want to leave the question with you.

MR. BRUNDAGE: Although, I think, the plants are much cleaner and much better arranged.

MR. FABRICANT: I was thinking of replacement.

MR. ALEXANDER: You have to have a bigger business in order to keep up with the level.

[A luncheon recess was taken.]

———————

The meeting reconvened at two o'clock.

255

MR. BRUNDAGE: The executive committee felt that the arguments in the monographs previously circulated all seemed to slant a little too much the same way; that is, they all emphasized the desirability of some change in the accounting presentation, and so we have tried to get someone to develop the other side.

Mr. Greer promised to do it, but he did not come through, so we have asked Mr. May to see if he could summarize the arguments against the change.

MR. FABRICANT: Would it be fair to say that we were afraid to ask him to add any additional arguments? (Laughter)

MR. MAY:

(Mr. May thereupon read a prepared manuscript on "The Case Against Change In Present Methods of Accounting For Exhaustion Of Business Property", a copy of which is attached hereto.)

Mr. WILCOX: I move a vote of thanks.

MR. BRUNDAGE: I do not know how much comment you would like to have or how long you would like to prolong the discussion of this one phase of the problem we have been considering.

MR. BROAD: I do not know whether it would be in order or not, but I would like to see someone who has opposite views put his own views in.

MR. BRUNDAGE: Mr. Greer promised to let us have it, and he did not come across. Then he said he would be here, but he could not get here.

MR. BROAD: I do not think there has been adequate explanation or theoretrical approach or discussion of the views of people who disagree with it.

I think our study would be improved if we could have just as strong a position on the other side. This to some extent goes on the defensive. I would like to see somebody go on the offensive and put his name to it, somebody who really believes it.

MR. SMITH: Does this represent your views, Mr. May?

MR. MAY: This is a statement of views against it.

MR. WILCOX: Is this going to be distributed?

MR. MAY: Yes.

MR. WILCOX: I would like to have it. I cannot remember it well enough from having heard it read.

MR. SMITH: It is a very convincing job, Mr. May. I do not see why you do not sign it.

MR. BRUNDAGE: Does anyone here wish to volunteer to go on the committee?

MR. BROAD: I think people who believe in it ought to sign it.

MR. BRUNDAGE: How about you, Mr. Wilcox?

MR. WILCOX: All right. I think I believe most of it.

MR. BRUNDAGE: How about you, Mr. Smith?

MR. SMITH: I believe most of it too, but I happen to be on four committees right now that are taking up a lot of travel and a lot of time.

MR. MAY: Maybe one of the economists would like to take it.

MR. WILCOX: The economists are all "agin" it.

MR. SMITH: I think Mr. Copeland would be interested, from what he said to us this morning.

MR. COPELAND: I would be glad to look it over.

MR. MAY: I think you ought to appoint Mr. Wilcox chairman of a committee of three with power to appoint the other two members.

MR. WILCOX: I was going to say that you ought to put Mr. Greer on as chairman. He is the man who will carry the ball on this. I would be glad to work with him.

MR. BRUNDAGE: I am not at all sure about that. If you agree to do it, it will be done. I am not sure about Mr. Greer.

MR. DEAN: Is Dr. Sanders a member of our group? He shares those views pretty strongly. I wonder if he would be interested.

MR. COPELAND: He might.

MR. BRUNDAGE: Mr. Wilcox will be chairman, and there will be Mr. Greer and someone else to be selected.

MR. WILCOX: All right. Thank you, Mr. Chairman. I guess thank you.

MR. MAY: I did the best I could.

MR. HOLME: A very good "best."

MR. FABRICANT: Mr. May, will you have additional copies prepared? I think we would all be interested in it.

MR. MAY: I did not think it would be important enough for that.

MR. FABRICANT: I think it is.

MR. BRUNDAGE: Would you like to have it circulated?

MR. WILCOX: I think it ought to be circularized. If this committee comes up with something different, it would be interesting to see where we depart from it.

MR. MAY: I have a note on the back of this, talking about this situation today, concerning traditional accounting.

Looking back over my life, I think we had an era in the first twenty-five years of the century, which was the era of the engineer and banker, of the single entry method, and the accountant was purely a recorder.

Then there was an era which perhaps is just about coming to an end, which I call the era of the accountant, in which we had income accounting and the accountant became an interpreter as well as a recorder.

I call those respectively the static and the dynamic approaches.

I think what we are entering on now is the era of the political and economic forecaster, which would relegate the accountant again to the role of recorder and justify the name of the era as the futuristic.

So we have the era of the static, the dynamic and the futuristic.

I think if I were to write a history of my personal accounting of the last sixty years, that would be the way I would call it.

MR. SMITH: As a historian you have done very well. As a prognosticator, I hope you are wrong.

MR. MAY: They used to call in the engineers. Now they call in the accountants. Next they will call in the prognosticators to forecast the income taxes.

MR. BROAD: Along the lines of discussion, the future income scream, I would like to hear some further remarks on that.

MR. BRUNDAGE: Mr. Alexander was there first. We are just supplementing this.

258

MR. ALEXANDER: I will just wait a while. That is all.

MR. HOLME: Mr. Chairman, in listening to a few comments along the same lines that Mr. May spoke about, I have heard this future era Mr. May described as that of the extrapolater.

MR. BRUNDAGE: Is there any other discussion, gentlemen, on what we have already heard?

MR. DEAN: This is not particularly a discussion of what we have heard, but in view of Mr. Cumberland's remarks this morning, I wonder whether we ought to consider having a paper which would sort of criticize our general papers, or put our papers in a frame of reference with relation to monetary theories.

Secondly (Mr. May has touched on this a number of times in the paper which he just read and in his other monograph), it seems to me we might also have a paper on the extent to which business decisions are dictated not because of business soundness, but because of what business men think they are forced to do because of the income tax laws, and what the general effect of that is going to be.

Heretofore it always seemed as though you ought to examine every proposition on the basis of whether it was sound from a reasonable business point of view, and examine its tax features later. Today you find people selling property and entering into long-term lease arrangements, not because they think they can prove what their business is going to be, or where the customers are going to be, twenty or thirty years from now, but because they think that the only way they can survive as managers is to produce more income for the stockholders.

MR. BRUNDAGE: I think that we should have one paper on the question of business income from the point of view of taxation. I feel that that really ought to be done, and that was referred to here under Item 4 below. I do not know who would be the best person to do it, but, as I understand it, Mr. Cumberland has committed himself to give us something on this first question. He certainly is chairman of a committee to do it. If he cannot do it, we will get somebody else to do it.

259

MR. CUMBERLAND: I will certainly try it. I know Mr. Tucker is very much interested in this thing.

MR. DEAN: You have six months.

MR. CUMBERLAND: I have committed myself to write a book in the next few months. I cannot do much outside of that, but I shall certainly try to get somebody to do it, Mr. Chairman, and report back to you.

MR. BRUNDAGE: Thank you.

MR. BRUNDAGE: On this Federal Tax problem, the discussion we had before the Trade and Industry Law Institute, a few weeks ago was broken down into "Our Federal Tax Policy" by Mr. May; "The Revenue Act of 1950" by Mr. Austin; and "A Long-Term Tax Program" by Mr. Darrell. This discussion is now in page proof and will be available shortly, and I have asked for fifty copies to distribute to the group.

This is not quite the point of view from which I thought it ought to be approached. I don't know whether it would be too much to ask Dr. Nourse to do that or not. What do you think?

MR. DEAN: I do not know what his commitments are. I think he would be interested in talking to me about it, but I do not know what previous commitments he has.

The Group then turned to consideration of procedural problems.

It was decided to hold another meeting on Nov. 4, 1950.

THE CASE AGAINST CHANGE IN PRESENT METHODS OF ACCOUNTING FOR EXHAUSTION OF BUSINESS PROPERTY

by GEORGE O. MAY

THE CASE AGAINST CHANGE IN PRESENT METHODS OF ACCOUNTING FOR EXHAUSTION OF BUSINESS PROPERTY

At its meeting on April 25, 1950 the Executive Committee requested that I present the case against changes in the concept of income of corporations engaged continuously in manufacture or trade to express revenue and charges against revenue as nearly as possible in terms of units of the same purchasing power.

This discussion, which is based largely on study of material submitted to the Study Group, will be related to Questions I, II and III which the Committee on December 19, 1947 decided to study:

QUESTION   I—Is LIFO accounting, as now applied, only a reasonable assumption as to the actual flow of goods and costs, or more broadly a means of bringing costs into account on approximately the same price level as revenues?

QUESTION   II—Should accounting procedures be revised so as to bring the cost of property exhaustion into account at approximately the same price level as the revenues and, if so, how should this object be accomplished?

QUESTION III—Should the situation be met by (1) changes in methods of accounting; (2) changes in methods of presentation; or (3) supplementary information, assuming social usefulness to be the objective?

It will be argued that Question I should be answered in favor of the second alternative, that Question II should be answered in the negative, with the suggestion that LIFO accounting should be abolished, and that Question III should be answered in favor of the third method.

261

In my monograph *Business Income and Price Levels* and my memorandum on LIFO Inventory Accounting I have already discussed some of the views expressed in favor of the position to be taken herein.

Just as opinions have differed on the point how objectives suggested in the three questions should be attained, so there have been differences in the fundamental approach of those opposed to changes in that direction.

The issues set forth were presented at a time when there was (as there still is) a wide difference of views of the proper function of financial accounts, and upon the question how they can attain the greatest usefulness. Objections to the proposals outlined in the questions are apt to differ according to the views held on this broader question.[1]

I shall accept the view adopted by the Institute in 1938 that: "A fair determination of income for successive accounting periods is the most important single purpose of the general accounting reports of a corporation."

Accounting thought on periodical income may for the present purpose be divided into three classifications:

The view that results from acceptance of the so-called "traditional cost principle."

The view that significance can best be attained by uniformity and as close adherence as possible to factual bases and objective evidence.

The view that significance can be attained only by having constant regard to substance, by the exercise of objective judgment, and by disclosure of the basis on which the accounts of the reporting entity are based.

As a preliminary to discussion therefore I reproduce here a brief statement of my views which appears in the current (May 1950) issue of the *Journal of Accountancy*:

---

[1] In this discussion the American Institute of Accountants, speaking through its Committee on Accounting Procedure, is referred to as the Institute, or the American Institute, and the Institute of Chartered Accountants in England and Wales as the English Institute.

"Perhaps the three most fundamental postulates of accounting presently accepted are:

1. That the entire income from sale arises at the moment when realization is deemed to take place;

2. That fluctuations in value of the monetary unit which is the accounting symbol may properly be ignored;

3. That, in the absence of actual evidence to the contrary, the prospective life of the enterprise may be deemed to be indefinitely long."

It will be assumed that the burden of proof is on those who advocate change, and that change should preferably be orderly and timely.

The Institute in *Accounting Research Bulletin No. 33* sought the tactical objective of preventing the adoption by corporations of a wide variety of inadequately considered methods of dealing with the problem of the greatly increased cost of repairing, renewing or replacing plant and equipment. It suggested that no action should be taken "at least until a stable price level would make it practicable for business as a whole to make the change at the same time"—a procedure analogous to moving the previous question. The Institute is in general, and doubtless was in this instance, deeply conscious of the importance attached by the Securities and Exchange Commission to uniformity in accounting (as indicated for instance in its *Accounting Release No. 53*). Its action, and the action of the Securities and Exchange Commission in relation to corporations such as United States Steel, duPont and Chrysler, which introduced new methods into their accounts for 1947, have had the result of preventing any general adoption of proposals such as are contained in my monograph; their tactical objective has been attained.

It can be fairly argued (as it was by Mr. Greer at the meeting on December 3, 1949) that the need for change is lessened as the years pass and the proportion of plant in use that was constructed at the prewar cost becomes less. It may also be claimed that industrial profits during the last three years have been high enough to ensure that no serious economic or financial harm has resulted from continuance of old accounting methods up to now. It would seem clear also that the public generally has discounted the significance of the reported "Net income for the year" in such cases, as the Institute contemplated.

The problem has become of less importance relatively because of the development of other major problems such as the proper treatment of pensions, lease-backs and accelerated depreciation on newly created property.

Inflation, high income taxes and artificial lowering of interest rates have had an effect on financial accounting not unlike that of prohibition on our drinking habits. Results are now being sought by artificial means which are not permitted to be attained naturally; in some cases the objectives are legitimate, in others they are not; their overall effect has been a decline in the significance of accounts, and an increase in the importance of the notes to accounts. All this operates to the advantage of the large investor and the shrewd speculator and to the disadvantage of the small investor and so discourages thrift.

It may with complete justice be pointed out that the variety of methods employed in present-day accounting is so great that a single change of the kind contemplated is relatively unimportant compared with that of creating a clearer understanding of the limits of the significance of accounts as they are now prepared.

A more informative classification of the income statement, accompanied by a description of methods of accounting, such as was contemplated by the Institute Committee of 1932 in its correspondence with the New York Stock Exchange, might achieve far more valuable results than any single modification of existing accounting practice.

It must be conceded that there is a regrettable disharmony in fundamental concepts as the result of the introduction and extension of LIFO accounting, and the denial of any corresponding modification of practice in relation to capital assets. But, as some who concede that this is so (e.g. Mr. E. B. Wilcox) have pointed out, one remedy is to discard, or limit the use of, LIFO accounting. Evidence afforded by the recent study made by Professor Butters shows that the adoption of LIFO has, in the main, been actuated by tax advantages rather than by theoretical economic or accounting considerations. (*Inventory Accounting and Policies*, Butters and Niland, Riverside Press, 1949, *passim*.)

The evidence indicates that the option to use the LIFO method has not resulted in inventory treatments best adapted to the nature of the business and the methods of conducting it. The inference may well be that a similar option in accounting for property exhaustion would have a similar result. The logical conclusion might be that LIFO accounting should be abolished and that the basis of plant accounting should remain unchanged, or that a consistent treatment of the two problems should be developed and made compulsory.

On the factual side, two arguments have been advanced. The first is that: "So far as it is possible to judge, the currency unit in the United States has been fairly stable over long periods. Its fluctuations have been marked at times, but to the extent that these fluctuations are temporary, income measured in terms of historical dollars ultimately becomes approximately equal to income in an economic sense." The evidence does not support this contention. The compilation of indexes of the Bureau of Labor Statistics covering wholesale prices from 1750 to 1949, which has been distributed to the Group, shows that in each twenty-five year period, the value of the dollar at its highest point has, on the average, been double its value at the low point of the period. The Snyder Index, which is perhaps the most comprehensive developed, shows, for the part of the period covered, results that are not materially different. Such fluctuations in the value of the dollar cannot be ignored without some very important consequences. But it does not follow that a change in the accounting use of the monetary unit is the only remedial step to be taken.

It is true, as the table in a general way shows, that in 1896 the index was substantially the same as in 1750. But I could not support the suggestion that as a result ultimately income determinations on an accounting basis have come into substantial conformity with those arrived at on an economic basis that takes into account the fluctuations in the value of the dollar. However, I do not think it necessary to argue the point further because I do not think that such an "ultimate" correspondence is of great significance as a practical matter. The value of annual accounting statistics declines at an accelerating rate as the period covered by them recedes into the past. Their importance lies mainly in their effect on contemporary action.

There is, however, evidence to support the other argument on the factual side, which is that (1) there is nothing new about wide variations in the value of money; (2) that prior to the first World War changes in the monetary value of capital assets were regarded as actually producing income or loss, and (3) that businessmen have traditionally acted upon the assumption that the value of the monetary unit was stable, although they knew this to be contrary to fact.

Upon the first point, the following from Jevons (*Money and the Mechanism of Exchange*, 1876) is relevant. Discussing the value of gold he said:

> "Between 1789 and 1809, it fell in the ratio of 100 to 54, or by 46 per cent. * * * From 1809 to 1849 it rose again in the extraordinary ratio of 100 to 245, or by 145 per cent., rendering government annuities and all fixed payments, extending over this period, almost two and a half times as valuable as they were in 1809. Since 1849 the value of gold has again fallen to the extent of at least 20 per cent.; and a careful study of the fluctuations of prices, as shown . . . in the Annual Reviews of Trade of the Economist newspaper . . . shows that fluctuations of from 10 to 25 per cent. occur in every credit cycle." (Ch. XXV.)

Upon the second point, the quotations from Dickinson and Montgomery, and discussion appearing in my monograph on

Business Income, beginning at page 2, may be cited. **The same** passages were quoted with approval by the economist Professor R. M. Haig in 1920. (*The Federal Income Tax*, Columbia Income Tax Lectures.)

To the same effect is the dictum of Lord Justice Fletcher-Moulton in the English case of *In re The Spanish Prospecting Co. Ltd.* (1911 1 Ch. 92) in which he discussed the general question of the meaning of profits; and a further passage from Dickinson immediately preceding that quoted in the monograph:

> "In the widest possible view, profits may be stated as the realized increment in value of the whole amount invested in an undertaking; and, conversely, loss is the realized decrement in such value. Inasmuch, however, as the ultimate realization of the original investment is from the nature of things deferred for a long period of years, during which partial realizations are continually taking place, it becomes necessary to fall back on estimates of value at certain definite periods, and to consider as profit or loss the estimated increase or decrease between any two such periods." (*Accounting Practice and Procedure*, 1920, p. 67.)

Upon the third point, which perhaps hardly needs confirmation or elaboration, a note from Thorstein Veblen's *Absentee Ownership* (1923) may be of interest:

> "It (the surplus of gold) * * * inflates the businessmen's expectations of gain, and thereby speeds up business and industry; for among the securely known facts of psychology, as touches the conduct of business, is the ingrained persuasion that the monetary unit is stable, the value of the money unit being the base-line of business transactions."

In a footnote, Veblen says of the presumption:

> "It is known not to accord with fact, but still it remains a principle of conduct. It has something like an instinctive force; or perhaps rather, it is something like a tropismatic reaction, in that presumption is acted on even when it is known to be misleading. And it is a necessary assump-

tion in business, since business is necessarily done in terms of price; so that money values unavoidably constitute the base-line to which transactions are finally referred, and by measurements upon which they are ultimately checked, controlled, adjusted, and accounted for." p. 179.

Such an ingrained habit should be recognized as a part of the setting in which accounts are presented and interpreted.*

Both economists and accountants join in the arguments which are stated as (4) on page 47 of my monograph:

"That no change should be made in either balance sheet values of capital assets or income charges for depreciation unless all assets, liabilities and income charges and credits are to be restated in terms of dollars of uniform purchasing power."

and which is discussed at pages 57-8.

I do not think there is any answer to the contention that property exhaustion should be expressed in terms of current purchasing power in any comparisons of the share of the fruits of industry received respectively by capital and by labor whose wages are by contract or in practice adjusted for any material change in purchasing power of the monetary unit.

That this course is not called for in order to put capital invested in plant or equipment on an equality with capital invested in a security such as Savings Bonds is however arguable, and has been argued by Professors Blough and Shoup, as well as by accountant members of the Group.

Three types of cases present different features:

(1) Railroads and utilities which are regulated on the basis of a fair return on monetary investment.

---

*Note—In *An Introduction to Corporate Accounting Standards* (New York: American Accounting Assoc. 1940), Paton and Littleton said: "The assumption that recorded dollar cost continues to represent actual cost permeates accounting thought and practice, as it does the law. * * * In periods of major price movements this assumption is clearly invalid for certain purposes * * *. Undoubtedly interpretative accounting faces a challenge at this point" p. 23.

268

(2) Heavy industries, such as steel, that are not strictly speaking regulated, but in which capital investment is relatively very large, and the public interest great.

(3) Lighter industries which are neither regulated nor of much public interest and in which capital assets are not an element of major importance.

In the case of the regulated industries some corporations may be able to earn the full return permitted and others may be unable to do so.

The theory of regulation is that the regulated companies should be permitted to earn sufficient to attract capital to the industry. This result can be achieved by varying any one or more of the factors which enter into the determination of the revenue regarded as permissible; viz., allowable costs, the rate base and the rate of return on that base. The revenue should in principle be sufficient to protect the capital invested and to be invested and to assure the financial stability of the enterprise.

If this were the only problem to be considered, it might be more convenient to accomplish it by varying the percentage of permitted return on the rate base than by changing the basis of computing the allowable costs. Apart from the effect of income taxation it would be immaterial whether the allowance appeared above or below the line at which the description "Net income for the year" might appear in the income statement or whether the corresponding credit might appear on the balance sheet as a "provision" for a cost made out of revenue before determining income, or as a "reserve" made out of income after that had been determined. The latter procedure would create less difficulty if the present trend should change and the situation should arise in which exhaustion measured in purchasing power would be less than the corresponding charge in terms of current monetary units.

The case of the less prosperous railroads and utilities (which today would include many railroads) might present more difficulty. But special tax relief would go far to meet that situation, and in the case of the recently reorganized railroads there are usually provisions which call for the financing of some debt retirement or capital expenditures out of revenue which might offset insufficiency in exhaustion charges.

The same line of reasoning might, in theory, be applied to the heavy industries. Even if no tax relief were given in such cases no great harm would result if providing for increased cost of replacement either out of revenue before determining income or out of income were effectively recognized as necessary to the preservation of the industries in a healthy condition.

In the case of the lighter industries, the problem is of minor importance. I conceded in my monograph it would not be necessary or worth while (except from the standpoint of uniformity) to require other companies to adjust their present methods of computing charges for exhaustion of property.

It may therefore be argued that the specific problems of the utilities and heavy industries can and should be made in other ways without disturbing the practice of companies whose exhaustion charges are relatively not of major importance. All accounting is a compromise between theory and practicability, and theoretically, the objective should be to find methods which produce the most useful results with the minimum expense, the minimum of change, and the maximum of simplicity.

In concluding this memorandum, I quote the following from Professor W. A. Paton in his Dickinson Lecture of 1940. Discussing LIFO accounting he said:

> "* * * the proponents of last-in, first-out commonly defend the notion that the basic or normal amount of the inventory is essentially a fixed asset like plant, apparently without seeing that the procedure they are supporting is not at all that which is considered proper for plant." p. 121

> "Whatever else may be said it remains true that last-in, first-out procedure does tend in some degree to minimize the fluctuations in reported net income. This leaves us facing the essential question: Is such stabilization desirable? As I have already tried to indicate, I feel that an answer in the negative is justified. A clear distinction

270

must, of course, be drawn between actual stabilization of business and apparent stabilization through accounts. I am offering no objection here to programs which attempt to reduce business fluctuations, but I am questioning efforts to alter the appearance of business affairs without modification of the objective conditions. Certain fields of business, it is generally agreed, are subject to sharp fluctuations in prices and volume of sales from year to year. Where this is the real situation, it is surely not desirable to introduce accounting methods which bring about an artificial averaging or smoothing. That is, if there are good years and bad years, this condition should be sharply disclosed, not obscured by the accounts and reports.

"The problem is one of adequately qualifying annual statements without creating misconceptions. The proper solution, I submit, lies in supplementing annual reports, not in doctoring them. As some of us have been recommending for a long time, accountants should make more use of comparative, cumulative, and average income statements, as a means of throwing the single-period statement into proper perspective. Further use of well-arranged statements of funds may also be helpful. But I object strongly to the presentation of an averaged statement as if it were the candid report of the course of operation in the particular year. Entire elimination of short-run reckoning is preferable to artifical modification of such reckoning." pp. 123-124.

The reasoning seems as relevant to the present discussion as to the consideration of the merits of LIFO.